COMPLEX WORDS, CAUSATIVES, VERBAL PERIPHRASES AND THE GERUND

ROMANCE LANGUAGES VERSUS CZECH (A PARALLEL CORPUS-BASED STUDY)

EDITED BY
**PETR ČERMÁK
DANA KRATOCHVÍLOVÁ
OLGA NÁDVORNÍKOVÁ
PAVEL ŠTICHAUER**

CHARLES UNIVERSITY
KAROLINUM PRESS, 2020

KAROLINUM PRESS
Karolinum Press is a publishing department of Charles University
Ovocný trh 560/5, 116 36, Prague 1, Czech Republic
www.karolinum.cz

EVROPSKÁ UNIE
Evropské strukturální a investiční fondy
Operační program Výzkum, vývoj a vzdělávání

MINISTERSTVO ŠKOLSTVÍ,
MLÁDEŽE A TĚLOVÝCHOVY

This work was supported by the European Regional Development Fund-Project
"Creativity and Adaptability as Conditions of the Success of Europe in an Interrelated World"
(No. CZ.02.1.01/0.0/0.0/16_019/0000734) and by the Charles University project Progres Q10,
Language in the shiftings of time, space, and culture.

A catalogue record for this book is available from the National Library of the Czech Republic.

ISBN 978-80-246-4554-4
ISBN: 978-80-246-4616-9 (pdf)

The original manuscript was reviewed by Bohumil Zavadil (Charles University)
and Jana Pešková (University of South Bohemia in České Budějovice).

Contents

1. EXPRESSIONS OF POTENTIAL PARTICIPATION, ITERATIVITY, CAUSATION, INGRESSIVITY AND ADVERBIAL SUBORDINATION IN THE LIGHT OF PARALLEL CORPORA

PETR ČERMÁK
DANA KRATOCHVÍLOVÁ
OLGA NÁDVORNÍKOVÁ
PAVEL ŠTICHAUER

1.1 INVESTIGATION PROJECT AND ITS HISTORY

The present monograph is the result of a long-term project, which started in 2013 when an investigation group was formed by experienced teachers (Petr Čermák, Pavel Štichauer, Jan Hricsina, Jaroslava Jindrová, Zuzana Krinková, Olga Nádvorníková), and their Ph.D. (MA, in one case) students (Leontýna Bratánková, Štěpánka Černikovská, Jiří Jančík, Dana Kratochvílová, Petra Laufková, Daniel Petrík, Eliška Třísková) from the Department of Romance Studies at the Faculty of Arts of Charles University. The objective of the investigation group was to explore the possible usage of the parallel corpus InterCorp (created by the Institute of the Czech National Corpus at the very same university; for further details refer to Nádvorníková this volume) for a contrastive analysis of Romance languages and Czech, the mother tongue of all the authors. The group was comprised of students and professors of Spanish, Italian, French and Portuguese. Four structurally different phenomena, which can be found in all these languages, were selected for analysis: complex words with the suffix -ble/-bile/-vel and the prefix re-/ri-, causative construction hacer/fare/faire/fazer + infinitive, ingressive verbal periphrases and the gerund. The primary objective was to study the Czech respondents of these language phenomena that can be found in the InterCorp corpus, thus testing its usefulness for this kind of study and formulating conclusions regarding the systemic Czech counterparts.

In the first stage, the analysis was conducted separately for each Romance language (with a shared introduction and conclusion) and was oriented primarily to Czech readers and Czech professors and students of Romance languages, i.e. their knowledge of Czech and the knowledge of at least one of the four Romance languages was taken for granted when analysing the linguistic material and presenting the results.

The first stage was concluded in 2015 with the publication of the collective monograph *Románské jazyky a čeština ve světle paralelních korpusů* (Čermák – Nádvorníková et al. 2015), which was published in Czech.

The project entered its second phase at the beginning of 2018, with the final result being the present monograph. This stage was conducted by four members of the original investigation group, who are now professors and assistant professors at the Department of Romance Studies (Petr Čermák, Dana Kratochvílová, Olga Nádvorníková, Pavel Štichauer). Building on the results of the first phase, on the original data and the illustrative examples that were prepared by the whole investigation group, the objective was to create a new monograph which, while sharing some of the original objectives with the Czech version, would present the results in a new light.

1.2 OBJECTIVES AND SCOPE OF THE PRESENT MONOGRAPH

While the monograph representing the result of the first stage of the project was written in Czech, the present book is oriented primarily to readers whose native language is not Czech and who might only have a primary or secondary interest in this Slavic language. It thus offers a corpus-based analysis of four research topics in four Romance languages in the light of their respondents in a typologically different language. The monograph is written in English and all Czech examples are translated or glossed. The anticipated audience for this book are primarily scholars interested in at least one of the Romance languages under scrutiny (Spanish, Italian, French, Portuguese). Therefore, while we do not expect readers to be well acquainted with all four languages and we present translations for Romance examples, we do not provide exhaustive glosses for them or detailed descriptions of what is the function of the analysed phenomena within the Romance language system in general. Where necessary, we concentrate solely on important differences that can be found between the four languages.

While analysing the same phenomena, i.e. complex words, causative constructions, ingressive periphrases and the gerund, the scope and point of view of these that are presented differ notably from the original Czech monograph. In the second stage, we decided to consider these phenomena as generally Romance,[1] meaning that we considered their function in Spanish, Italian, French and Portuguese as being largely comparable (while mentioning some partial differences that were significant for our research) and then contrasted these phenomena with Czech as a whole. Thus, from the contrastive point of view, this monograph compares the representation of potential (non-volitional) participation, iterativity, causation, ingressivity and adverbial subordination in Romance and in Czech (rather than presenting partial analyses concentrating solely on one of the four languages, i.e. Spanish vs Czech, Italian vs Czech, French vs Czech and Portuguese vs Czech, as in the first stage of the research).

The second important difference is closely related to the above-presented point. Since we consider the phenomena as generally Romance, we also approach them on a more abstract level than we did in the first stage. At this point, we are not concerned primarily with the formal manifestation of the phenomena under scrutiny; we rather consider the suffix *-ble/-bile/-vel*, the prefix *re-/ri-*, the construction *hacer/fare/faire/fazer* + infinitive, the ingressive periphrases and the gerund as prototypical or "pure"

---

[1]   However, as in the first stage, we excluded Romance languages other than Spanish, Italian, French and Portuguese from our research.

expression form of abstract categories of potential (non-volitional) participation, iterativity, causativity, beginning of an action and adverbial (or circumstantial) subordination. Ranging from complex words through causatives and periphrases to the gerund, we aim to explore the extent to which the abovementioned linguistic categories are systemically encoded in Czech and on which language levels these can primarily be found. Therefore, our primary goal is to present a corpus-based contrastive analysis of these highly abstract categories and their manifestation in Czech, thus moving toward presenting the semantic notions generally attributed to them in a new light. This is based on concrete language data, rather than on intuition or formal manifestation.

1.3 ORGANISATION OF THE MONOGRAPH

This monograph is organised into seven sections, including the present introductory chapter, i.e. **Chapter 1**.

Chapter 2 is devoted to a detailed description of the corpus we work with and the method. It is the only chapter that has one single author, Olga Nádvorníková. In the rest of the book, this chapter is referred to as **Nádvorníková (this volume)**.

Chapters 3–6 represent the core of this monograph. As stated previously, these chapters are based on the original data and incorporate some of the observations made in the Czech version of the book. The following list briefly presents the topic of each chapter, the name of the person preparing the English version and the names of the authors of the original Czech subchapters, which have been incorporated into the new version. All contributors to the original Czech monograph are also listed as co-authors of the new version.

Chapter 3 focuses on complex words, more specifically, on the suffix -ble/-bile/ -vel and the prefix re-/ri-, the function of these affixes and the representation of these functions in Czech. The English version was written by Pavel Štichauer, who is also the main author of the original Czech version. The authors of the original Czech subchapters referring to Spanish, French and Portuguese were Jan Hricsina (Pt., suffix -vel), Jaroslava Jindrová (Pt., prefix re-), Jiří Jančík (Fr.), Zuzana Krinková (Es., prefix re-) and Daniel Petrík (Es., suffix -ble). This chapter is referred to as **Štichauer et al. (this volume)** in the rest of the book.

Chapter 4 deals with the causative construction hacer/fare/faire/fazer + infinitive and the expression of causativity in Czech. The English version was written by Petr Čermák and Dana Kratochvílová, Petr Čermák was also the main author of the Czech version. The authors of the original subchapters referring to Italian, French and Portuguese were Petra Laufková (Fr. and Pt.) and Pavel Štichauer (It.). In the rest of the book, this chapter is referred to as **Čermák – Kratochvílová et al. (this volume)**.

Chapter 5 analyses ingressive verbal periphrases and the expression of the beginning of a process in Czech. The English version was written by Dana Kratochvílová, while the main author of the Czech version was Jaroslava Jindrová. Dana Kratochví-lová was also the author of the original Czech subchapter referring to Spanish. Authors of the original subchapters referring to Italian and French were Pavel Štichauer (It.) and Eliška Třísková (Fr.). This chapter is referred to as **Kratochvílová – Jindrová et al. (this volume)** in the rest of the book.

Chapter 6 is devoted to the Romance gerund and its Czech respondents. The English version was written by Olga Nádvorníková, who is also the main author of the Czech version. The original subchapters dedicated to Spanish, Italian and Portuguese were written by Leontýna Bratánková (It.), Štěpánka Černikovská (Es.) and Jan Hricsi-na (Pt.). In the rest of the book, this chapter is referred to as **Nádvorníková et al. (this volume)**.

Finally, **Chapter 7** presents the conclusions and possibilities for future study in the area of contrastive corpus-based analysis and the study of abstract linguistic categories and their formal manifestation. This chapter was written by Petr Čermák, Dana Kratochvílová, Olga Nádvorníková and Pavel Štichauer and is referred to as **Čermák – Kratochvílová – Nádvorníková – Štichauer (this volume)**.

1.4 TERMINOLOGICAL REMARKS

In order to conclude this introductory chapter, we consider it important to present the most important terms that are used throughout this whole monograph and to specify the meaning we attributed to them.

1.4.1 ROMANCE LANGUAGES UNDER SCRUTINY AND USE OF THE TERM *ROMANCE*

As previously mentioned, this monograph is concerned solely with Spanish, Italian, French and Portuguese. For the sake of simplicity, we often use terms such as Romance construction, Romance prefix etc. when referring to a phenomenon we have analysed. It is important to bear in mind, that to a certain level, this is an oversimplification since we do not consider at all the Catalan and Galician language, minor Romance languages and dialects, and more importantly, we do not analyse Romanian, which displays greater structural differences from Spanish, Italian, French and Portuguese. Therefore, throughout this whole monograph, the use of the term *Romance* is identified exclusively with the four analysed Romance languages.

When referring to Spanish, Italian, French and Portuguese separately, we use the following abbreviations: Es., It., Fr. and Pt.

1.4.2 USE OF THE TERMS *COUNTERPART* AND *RESPONDENT*

We often come across situations in our analyses where the expected systemic functional counterpart of a Romance phenomenon does not appear among the prevailing translational solutions found in the InterCorp parallel corpus. Since this distinction is crucial to us, we use the term *counterpart* when discussing the theoretical Czech systemic equivalent of a specific Romance phenomenon while the term *respondent* is reserved for specific Czech translations found in the corpus. The opposition between counterpart and respondent can thus also be understood in terms of langue (typological counterpart) and parole (used respondent).

2. CORPUS DESIGN & CORPUS-BASED CONTRASTIVE RESEARCH METHODOLOGY

OLGA NÁDVORNÍKOVÁ

2.0 INTRODUCTION

Multilingual corpora strongly changed the research paradigm in contrastive studies, making it possible to base the contrastive statements not only on intuition but on large corpus data. As pointed out by Altenberg – Granger (2002, 7), bilingual and multilingual corpora have brought about a revival of interest in contrastive linguistics, since they opened up new possibilities of research, based on empirical data. According to these authors, "the information gained from corpora is both richer and more reliable than that derived from introspection" (ibid.).

Specific methods and approaches subsequently developed, e.g. bi-directional analysis ('Johansson's procedure', see Johansson 2007) or the use of 'translation counterparts as markers of meaning' (Malá 2013 and 2014). With the analysis of the overall pattern of translation correspondence, we can 'see through multilingual corpora' (Johansson 2007) and shed new light on the differences and similarities between the languages compared.

These developments would not be possible without the constitution of a rigorous methodology of the exploitation of multilingual corpora, taking into account, on the one hand, the limitations of the representativeness of these corpora in terms of size and composition, and, on the other hand, the potential specific features of the language of translation (see Nádvorníková 2017a and 2017b). This chapter first provides a brief summary of the basic methodological principles of corpus-based contrastive research (**Section 2.1**) to subsequently explain the strengths and the limitations of the corpora used in the research introduced in this book (**Section 2.2**).

2.1 CORPUS-BASED CONTRASTIVE RESEARCH METHODOLOGY

Most corpora used in contrastive corpus-based research is comprised of original, non-translated texts and the corresponding translations. These corpora are mostly called 'parallel' (see Xiao – Yue 2009, 241–242; Aijmer 2008, 276; Granger 2003, 21), with a potential distinction between unidirectional parallel corpora (i.e. containing translations only in one translation direction, e.g. from English into Norwegian and not from Norwegian into English) and bi-directional ones (i.e. comprising source and target texts in both directions of translation).[2] If in a bidirectional parallel corpus, the non-translated components have the same characteristics in terms of size and composition (and, eventually, sampling techniques), the parallel corpus may be called 'comparable'.[3]

Nevertheless, the use of the terms 'parallel corpus' and 'comparable corpus' in contrastive corpus-based research is not consistent. First, a comparable corpus cannot contain translations or cannot be multilingual. In the former, the corpora in the two (or more) languages are of the same size and composed of the same text types, but are not translations of each other.[4] In the latter, the comparable components are written in the same language but differ in specific properties: e.g. the corpus *Jerome*, comprising translated and non-translated texts in the same language – Czech (see Chlumská 2013 and 2017 and an example of its exploitation in 2.2). A similar terminological confusion can be observed in the term 'parallel': Granger (1996, 38) used the term 'parallel corpus' for corpora comparable in terms of size and composition.

In this research, we will follow the most consensual use of the aforementioned terminology, reserving the term 'parallel' for bilingual or multilingual corpora containing translationally equivalent texts (see e.g. Peters – Picchi – Biagini 2000, 74) and the term 'comparable' for corpora with the same size and composition (see also Xiao and Yue 2009, 240–241 or Aijmer 2008, 276).

However, more important issues discussed in the literature related to the use of parallel corpora in contrastive research concern methodological principles and restrictions that have to be taken in consideration while making contrastive statements on the basis of the comparison of original texts and the corresponding translations.

The first question that arises in this context is the delimitation of the units compared: what is the source item and what is its 'equivalent' in translation? The identification of the source unit and its potential counterparts requires a deep insight into their *valeur*, i.e. their position in the system of all the languages under scrutiny. In the research introduced in this book, based on the comparison of four different Romance languages and Czech, this question becomes even more pressing since the language units entering the comparison may have a different *valeur* in the source Romance languages. The gerund, for example, has a different frequency, different functions and a different position in the system of non-finite verb forms in Italian, French, Spanish and Portuguese. For this reason, a *tertium comparationis* of the cross-linguistic term

---

2   Xiao and Yue (2009, 241) also mention multidirectional corpora where the same source text can be compared with its translations into several languages.

3   The most prominent example of comparable parallel corpus English-Norwegian Parallel Corpus (ENPC, see Johansson 2007).

4   See the definition of a comparable corpus in Aijmer (2008, 276): "A comparable corpus on the other hand does not contain translations but consists of texts from different languages which are similar or comparable with regard to a number of parameters such as text type, formality, subject-matter, time span, etc."

converb was suggested for its comparison with Czech (see Nádvorníková et al. this volume).[5]

The identification of the 'equivalent' of the source unit in translation has to address numerous issues. First, from the point of view of translation studies, the analysis of 'translation equivalence' at the level of only words or sentences is inaccurate since translators do not translate words or sentences but texts. In addition, the term 'equivalence' is itself questionable, as it can be understood both in a descriptive and prescriptive meaning (what corresponds to the source item or what *should* correspond, see e.g. Guidère 2011, 83). Thus, in our book, we distinguished the two meanings by using the term 'respondent' for concrete translation solutions in Czech, and by reserving the term 'counterpart' for potential systemic equivalents, see Čermák – Kratochvílová – Nádvorníková – Štichauer (this volume, **Section 1.4.2**).[6]

However, in the actual analyses of bilingual parallel concordance, a researcher has to encounter a large range of respondents, i.e. also multiple candidates to the systemic counterparts of the search unit. The crucial issue, in this case, is the distinction between the particular translation solutions and the prevailing types of respondents (*recurrent translation patterns*, see Krzeszowski 1990, 27), which potentially reveal the systemic equivalences. In fact, solid contrastive statements can only be formulated on the latter, whereas the former can be used in a study in the domain of translation studies focussed on special translation techniques (e.g. modulation or transposition, see Vinay – Darbelnet 1995) or translation quality assessment (e.g. omissions or additions).[7]

The last issue defining the usability of parallel (translation) corpora in contrastive research is related to potential specific features of the language of translated texts, different from the non-translated ones. These differences may be due to the influence of the source language (interference, shining through), but also due to the translation process itself (so-called translation universals, see Baker 1996, 176–177 for the definitions given below). The specific features of translation that are the most discussed in literature are simplification ("The idea that translators subconsciously simplify the language or message or both"; for research see e.g. Vanderauwera 1985; Laviosa 2002, or Cvrček – Chlumská 2015), explicitation ("The tendency to spell things out in translation, including, in its simplest form, the practice of adding background information", see e.g. Blum-Kulka 1986; Olohan – Baker 2000; Pápai 2004, or Nádvorníková 2017c) and normalisation ("The tendency to conform to patterns and practices that are

---

5   The necessity of *tertium comparationis* in contrastive linguistics is mentioned e.g. in Goddard – Wierzbicka (2008); see also Altenberg – Granger (2002, 15–18). Barlow (2008) points out that without a common basis for the comparison of the analysed phenomena, the contrastive analysis will always compare pears and apples; in the best of the cases, however, contrastive analysis compares different kinds of apples (Barlow 2008, 101).

6   See a similar distinction in Johansson (2007, 5; translation *correspondence* vs systemic *equivalence*).

7   Missing equivalents in translation may be due not only to the (voluntary or involuntary) omissions performed by the translator, but also to technical issues (misaligned segments). Moreover, the missing counterpart may be compensated outside the given parallel segment.

typical of the target language, even to the point of exaggerating them", see e.g. May 1997 or Kenny 2001).[8]

Contrastive research based on parallel (translation) corpora implemented several methodological principles designed to identify and/or avoid the influence of the specific features of translation. The basic principle is the systematic identification of the direction of translation: indeed, in a corpus of mixed directions of translation, potential sources of interference are multiplied. This principle is often combined with the bi-directional analysis, which also compares the translation respondents of a given item in the opposite direction of translation. A bi-directional analysis is especially in use in comparable corpora, where the components in all the directions of translation are comparable in size and composition (see above). We did not apply the bidirectional analysis systematically to all the topics in our analysis because the subcorpora of translations from Czech into Romance are much smaller than those in the opposite direction of translation and thus not comparable. Therefore, the bidirectional analysis was tested only in the case of the gerund, in order to establish to what extent the Czech transgressive corresponds to the Romance gerund (see Nádvorníková et al. this volume).

The specificities of parallel corpora (both in the translated and non-translated parts) can also be identified by the comparison with the corresponding monolingual reference corpora. In fact, parallel (translation) corpora, by definition, cannot be representative of the entirety of the language use, since they are limited to texts and the types of text being translated (some types of text, e.g. letters or e-mail messages, are rarely translated) or because there are more translations in one direction of translation (e.g. from English into Czech) than in another (e.g. from Czech into English), cf. Granger – Lerot – Petch-Tyson (2003, 20). For this reason, it is recommended to compare the results obtained from parallel corpora to those extracted from monolingual corpora, referential for the given languages (see e.g. Altenberg – Granger 2002, 9). However, we did not apply this procedure to our study, since a systematic comparison of the results in the four topics to five reference corpora (in Czech and in the four Romance languages) would be to go beyond the scope of this book. Nevertheless, we decided to verify the potential specificity of the language of translation in our research at least in the first topic addressed in this book: causative constructions (see Čermák – Kratochvílová et al. this volume). As explained in that chapter, the Romance causative construction (*hacer/fare/faire/fazer* + infinitive) has a wide range of types of respondents in Czech (synthetic as well as analytic, see **Section 4.3**). If the Czech translations were influenced by the source language, we could expect there to be a higher frequency of the analytic respondent *nechat* + infinitive (the closest by its form to the Romance causative constructions), in comparison with the non-translated texts. In order to test this assumption, we used the corpus *Jerome* (comparable translation

---

8   The specific language of translation is sometimes called 'translationese' (see e.g. Baker 1993 or Mauranen 1999). However, as pointed out by Chlumská (2017, 23), 'specific features of translation' and 'translationese' are not synonymous, since the latter conveys a negative evaluation.

corpus of Czech, see Chlumská 2013 and http://wiki.korpus.cz/doku.php/en:cnk:je-rome). The corpus comprises translated and non-translated texts in equal amounts (mostly fiction, but also a subcorpus of non-fiction). The whole corpus contains 85 million tokens but also includes a smaller subcorpus (5 million tokens) balanced according to the source languages (14 languages, including the four Romance languages under study in this book).[9] The proportions of source languages in the unbalanced corpus correspond to their proportion in the Czech publishing market; consequently, English as a source language prevails. For our experiment, we used both variants of the Jerome corpus – balanced as well as unbalanced. The results of the corpus search are shown in **Table 2.1**:

Tab. 2.1. Comparison of the frequency of Czech causative construction nechat + infinitive *in the Jerome corpus*

Jerome corpus (*nechat* + **infinitive**)[10]	Unbalanced corpus		Balanced corpus	
	Non-translated texts	Translated texts	Non-translated texts	Translated texts
Size of the corpus (in tokens)	42,401,470	42,563,842	2,547,367	2,540,043
Abs.fq.	5,107	6,389	401	297
Rel.fq. (ipm)	120	150	157	117
Dice coefficient	0.22		−0.30	

Table 2.1 shows that in absolute as well as in relative frequencies (ipm), the frequency of the construction *nechat* + infinitive in translated and non-translated texts are different. In the unbalanced corpus, the frequency is higher in the translated texts, whereas in the balanced corpus, the result is the opposite. According to the chi-squared test, both differences are statistically significant (at p<.001). However, as shown in Cvrček – Kodýtek (2013), the statistical significance does not necessarily mean the statistical *relevance* (the so-called *effect size*), i.e. whether it is possible to identify a relevant factor behind it. In order to test the effect size, we used the Dice coefficient, based on the comparison of the relative frequencies:

Dice = 2x (ipm1 – ipm2) / (ipm1 + ipm2)

The Dice coefficient results vary between –2 and 2, which are both extreme values signalling high relevance of the difference in frequency. However, in our analysis of

---

9   Since the design of the corpus is synchronic, it only includes translations published after 1992. In addition, it avoids the potential influence of the authors' idiolects by limiting the number of texts written by one author to three books only. More books translated by one translator are accepted although the authors of the originals must be different.

10 In order to reduce the amount of extraction noise and increase the comparability of the results in the two subcorpora, we used a simplified regular expression *[lemma="nechat"] [tag="Vf.*"]*, without potential elements between the verb nechat and the infinitive. Despite this limitation, we consider the results reliable.

the frequency of the Czech causative construction *nechat* + infinitive in translated and non-translated texts, the Dice coefficient is 0.22 in the unbalanced corpus and –0.30 in the balanced corpus. These results show that the statistical relevance of the differences observed in **Table 2.1** is minimal, which means that the influence of the translated text on the frequency of *nechat* + infinitive is not found.

Although the detailed analysis in the Jerome corpus was conducted on only one topic addressed in this book (causative constructions), we dare say that the other domains under examination in this study are not substantially influenced by the specificities of the translated language either. However, other limitations of the corpus, especially those related to the composition of the corpus and the size of the different language subcorpora, may come into play. For this reason, we introduce below (**Section 2.2**) a detailed description of the corpus used in this study and take into consideration its possible limitations throughout this book.

2.2 CORPORA USED IN THIS STUDY

Data for the research in the four topics introduced in this book was drawn from a large multilingual (parallel) corpus named InterCorp (http://ucnk.korpus.cz/intercorp/?lang=en, Čermák and Rosen 2012 or Nádvorníková 2016 in French).

The InterCorp parallel corpus project was started in 2005 by the Institute of the Czech National Corpus (http://ucnk.ff.cuni.cz) with the first version of the corpus published on the internet in 2008. Since then, a new version of the corpus has been launched every year, which has improved the corpus interface functions and added new texts and sometimes new languages to the corpus (see the versions listed at http://wiki.korpus.cz/doku.php/en:cnk:intercorp). The present study was carried out on data extracted from version 6 of the corpus (see http://wiki.korpus.cz/doku.php/en:cnk:intercorp:verze6 and the detailed description below).[11]

The search in the corpus is free for non-commercial uses after registration (https://www.korpus.cz/signup)[12] and extensive research has already been conducted on it (see the database of publications at https://www.korpus.cz/biblio). Nevertheless, the corpus is not used only in (contrastive) linguistic research but also in everyday practice by translators, students and language teachers (see e.g. https://korpus.cz/proskoly). In addition, in 2015, an online dictionary based on the InterCorp data was made available on the internet (http://treq.korpus.cz/, see Škrabal – Vavřín 2017).

---

11 As mentioned in Čermák – Kratochvílová – Nádvorníková – Štichauer (this volume, Introduction), the first (Czech) version of this book, resulting from the first stage of our research, was published in 2015, and the data was extracted in 2013, from the latest version of the corpus available at that time (version 6). The InterCorp parallel corpus is nowadays (in 2020) at version 12, which is obviously larger than the previous versions. However, for the present monograph, it was not possible to extract and examine completely new data.

12 After signing a non-profit licence agreement, the Institute of the Czech National Corpus can also provide texts from the InterCorp parallel corpus as bilingual files including shuffled pairs of sentences.

InterCorp parallel corpus contains the originals and the corresponding translations in 40 languages, including the four Romance languages under study in this book (Spanish, Italian, French, and Portuguese).[13] For more than half of the languages included in the corpus, the texts were lemmatised and POS-tagged (with the exception of e.g. Arabic, Hindi, Hebrew, Chinese, Vietnamese etc.). For all the four Romance languages under examination in this study, both lemmatization and POS-tagging are available in the corpus. Nevertheless, in order to exclude potential mistagged tokens, we preferred regular expressions to the POS-tags in the specific corpus searches, wherever it was possible (for example, the gerund was searched via the suffixes in the four Romance languages, see Nádvorníková et al. this volume).[14]

The originals and the translations in the corpus are aligned at the sentence level using the sentence aligner *hunalign* (http://mokk.bme.hu/resources/hunalign/, see Varga et al. 2005).[15] Since Czech is the pivot language of the project, all texts are aligned with this version, and through this version to other languages, which makes it possible to perform a multilingual search in the corpus interface (KonText). Among the fiction texts available in most language versions, are obviously translations from English,[16] but, surprisingly, the text available in the InterCorp parallel corpus in most of the translations was not written in English, but in French: it is *Le Petit prince* by Antoine de Saint-Exupéry (available in 29 translations):[17]

[FR]   « *Moi, se dit le petit prince, si j'avais cinquante-trois minutes à dépenser, je marcherais tout doucement vers une fontaine…* » (Antoine de Saint-Exupéry, *Le Petit prince*)

[CS]   „*Kdybych já měl padesát tři minuty nazbyt,*" *řekl si malý princ,* „*šel bych docela pomaloučku ke studánce…*" (transl. Zdeňka Stavinohová)

[DE]   „*Wenn ich dreiundfünfzig Minuten übrig hätte*", *sagte der kleine Prinz,* „*würde ich ganz gemächlich zu einem Brunnen laufen…*" (transl. Grete Leitgeb; Josef Leitgeb)

---

13   Arabic (ar), Belarussian (be), Bulgarian (bg), Catalan (ca), Czech (cs – pivot language), Danish (da), German (de), Greek (el), English (en), Spanish (es), Estonian (et), Finnish (fi), French (fr), Hebrew (he), Hindi (hi), Croatian (hr), Hungarian (hu), Icelandic (is), Italian (it), Japanese (ja), Lithuanian (lt), Latvian (lv), Macedonian (mk), Malay (ms), Maltese (mt), Dutch (nl), Norwegian (no), Polish (pl), Portuguese (pt), Romany (rn), Romanian (ro), Russian (ru), Slovak (sk), Slovene (sl), Albanian (sq), Serbian (sr), Swedish (sv), Turkish (tr), Ukrainian (uk), Vietnamese (vi).

14   The amount of mistagged tokens is minimal in the corpus, with the exception of the past transgressive in Czech, where 50% of the occurrences were noises (see Nádvorníková et al. this volume).

15   For details about the design of the InterCorp parallel corpus and technical aspects of its constitution, see Vavřín – Rosen (2008) or Čermák (2010).

16   E.g. Harry Potter's stories by J.K. Rowling or books by Lewis Carroll, Georges Orwell, Douglas Adams or J.R.R. Tolkien.

17   *Le Petit prince* is available in Czech, Belarussian, Bulgarian, Catalan, Danish, German, Lower Sorbian, Greek, English, Spanish, Finnish, Hindi, Croatian, Upper Sorbian, Hungarian, Italian, Latin, Latvian, Macedonian, Dutch, Polish, Portuguese, Romanian, Russian, Slovak, Slovenian, Swedish, Serbian Cyrilic, Ukrainian. On the top list of texts available in the most translations in the core of InterCorp, are other texts also written in Romance languages: *Il nome della rosa* by Umberto Eco (in 22 translations, the 9th position) and Paulo Coelho's *O Alquimista* (also 22 translations).

[EN]   *"As for me,"* said the little prince to himself, *"if I had fifty-three minutes to spend as I liked, I should walk at my leisure toward a spring of fresh water."* (transl. Katherine Woods)

[ES]   —*Si yo dispusiera de cincuenta y tres minutos* —pensó el principito— *caminaría suavemente hacia una fuente...* (transl. Bonifacio del Carril)

[HIN] "अगरमेरेपासतरिपनमनिटबतिानेकोहोते" छोटेराजकुमारनेसोचा, , तोमैंधीरे - धीरेएकजलाशयकीओरचलपड़ता ... l" (transl. कशोिरबलवीर, जगवंश)

[IT]   *"Io",* disse il piccolo principe, *"se avessi cinquantatré minuti da spendere, camminerei adagio adagio verso una fontana..."* (transl. Nini Bompiani Bregoli)

[PT]   *"Eu, pensou o principezinho, se tivesse cinqüenta e três minutos para gastar, iria caminhando passo a passo, mãos em o bolso, em a direção de uma fonte..."* (transl. Frei Betto)

The corpus is divided into a core part and so-called collections. The core consists mostly of fiction and partly of non-fiction. The collections are comprised of various types of texts: movie Subtitles, Acquis communautaire, transcripts of debates in the European Parliament and journalistic texts (collections SYNDICATE and Presseurop).[18] The core of the corpus and the collections differ not only in the text types included but, more importantly for our research, in the quality of the data: unlike the collections, the texts in the core of the corpus are all proofread and the quality of their alignment is semi-manually checked using the InterText editor for aligned parallel texts (see Vondřička 2014). Moreover, texts in the core of the corpus are mostly translated by professional translators and revised in publishing houses, unlike e.g. the collection of movie subtitles, and the direction of translation is identified with certainty in this part of the corpus. As can be seen in **Section 2.1**, the distinction between the source and the target languages is a crucial factor in corpus-based contrastive research; consequently, we limited the data for the research introduced in this book only to original texts in the core part of the corpus, in the four Romance languages under examination.[19] Thus, the research in the four topics introduced in this book was conducted on the same subcorpora, as defined in **Table 2.2**.

Table 2.2 shows that the core of the corpus represents only a minor part of the InterCorp parallel corpus (cf. columns 2 and 3 in the table) and none of the core subcorpora can be considered by its size as representative for the given language. For this reason, in the analyses introduced in this book, the frequency counts were limited to the minimum, and if introduced, their main purpose is to identify the size of the dataset examined. In addition, the four subcorpora are not comparable one to each other: the largest, for Spanish, is six times larger than the others. For this reason, in the analyses, datasets in Spanish may prove to be more quantitatively valuable and reliable than in the other three languages (see e.g. Štichauer et al. this volume, **Section 3.4.1**).

---

18   In 2017, a new collection was added to the corpus:18 translations of the Bible.

19   This means that we excluded from the core of the corpus the texts translated from a third language (e.g. all translations from English), since different source languages may give rise to other interferences.

Tab. 2.2. Subcorpora of the InterCorp parallel corpus used in this research

Sub-corpus	Total N° of tokens (collections & core)	Subcorpus used in this study (the core of the corpus limited to translations from the four Romance languages into Czech)			
		N° of tokens	N° of texts	N° of (different) authors	N° of (different) translators
ES>cs	73,002,746	9,326,150	105 (36 Europ. / 69 Am.)	43 (21 Europ. / 22 Am.)	44
IT>cs	54,564,618	1,631,204	17	11	9
PT>cs	58,531,766	1,485,541	15	11 (8 Port. / 3 Braz.)	9
FR>cs	62,288,229	1,533,451	31	23	24

As mentioned above, most of the texts in the core part of the InterCorp parallel corpus are classed as fiction; in the four Romance languages under scrutiny in this study, non-fiction is mostly represented by history: Giuliano Procacci *Storia degli italiani* in Italian or *Dames du XIIe siècle* by Georges Duby or books about history for young people (*Marco Polo, Alexandre le Grand*) in French. In Spanish, we find in non-fiction e.g. *La rebelión de las masas* by José Ortega y Gasset. In fiction, the most represented authors (in number of tokens) are, for example, Arturo Pérez-Reverte, Isabel Allende or Gabriel García Márquez in Spanish; Umberto Eco, Elsa Morante or Alessandro Baricco in Italian; Louis Ferdinand Céline, Michel Houellebecq or Bernard Werber in French; and José Maria Eça de Queirós, Jorge Amado or João Giumarães Rosa in Portuguese. Since the InterCorp parallel corpus is synchronic, most texts were published after 1950, with the exception of major works in the given literature, e.g. Marcel Proust in French or the above-mentioned José Maria Eça de Queirós in Portuguese. In addition, both European and American authors are represented in Portuguese and Spanish. In the analyses presented in this book, we attempt to identify and minimise the potential impact of the authors' or translators' idiolects by systematically mentioning the name of the author and the translator in the examples.[20]

Despite the aforementioned limitations in size and in composition of the subcorpora of the InterCorp parallel corpus used in this research, we believe that the results obtained in the four topics introduced in this book (complex words with the suffix *-ble/-bile/-vel* and the prefix *re-/ri-*, causative construction *hacer/fare/faire/fazer* + infinitive, ingressive verbal periphrases and the gerund) are reliable and provide a good example of the use of parallel corpora in contrastive research. Future research may verify and refine our findings on larger corpora (not only a new version of the InterCorp parallel corpus but on monolingual reference corpora for the four Romance languages as well) and develop further contrastive analyses comparing the four Romance languages.

---

20 Olohan (2004, 28) points out that not mentioning the name of the translator in a corpus-based contrastive study may be a signal of the underestimation of the translation task and process.

3. MORPHOLOGICALLY COMPLEX WORDS IN ROMANCE AND THEIR CZECH RESPONDENTS

PAVEL ŠTICHAUER

JAN HRICSINA

JIŘÍ JANČÍK

JAROSLAVA JINDROVÁ

ZUZANA KRINKOVÁ

DANIEL PETRÍK

3.0 INTRODUCTION

This chapter explores the nature of morphologically complex words, such as derived words and compounds, and aims to investigate the Czech respondents of selected derivational means, which are introduced below. Unlike syntactic constructions, such as the causatives dealt with by Čermák – Kratochvílová et al. (this volume), we go deeper into the realm of the lexicon where various unpredictable factors come into play. In this chapter, we intend to explore the question of whether morphological complexity, i.e. the fact that a word is derived by means of a derivational affix, might be relevant to its Czech translational respondents. This is defined in the introduction as concrete realisations of more abstract typological counterparts. We will argue that this type of morphological complexity can indeed determine the translator's choice solely because a particular derivational form, such as a suffix, displays what we will call a *semantic instruction*, which can sometimes be easily expressed by way of a paraphrase or a gloss. We will demonstrate that such a semantic instruction in a translation can be maintained, modified, or avoided, depending on the particular means of the word-formation that we will be discussing. We intend to show that a translational solution – a Czech respondent – will overtly reflect such morphological complexity. We put forward the following two questions, which represent two different typological situations:

1) If in the target language, Czech in our case, there is a structurally identical word--formation means with a more or less identical semantic instruction, can we expect a tendency to adopt a structurally identical solution, i.e. to maintain the same derivational pattern? This question will be explored on the basis of the suffix *-ble/-bile/-vel* used to derive modal adjectives such as Es. *insoportable* ('unbearable').

2) If in the target language there is no structurally analogical word-formation pattern or if the pattern is constrained in a radically different way, can we nonetheless arrive at a typology of translation solutions, which will tend to be adopted in a quantifiable way? This question will be discussed on the basis of the prefix *re-/ri-*, which is used to derive verbs with an iterative meaning.

This chapter is structured as follows. In **Section 3.1**, we briefly review some of the basic notions of word-formation, such as the distinction between simple and complex words. In **Section 3.2**, we introduce a contrastive perspective focussing on common and different word-formation patterns. In **Section 3.3**, we put forward a typology of the Czech respondents, first for the suffix -ble/-bile/-vel and subsequently for the iterative prefix re-/ri-. In **Sections 3.4** and **3.5**, we proceed to a detailed presentation of the data for the suffix -ble/-bile/-vel and the prefix re-/ri-, respectively. We discuss the data for all four Romance languages under scrutiny, pointing out, where necessary, particular differences. In **Section 3.6**, we draw various conclusions highlighting interesting outcomes as well as some of the obstacles and problems left for future research.

3.1 WORD-FORMATION: COMPLEX *VS* SIMPLE WORDS

We take the notion of a *complex word* simply as a lexeme created by way of a combination of a base and an affix (derivation) or by way of a combination of two autonomous lexemes (compounding). Following, among others, Lieber (2004), we maintain that the semantics of complex words, except for truly opaque, baseless formations (see below for details), is to a large extent compositional, i.e. the meaning of a complex word can be computed on the basis of two semantic elements, that of the base and that of the affix. Even though the semantics of affixes represents a controversial issue, to which much discussion has recently been devoted (see, Lieber 2004, 2 for derivation, and, e.g., Bauer 2017, Chap. 4 for compounding), we adopt, in what follows, the notion of *semantic instruction*, inspired by Corbin (1987).

While Lieber (2004) attempts to formalise the semantic instruction of the affixes on the basis of sufficiently fine-grained semantic features, we follow a traditional view according to which we can capture the meaning of an affix by way of an explicit paraphrase or gloss, such as those applied to agent or action nouns, defined as *the one who carries out an action expressed by the verb* or *the activity or state expressed by the verb*, respectively. Of course, in some cases, the semantic contribution of an affix is so straightforward that we can use a semantic feature such as *iterativity* or a general notion of *repetition*, as will be seen in the case of the prefix re-/ri-.

We will show that such a paraphrase might also be exploited by the translator when presented with a complex word if the word is not entirely opaque and non-compositional (we will also be discussing this type of apparently complex words).

3.2 ROMANCE AND CZECH: COMMON AND DIFFERENT WORD-FORMATION PATTERNS

Since our primary aim is an empirically oriented parallel corpus-based study and not a theoretical discussion of word-formation, we present, at the very outset, two concrete examples, already hinted at above, which will be addressed in the following sections. The first is the modal suffix -ble/-bile/-vel used to derive adjectives such as Es. *destru-*

ible ('destructible'), It. *prevedibile* ('foreseeable'), Fr. *insupportable* ('unbearable'), Pt. *inevitável* ('inevitable'). The second is the iterative prefix *re-/ri-* as is found in verbs such as Es. *repintar* ('to re-paint'), It. *riaprire* ('to re-open'), Fr. *recharger*, Pt. *recarregar* ('to re-load'). We now briefly characterise these two affixes.

First, the suffix *-bile/-ble/-vel* is paralleled in Czech by an analogical suffix with presumably the same semantic instruction, *-telný*, as found in adjectives such as Cs. *nepřekonatelný, neporazitelný* ('unbeatable'). Thus, we have an example that will be investigated in order to answer the first of the above questions, namely whether a strong tendency to a kind of morphological equivalence can be expected (at least where entirely opaque formations are not taken into account, such as *possible*; see below for a detailed discussion of such adjectives). In general, we can say that such a straightforward correspondence is far from being the case because we find, on the one hand, specifically synonymous adjectives differentiated by their distribution, and, on the other hand, syntactic solutions which render the semantic instruction of the suffix in a different – syntactically based – way. For instance, in the parallel corpus, we find a wide range of respondents such as the It. *ed è **un moto invincibile** perché comune a tutti... a je to [vzestup], který **se nedá zastavit**, protože je společný všem...*, where the adjective *invincibile* is translated by way of a modal construction corresponding to English 'that cannot be stopped'.

Second, the prefix *re-/ri-* is considered to be a polysemous affix whose major semantic instruction is *iterativity*, i.e. repetition of the action or activity expressed by the verb base[21]. Apart from this semantic instruction, which is obviously the most productive, we also find adjectives where the prefix *re-/ri-* does not seem to display any iterativity. Various frequentative and reinforcing connotations can thus be found, such as It. *richiudere* ('to close almost entirely') or Es. *recortar* ('to shorten a bit more'). There are also entirely lexicalised verbs, often used in more or less fixed collocations, such as the It. *rientrare in una classifica* ('to enter in a ranking, to rank'). It is well known that verbs with these unpredictable meanings are usually the most frequent, while those we would be most interested in, i.e. those with a totally compositional iterative meaning, tend to appear as low-frequency items (e.g., It. *riaccompagnare* 'to go with, to take sb, to see sb home again', cf. Baroni 2007). As we shall see, this is also the case for the data we will be presenting below.

The notion of iterativity can be characterised as an aspectual-qualitative characteristic of a process and as such, it belongs to the sphere of Aktionsart or manner of action, see Kratochvílová – Jindrová et al. (this volume) for an extended discussion regarding these terms. It is also worth noting that in Spanish, Italian and Portuguese, there is also a second important means of its expression: the periphrasis Es. *volver a* / It. *tornare a* / Pt. *tornar a* + infinitive. Problems related to periphrastic constructions and the reflection of notions associated with Aktionsart (manner of action) are further discussed by Kratochvílová – Jindrová et al. (this volume).

---

21   For an extended discussion regarding the polyfunctionality of Czech prefixes, see Kratochvílová – Jindrová et al. (this volume).

Unlike the suffix *-ble/-bile/-vel*, the prefix *re-/ri-* is not exactly paralleled in Czech by an analogical prefix with the same semantic instruction. If we leave aside technical verbs, such as *reformulovat* ('to reformulate'),[22] which are clearly direct borrowings, the semantic feature of iterativity is expressed in a different way, for example, by using various iterative adverbs such as *opětovně, znovu* ('repeatedly, once again'). Therefore, we have an example which we will discuss in relation to the second question as to how the morphological complexity is rendered whereas, in the target language, there are no structurally similar means.

3.3 THE TYPOLOGY OF CZECH RESPONDENTS

As we have already seen in the preceding section, our aim is to arrive at a sufficiently fine-grained typology of Czech respondents for selected constructions. Such a typology is useful not only from the qualitative viewpoint but also from the quantitative viewpoint, as we also put forward an overall quantification of individual types. In this chapter, we present a typology of Czech respondents for the adjectives with the suffix *-ble/-bile/-vel*, and for the verbs prefixed with *re-/ri-*.

3.3.1 TYPOLOGY OF CZECH RESPONDENTS OF THE ADJECTIVES WITH THE SUFFIX *-BILE/-BLE/-VEL*

The typology put forward for the suffix *-ble/-bile* has already been presented in our earlier work (see Štichauer – Čermák 2011, 128–129) and exemplified on the data from Spanish and Italian only; here we intend to extend the analysis to include the data from French and Portuguese.

We define four major respondents, referred to as *types* A, B, C, D. The types A/B are synthetic, the types C/D, which can further be divided into two or three subtypes, are analytic or syntactic in nature.

TYPE A. This type is defined as the closest respondent both formally and semantically. An adjective with the suffix *-ble/-bile/-vel*, such as, e.g., the above mentioned It. *insopportabile* is exactly paralleled by the Cs. *nesnesitelný*, where we have the formal and semantic correspondence between the suffixes, and we also have the same relationship with the verb, which can be easily isolated and used autonomously in the syntax.

TYPE B. This type is defined as partial correspondence between the two adjectives, both formally and semantically. To an adjective with the suffix *-ble/-bile/-vel* an

---

22   This is proven by the impossibility to use the prefix *re-* with the common verbs, cf. *reotevřít, *reozdobit ('to re-open, to redecorate') vs *rekvalifikovat, reloadovat* ('to requalify, to reload').

adjective (that is a necessary, typological condition) also corresponds, but this respondent displays a different suffix and only partially maintains the modal semantics. Thus, in cases such as Es. *imprevisible* ('unpredictable', 'unforeseeable') we often find not the straightforward adjective *nepředvídatelný*, in which case we would have a type-A respondent, but an adjective such as *neočekávaný, nečekaný* ('unexpected'). This adjective is also semantically a little more nuanced in that the meaning is not glossed as 'what cannot be expected', but rather 'what is not expected'.

TYPE C. This type is broadly defined as a syntactic respondent. Depending on whether the syntactic roles are maintained or inverted and whether the modal meaning is maintained or eliminated, a further distinction is made between the following three subtypes:

C1. This respondent is delimited as a syntactic solution where the modal adjective is rendered by an active, subject-based clause, where the modality is also maintained. For instance, the Es. *algo es insoportable para alguien*, lit. 'something is unbearable for somebody' can be transformed into the Cs. *někdo nemůže něco snášet*, lit. 'somebody cannot bear something'. Therefore, what is important for this subtype C1, is the subject-oriented reading and, at the same time, the overt expression of the modality by way of the modal verb.

C2. This type is also subject-oriented in exactly the same way as the C1-type but differs from it by the absence of the overt expression of the modality. For instance, we can find cases such as the Pt. *é-me incompreensível*, lit. 'it is to me incomprehensible', which is translated by subject-oriented bare-verb constructions of the type *ale tomu já nerozumím*, lit. 'but I don't understand that'.

C3. With this type, we have no change in the syntactic roles as above; the subject of the adjectival construction remains the same. However, the translation does not introduce a similar adjective but a verb-based solution where a verb such as *dát se* (difficult to gloss without an appropriate context) typically appears. An example is It. *l'età era indefinibile*, lit. 'the age was undefinable', where we sometimes find in Cs. *věk se nedal určit* 'it was not possible to determine the age', or 'the age couldn't be determined'.

TYPE D. This type represents a somewhat residual group that includes both syntactical as well as various lexical solutions. It is clear that this type is extremely heterogeneous, and it is thus difficult to determine to what extent the modality inherent in the suffix is expressed. Nonetheless, there are two identifiable respondents:

D1. This type captures various analytic alternatives, often bordering on idiomatic constructions. We thus find, for adjectives such as the already mentioned It. *insopportabile*, prepositional constructs based on deverbal nouns, such as *k nesnesení, k nevydržení*, lit. 'to not bearing, to not sustaining'.

D2. This type is even more elusive since it represents solutions where there is virtually no translation of the adjective. Indeed, we can sometimes find cases such as the Pt. *uma considerável vantagem* 'a considerable advantage', which is rendered in our corpus simply as *výhody* 'advantages'. We have also decided to include in this group cases where the adjective is translated by way of an adverb derived directly from the adjective. For instance, in It. (...) *il cielo che io e Antonio vediamo come un tappeto buio steso, sui nostri capi, da uomini* **invisibili** – (...) *oblohu, kterou pak já a Antonio vidíme jako nějaký tmavý koberec, který nám někdo* **neviditelně** *rozprostřel nad hlavou*, literally: 'the sky that I and Antonio see as a dark carpet that someone **invisibly** unfolded above our heads', the adjective *invisibile* is quite transparently rendered by the derived adverb corresponding to *invisibilmente* 'invisibly'.

Of course, this decision is especially problematic from a semantic point of view because the modal semantics is clearly maintained. However, morphologically and syntactically we do have a differently constructed respondent. It is clear that such problems arise mainly because we restrict ourselves to short segments, ignoring larger portions of text which can be involved in the translational process. However, since we wish to investigate well-defined typological differences between Romance and Czech, without indulging in translation criticism, we are bound to accept this kind of limitation.

3.3.2 TYPOLOGY OF CZECH RESPONDENTS FOR VERBS WITH THE PREFIX *RE-/RI-*

The typology of Czech respondents for verbs prefixed with *re-/ri-* appears to be less elaborated than that presented for modal adjectives. In fact, we can delimit three well-defined structural correspondences, which, as will be seen, display a wide range of concrete, and sometimes unpredictable, realisations. As above, we also build on a previously presented typology (see Bratánková – Štichauer 2011; Čermák 2013) extending it to French and Portuguese. Here there is the first distinction between types A and B, where the former are analytic solutions, the latter synthetic ones, and a negatively defined type C, where no iteration or repetition is overtly expressed.

TYPE A. This type is represented by analytic constructions where a verb is combined with an adverb overtly expressing repetition, such as *zase, znovu, opět, opětovně* 'again', 'repeatedly'.

TYPE B. This type is defined on the basis of a synthetic solution with two possible realisations. The first is a single verb which already expresses, inherently, some kind of repeated action, e.g. It. *riaprire il caso* 'to reopen the case' – *obnovit případ* 'to renew the case'. The second captures cases where iterativity is expressed not by the verb-modifying adverb, but by a different part of speech, as in It. *riaprire le indagini* 'to reopen the investigation' – *zahájit* **nové** *vyšetřování* 'to initiate a **new** investigation'.

TYPE C. In this type, as already mentioned, no repetition seems to be overtly expressed. There appear to be two reasons for this. First, the opposition between, say, *aprire – riaprire* 'to open – to reopen' is sometimes neutralised or it is covertly expressed by larger contextual information. This is what we particularly find with polysemous verbs where other semantic features are also connected with the prefix re-/ri-.

We now turn to a detailed presentation of the quantitative distribution of the single types discussing some of the peculiar cases. We begin with the suffix -ble/-bile/-vel and, subsequently, we move on to the prefix re-/ri-.

3.4 THE MODAL SUFFIX -BLE/-BILE/-VEL

The Latin suffix -abilis/-ibilis gave rise, in Romance, to various outcomes, such as both -abile and -evole, in Italian, where eventually the only Latinate form -abile prevails and can be said to be the only productive suffix. In Es., Fr. and Pt. we find a similar evolution with -ble and -vel being the forms of interest. In fact, we restrict ourselves, in what follows, to a synchronically active pattern where the prototypical group of formations are adjectives derived from transitive verbs with a clear modal meaning glossed as 'what can/cannot be done'. Nevertheless, we are forced to take into account all kinds of deviations from this core semantics as the range of possible meanings (as well as the type of verbs required for the derivation) is larger. We first briefly characterise the suffix (we follow here, e.g., Grossmann – Rainer 2004, 422–426; Bisetto 2009; Val Álvaro 1981; Grevisse – Goosse 2007, 169–173; Mateus 2003, 945; Pires de Oliveira – Ngoy 2007).

As previously mentioned, the suffix requires transitive verbs with agentive subjects; we thus find the following restrictions on the base verbs:

1) Psychological verbs (whose subject can be broadly defined as *experiencer*) are ruled out, as witnessed by the impossibility to have, for instance, It. *preoccupabile (from preoccupare). This constraint is not absolute as, for example, in French where we do find examples of adjectives also derived from these verbs, such as *affligeable, agaçable, aguichable, attristable* (cf., e.g., Leeman – Meleuc 1990, 33).
2) Stative verbs, especially those where the subject assumes the role of a *possessor*, as can be seen in It. *possedere* → *possedibile, Fr. *posséder* → *possédable.

As for the semantic interpretation, we can also find specific nuances, which go beyond the simple passive potentiality, as in Fr. *souhaitable* 'desirable', It. *pagabile* 'payable' while their meaning is rather deontic, paraphrasable as 'what deserves to be desired', 'what must be paid'. We will discuss further issues relative to formal and semantic aspects below when addressing the corpus data.

3.4.1 DATA ELABORATION AND ANALYSIS

In order to obtain a frequency list of all adjectives with the suffix, we ran a simple tag-based query which had an identical form for all four subcorpora, depending on the exact form of the suffix. We thus have three basic queries:

> Es. + Fr. *[lemma=".*ble" & tag="ADJ.*"]*
> It. *[lemma=".*bile" & tag="ADJ.*"]*
> Pt. *[lemma=".*vel" & tag="ADJ.*"]*

Of course, such a query yields a raw frequency list where all adjectives ending in the sequence in question appear. In a subsequent step, we have therefore proceeded to manually elaborate the frequency lists to weed out some of the particular lemmas, which we will now briefly discuss.

It is possible to delimit four groups of these adjectives, depending on the formal and semantic transparency. Therefore, we define four classes, inspired by Tekavčić (1972, 75–76), where the transparency (referred below as T) is complete, partial or there is none:

1) Group T(1). In this class, we can find exactly what we are interested in: morphologically and semantically transparent adjectives, i.e. formations where the verbal base and the suffix *-ble/-bile/-vel* can be clearly discerned. Morphologically, this group is required to display no allomorphy between the verbal stem and the stem of the derived adjective. We thus have pairs like It. *leggere – leggibile* 'to read – readable'. Semantically, the semantics of the adjective must satisfy, in a reproducible way, the potential reading (regardless of possible contextual nuances) glossed as 'what can/cannot be done'.

2) Group partial-T(2). This group comprises adjectives, which are semantically compositional in the same way as those in group T(1), but formally they display a kind of allomorphy, as is found in pairs such as Es. *ver – visible* 'to see – visible'. Of importance here is not only the straightforward semantic relationship between the base verb and the derived adjective but also the systematic formal relationship in that the allomorphy in question is not confined to just one pair but is found across a wide range of patterns (this requirement comes close to what Corbin 1987, 342 called *allomorphic projection*).

3) Group partial-T(3). In this group, there is also semantic transparency in that this class of adjectives show the basic modal meaning defined above although what is crucially lacking is the morphological motivation. We find what we could call *baseless formations*, i.e. adjectives that lack a verbal base altogether. This is the case, for example, of the adjective Es. *vulnerable* (along with the other Romance respondents), which may be linked to the verb *herir* (It. *ferire*, Fr. *blesser*). These adjectives are direct loanwords from Latin.

4) Group non-T(4). This negatively defined group comprises adjectives which, synchronically, do not display any semantic and morphological transparency. They lack a verbal base and do not satisfy the general meaning instruction. Examples, also current in English, which typically illustrate this group are *probable, possible,* etc.

It is clear that, as mentioned above, class T(1) comprises those adjectives that we are interested in. However, it would be too hasty to immediately rule out the other three classes away as the semantic transparency in class T(3) and the morphological transparency in class T(2) might be a relevant factor. Therefore, we have weeded out the adjectives in class T(4) while selectively maintaining some of those pertaining to classes T(2) and T(3). Unsurprisingly, these formations are some of the most frequent adjectives. Their elimination, which in type frequency is not so relevant, affects the overall token frequency in that they represent between 40–50% of all the tokens. We now briefly describe these adjectives for all four languages under investigation.

First, it needs to be said that in order to identify and discuss the typology presented above, we set up, as in the other case studies present in this book, a frequency limit of 10 (or 11, depending on the size of the four subcorpora) tokens. Such a limit is comprehensible as we are interested in recurrent translational patterns, and not in nonce-formations (although these are, of course, extremely important for other aspects such as productivity). As a result, there are four datasets for Es., It., Fr. and Pt.

For Spanish, which is quantitatively far more represented than the other languages, we obtained a raw frequency list of 197 adjectives with the overall token frequency equal to 16,362. The elimination of 70 adjectives pertaining to classes T(4) and partly to T(2) and T(3) produces a reduced list of 122 adjectives with the token frequency equal to 7,959. Examples of the eliminated adjectives – almost identical for all languages under scrutiny – are *posible, estable, irresponsable, temible* etc. (for the complete list, see Čermák – Nádvorníková et al. 2015, 110–111).

For Italian, we had a significantly smaller dataset with 50 adjectives each having more than 11 tokens with the overall token frequency equal to 1791. Eliminating 23 adjectives of the classes T(4) and, partly, T(2), T(3), we arrived at the list of 27 adjectives with the overall frequency equal to 622 (again, for details, see Čermák – Nádvorníková et al. 2015, 98–99).

In the French dataset, the situation is much the same with a raw list including 76 adjectives (each again with the frequency of 11 and more tokens), with the overall frequency of 2,978. Elimination of 52 formations (such as *invraisemblable, impassible, implacable, pitoyable* etc., see Čermák – Nádvorníková et al. 2015, 140–141) yields a list of 24 adjectives whose overall token frequency equals 587.

Finally, Portuguese represents the smallest dataset with 44 adjectives each having more than 10 tokens with the overall token frequency of 1,478. Again, the elimination of the undesired formations yields a list comprising 17 adjectives with the overall frequency equal to only 342 tokens (see Čermák – Nádvorníková et al. 2015, 124).

The summary of all four datasets is given in **Table 3.1**.

Tab. 3.1. Frequency data for adjectives with the suffix -ble/-bile/-vel

Language	Type frequency	Overall token frequency
Spanish	122	7,959
Italian	27	622
French	24	587
Portuguese	17	342

As is clear from this direct comparison, the only quantitatively valuable dataset is that of Spanish, which is due, as for the other phenomena investigated in this book, to the larger size of the Spanish-Czech parallel corpus. Taking into account this serious limitation, which will be overcome in the future enlargement of the Italian, French and Portuguese subcorpora, we can nevertheless present the quantitative distribution of the types defined above.

3.4.2 QUANTITATIVE DISTRIBUTION OF THE TYPES

Beginning with the absolute figures, which are not particularly telling since they do not allow for direct comparison, we summarise the results in **Table 3.2**:

Tab. 3.2. Distribution of types for adjectives with the suffix -ble/-bile/-vel in the four subcorpora – absolute frequencies

Language	Frequency	A	B	C1	C2	C3	D1	D2
Spanish	7,959	4,116	2,575	120	114	249	108	677
Italian	622	370	86	11	29	39	30	56
French	587	392	76	4	3	16	27	69
Portuguese	342	141	127	16	29	8	4	17

While acknowledging that the figures, especially for French and Portuguese, are so low, mainly because we have restricted ourselves to only those adjectives that reach the minimum of 10 or 11 tokens, we still have to acknowledge the basic difficulty when directly comparing these results. A better overview is obviously provided by relative frequencies. In **Table 3.3** is the percentual distribution of the types according to the above-defined typology.

Overall, the relative frequencies, though they must be taken with extreme caution, clearly show as a predominant solution type A, where the direct correspondence between the adjective with -ble/-bile/-vel and the Czech respondent with the suffix -telný is maintained. Indeed, more than half of the identified respondents belong to type A. The second more frequent type is B, where, as defined above, we still find an adjective,

Tab. 3.3. *Distribution of types for adjectives with the suffix* -ble/-bile/-vel *in the four subcorpora – relative frequencies (%)*

Language	%	A	B	C1	C2	C3	D1	D2
Spanish	100	52	32	2	1	3	1	9
Italian	100	60	14	1	5	6	5	9
French	100	67	13	1	1	3	5	12
Portuguese	100	42	37	5	8	2	1	5

but with a different suffix and with a slightly different semantic instruction. What is quite striking is that the syntactic solution of type C, further differentiated in three subtypes, is by far the least exploited respondent. On the contrary, the residual type D, with especially high figures for D2, represents an interesting, albeit a hardly generalisable, group of individual solutions, to which we will turn below. But before doing so, a mention is required of the important correlation between the typology and the four classes T(1), partial-T(2)/T(3), and non-T(4).

Indeed, there appears to be a strong correlation between the type and the adjectival class defined in terms of total, partial or null transparency. It is perhaps not a surprising fact that adjectives of class T(1), i.e. those entirely transparent and compositional, cover almost 90% of the type-A respondents while those belonging to class partial-T(2), cover only 25% of the type-A respondents. Conversely, adjectives of the class partial-T(3), i.e. those where the semantic instruction is maintained but the verb base is entirely lacking, tend to be translated by the respondents defined as type-B. This correlation can safely be demonstrated for the Spanish dataset, not just because we have a large amount of data, but in the case of the other languages, this dependency turns out to be less significant. Therefore, we do not dwell on the details. Instead, we move on to the discussion of concrete examples, especially those deserving particular attention.

3.4.3 DISCUSSION OF VARIOUS EXAMPLES

As we have already seen, in the majority of cases (between 42% and 67% of all the tokens, depending on the dataset), there is the hypothesised correspondence between the suffix -ble/-bile/-vel and the Czech suffix -telný. Thus, we find a wide range of examples where adjectives, such as Es. *invisible* 'invisible' (along with the other Romance respondents), *increíble* 'incredible' or *insoportable* 'unbearable' match the Czech adjectives *neviditelný* 'invisible', *neuvěřitelný* 'incredible' or *nesnesitelný* 'unbearable'. This is probably an uninteresting situation and it is worth exploring the marginal respondents of the other types.

We mostly leave aside type B, since in this case, we have a synonymous adjective where not only the modality is coded in a less explicit way, but the choice of the adjective appears to be entirely unpredictable, as shown in example (1).

(1) Pt.
Tenho uma pessoa **respeitável**, com bom paladar, muito escrupulosa em contas.
→ Mám **spořádanou** osobu, chutně vaří a je pečlivá v účtech.
Literally: *I have an **orderly** person*.
Eça de Queiroz, *Bratranec Basilio* (*O Primo Basílio*), transl. Zdeněk Hampl, Prague: Odeon, 1989.

We pay some attention to the type-C respondents, simply because these require a kind of lexical transformation in that the adjective is translated by way of a syntactic construction. For instance, adjectives such as It. *riconoscibile* 'recognisable' are rendered here by way of *byl k poznání* (lit. 'he was to recognising'), *dal se poznat*, which is a reflexive form of causative construction 'he made himself recognise'. A similar, C1-type solution can be seen in example (2).

(2) Fr.
Deux, que vous restiez absolument **invisible**. → Zadruhé: aby vás **nebylo** vůbec nikde **vidět**.
Literally: *so that it **won't be possible to see** you*.
Michel Tournier, *Tetřev hlušec* (*Le Coq de bruyère*), transl. Václav Jamek, Prague: Odeon, 1984.

Within type D, which is a heterogeneous group with hardly classifiable respondents (see Čermák – Nádvorníková et al. 2015, 118 for some examples from Spanish), we have identified at least two recurrent situations worth discussing. The first, D1, corresponds to a solution where some nominal, often deverbal, construction appears, sometimes bordering on idiomatic phrases, as in example (3):

(3) Es.
Después Rosario me secó, se secó, arregló el cuarto en un santiamén (es **increíble** lo hacendosa y práctica que es esta mujer) y se puso a dormir pues al día siguiente tenía que trabajar. → Pak mě Rosario utřela, sebe taky utřela, v cukuletu uklidila pokoj (je **k nevíře**, jak je přičinlivá a praktická) a šla spát, protože další den musí pracovat.
Literally: *it is to **not-belief***.
Roberto Bolaño, *Divocí detektivové* (*Los detectives salvajes*), transl. Anežka Charvátová, Prague: Argo, 2009.

The second, type D2, comprises cases where the meaning inherent in the suffixed adjective is coded by way of a completely different construction. A case in point is example (4):

(4) It.

Poi incominciarono a muoversi in modo **visibile** anche Mecenate e Virgilio; (...).
→ Pak **jsem uviděl**, že se začali hýbat i Maecenas a Vergilius; (...).
Literally: *I saw that they started moving.*
Sebastiano Vassalli, *Nespočet* (*Infinito numero*), transl. Kateřina Vinšová, Prague: Paseka, 2003.

This example, which is not infrequent within the D-type respondents, involves an interesting overhaul of the original text. In Italian, we have an adjective-based sequence *they started to move in a visible way*, and the "visibility" meaning is taken over by the verb-based construction with *see*. A similar example is in (5), where again, the "visibility" meaning is expressed by the negative form of the verb *escape*:

(5) Pt.

A mudança de tom, **visível** na forma como dissera a última frase, não escapou a Luís Bernardo. → Luísi Bernardovi **neunikla** změna tónu v poslední větě.
Literally: *to Luís Bernard **did not escape** the change of tone.*
Miguel Sousa Tavares, *Rovník* (*Equador*), transl. Lada Weissová, Prague: Garamond, 2006.

Finally, as hinted at above, we also classify within the D2 types those respondents where the adjective with the suffix *-ble/-bile/-vel* is translated into Czech by way of a directly derived adverb, in which the modal meaning is clearly maintained, as can be seen in examples (6) and (7).

(6) It.

Ma il cuore di colui, frattanto, s'involava **irresistibile** verso Bella, (...). → Chlapcovo srdce se však **nezadržitelně** rozběhlo k Belle (...).
Literally: *irresistibly.*
Elsa Morante, *Příběh v historii* (*La storia*), transl. Zdeněk Frýbort, Prague: Odeon, 1990.

(7) Es.

Ante la necesidad de consolarme Paulina del Valle cambió **de manera imperceptible** para todos, menos para Frederick Williams. → Paulina del Valle se tím, jak mě musela utěšovat, změnila – i když tak **nepostižitelně**, že si toho všiml jen Frederik Williams.
Literally: *imperceptibly.*
Isabel Allende, *Sépiový portrét* (*Retrato en sepia*), transl. Monika Baďurová, Prague: BB Art, 2003.

These examples are of interest because they show the limits of the proposed typology. If we insist on the part-of-speech correspondence, we are bound to rule out these respondents from the A-type group. However, the formal and semantic correspondence is so strong that it might be more reasonable to split the A-type into an A1, the adjectival type, and an A2-type, the adverbial type. Such a modification of the typology would lead to a slightly different quantitative distribution, leaving in the D-type group only those respondents that resist straightforward classification.

3.5 THE ITERATIVE PREFIX *RE-/RI-*

In the four Romance languages under investigation, we find the prefix *re-/ri-* whose major semantic instruction, as mentioned above, is a broadly defined *iterativity*, i.e. repetition of the action, activity expressed by the base verb. It is widely held that this general meaning of repetition also assumes different semantic realisations, some of them contextually induced rather than inherently present in the prefix itself. There appears to be an agreement in the literature that these semantic specifications can be as follows (cf. for Es. Martín García 1998, 45–51, Varela – Martín García 1999, 5012–5013; for It. Grossmann – Rainer 2004, 155; for Fr. Grevisse – Goosse 2007, 186; Jalenques 2002, 84–87; Mok 1964, 106–109; for Pt. Vilela 1994, 117; Cunha – Cintra 1999, 88; Said Ali 2001, 188; Bechara 2009, 367):

1) Simple iterativity (i.e. a single, repeated instance of an action), e.g. Es. *abrir – reabrir* 'to open – to reopen'.
2) Reversibility (i.e. a return to a preceding state of affairs), e.g. Pt. *construir → reconstruir* 'to construct – to reconstruct'.
3) Movement in the opposite direction, e.g. Pt. *fluir → refluir* 'to flow – to reflow'.
4) Reciprocity, e.g. It. *abbracciare → riabbracciare* 'to embrace – to reembrace'.
5) Intensification (i.e. those cases where there appears to be no repetition of the action, just a reinforcing connotation), e.g. Fr. *doubler – redoubler* 'to double – to redouble'.

While we maintain that some of these semantic nuances are rather context-induced (for example, *to reembrace* can, in fact, be a repeated action by one and the same person and not just the reciprocal action of the other person), we view the semantic feature of intensification as something that often coexists with the basic meaning of iteration. These polysemous verbs tend to be quite frequent so it is important to keep the two meanings apart (as far as possible).

3.5.1 DATA ELABORATION AND ANALYSIS

As in the case of the adjectives with the suffix *-ble/-bile/-vel*, we ran a series of combined regular and tag-based queries, which had a similar form for all four subcorpora, depending on the exact form of the suffix and on the tagset. In its basic form, the query had the following shape *[lemma="re.*" & tag="V.*"]* with obvious modifications according to the language in question. Of course, as above, we obtained raw frequency lists from which much extraction noise was to be eliminated. In particular, we weeded out the following two types of formations:

1) Various forms containing the sequence *re-/ri-* that cannot be said to be a verbal prefix.
2) Verbs which are not synchronically segmentable in such a way that a verbal base and a prefix can be clearly discerned. This is obviously the case of verbs such as Es. *recordar* (cf. **cordar*) 'to remind', It. *ricevere* (cf. **cevere*) 'to receive' etc.

Conversely, all verbs that are also polysemous and display an intensifying meaning have been maintained as they can all assume, in a particular context, an iterative interpretation. However, it is clear that these verbs reach high frequencies where the simple iterative meaning represents a marginal case. This is the reason why, as we shall see, type C is by far the most frequent respondent.

Once the frequency lists have been elaborated in this way, we obtained the following datasets summarised in **Table 3.4**.

Tab. 3.4. Frequency data for verbs with the prefix re-/ri-

Language	Type frequency	Overall token frequency
Spanish	69	7,287
Italian	56	3,526
French	84	7,099
Portuguese	34	1,037

It must be noted that, as in the preceding case, these figures include only those verbs whose token frequency is equal or higher than 10 tokens. Moreover, we should also note an apparently unexpected high type and token frequency of the French prefixed verbs despite the smaller size of the corpus. Although we would need to be reassured about this fact independently (on the basis of comparable frequency lists), we can say that French typically displays a large amount of such prefixed verbs, which thus seem to be particularly productive.

3.5.2 QUANTITATIVE DISTRIBUTION OF THE TYPES

Table 3.5 shows the absolute figures which, as above, are misleading in that they do not take into account the different sizes of the four subcorpora.

Tab. 3.5. *The distribution of types for verbs with the prefix re-/ri- in the four subcorpora – absolute frequencies*

Language	Frequency	A	B	C
Spanish	7,287	881	2,983	3,423
Italian	3,526	475	640	2,411
French	7,099	1,178	1,431	4,490
Portuguese	1,037	202	98	737

Moving on to the relative frequencies, summarised in **Table 3.6**, we can see that although the clearly dominant type is the C-respondent, where no overt iterativity is explicitly expressed, a less evident situation is in the interplay between the A and B types.

Tab. 3.6. *The distribution of types for verbs with the prefix re-/ri- in the four subcorpora – relative frequencies (%)*

Language	Frequency	A	B	C
Spanish	100%	12	41	47
Italian	100%	14	18	68
French	100%	17	20	63
Portuguese	100%	19	10	71

In fact, Spanish – which is, due to the corpus size, the most reliable dataset – displays a distribution where the analytic expression of repetition by way of an extra adverb turns out to be the least exploited. The B-type, where iterativity is inherently coded in the selected verb (or otherwise within the clause), reaches the same frequency as the previously mentioned C-type respondent. This situation, where direct comparison appears difficult, also arises because some verbs that would be clearly iterative in one Romance language are less so in the other languages. A case in point is It. *riuscire*, which has the dominant, lexicalised meaning 'to succeed' but is susceptible to be also used in the iterative meaning 'to go out again'. The same case can be made for *riguardare* 'to concern, to regard' or 'to look up again'. It is now obvious that the inclusion or exclusion of such verbs affects the frequencies in a sensible way (see the lists of verbs included for each language in Čermák – Nádvorníková 2015 et al., 94–95, 104–106, 121, 132–134). We now consider various examples.

3.5.3 DISCUSSION OF VARIOUS EXAMPLES

We begin with the type-A respondents. As defined above, we view this type as an overt analytic solution that combines the base verb with an adverb carrying the iterative meaning, such as *znovu, opět, zase* etc. Examples (8) and (9) illustrate this.

(8) Es.
Jacob **había replegado** el cuerpo. → <u>Jacob **znovu složil** své tělo na zem</u>.
Literally: *Jacob has **reposed again** his body on the ground*.
Juan Carlos Onetti, *Bezejmenný hrob a jiné příběhy* (*Para una tumba sin nombre*), transl. Hedvika Vydrová, Prague: Mladá fronta, 1987.

(9) It.
Il giudice si solleva dai cuscini, mette giù le gambe dal letto, **rilegge** per bene il foglio. → Soudce se zvedne z polštářů, sundá nohy z postele, **přečte si znovu** a důkladně <u>ten lísteček</u>.
Literally: *he carefully **reads again** that sheet of paper*.
Alessandro Baricco, *City* (*City*), transl. Alice Flemrová, Prague: Volvox Globator, 2000.

We also find a wide range of examples where there is one of the above-mentioned semantic concretisations, such as the movement in the opposite direction, as example (10) shows:

(10) It.
Non era san Macario quello che viveva su una colonna e, quando i vermi gli cadevano di dosso, li raccoglieva e se li **rimetteva** sul corpo perché anch'essi, creature di Dio, avessero il loro festino? → Nežil snad svatý Makarius na sloupu a nesbíral červy, kteří z něho padali, **nevkládal je zpátky** do ran, že jsou to boží stvoření a chtějí se taky nějak nasytit?
Literally: *he **inserted back** into the wounds*.
Umberto Eco, *Foucaultovo kyvadlo* (*Il pendolo di Foucault*), transl. Zdeněk Frýbort, Prague: Český klub, 2001.

A clear example of a B-type respondent, where iterativity is inherently included in the meaning of the verb, can be seen in example (11):

(11) Fr.
Quant à notre ami, il **redescendit** vers Jonathan Absalon Varlet qui, en le voyant revenir, s'écria (...). → <u>Náš přítel **se vrátil** dolů k</u> Jonatánu Absolónu Barletovi, který jakmile ho uviděl, vykřikl (...).
Literally: *our friend **returned** down to*.
Frédéric Tristan, *Hrdinné útrapy Baltazara Kobera* (*Les Tribulations héroïques de Balthasar Kober*), transl. Oldřich Kalfiřt, Prague: DharmaGaia – Dauphin, 2003.

However, within the type-B we can also find solutions that are hardly predictable especially in those cases where iterativity is expressed outside the verbal domain and is instead coded by way of a different construction, as can be seen in the interesting example (12):

(12) It.
Dovette essere per lui una tale ossessione, dipingere il niente che, **riletti** a posteriori, tutti i suoi ultimi trent'anni di vita ne sembrano posseduti come interamente assorbiti. → Musela to pro něj být taková obsese, namalovat nic, že **ze zpětného pohledu** se těch posledních třicet let jeho života tím zdá být posedlých – jakoby zcela pohlcených.
Literally: ***from a retrospective look***.
Alessandro Baricco, *City* (*City*), transl. Alice Flemrová, Prague: Volvox Globator, 2000.

Finally, within the C-type respondents, we find virtually no iterativity. This is because the verb in question is either polysemous, with, for instance, an intensifying connotation, or entirely lexicalised with a specific meaning, as can be seen in example (13) from Portuguese (although analogical examples could easily be found in the other languages under investigation):

(13) Pt.
Remetia as cartas a Jorge, ou entregava-lhas ela mesma, no portal! → Dopisy Jorgovi **pošle**, nebo mu je sama u dveří odevzdá?
Literally: *will she **send** the letters to Jorge*.
Eça de Queiroz, *Bratranec Basilio* (*O Primo Basílio*), transl. Zdeněk Hampl, Prague: Odeon, 1989.

3.6 CONCLUDING REMARKS

In the opening of this chapter, we put forward two questions regarding two opposing extremes of correspondence between Romance and Czech at the level of word-formation processes. On the one hand, we have formulated a view according to which having two analogical, structurally identical word-formation means could be reflected in a systematic translational strategy. On the other hand, we have also pointed out that where there is no such morphological isomorphy, there still might be a quantifiable tendency towards coding the morphological meaning in a predictable way.

In the first instance, we have dealt with the adjectives derived by the suffix *-ble/ -bile/-vel*, which carries a clear modal semantic instruction, defined by Plag (2003, 94) as "potential non-volitional participation in an event". Czech also possesses such a suffix with a wide range of derived adjectives that look like direct correspondences of their Romance respondents. We have demonstrated that this correspondence is indeed reflected in the overwhelming dominance of the type-A respondents (67% for French, 60% for Italian, 52% and 42% for Spanish and Portuguese, respectively). The second most numerous type, the B-group, represents those respondents that maintain the part-of-speech correspondence while carrying the modal meaning in a less explicit way. Interestingly, a syntactically coded modal meaning, defined within the C-typed respondents turned out to be the least exploited solution.

The quantitative analysis also revealed some shortcomings of the proposed typology. In particular, adverbs in -telně directly derived from such modal adjectives, have been lumped together with the residual group of D-typed respondents. This is undoubtedly a problematic move as discussed above. In fact, splitting the type A into two sub-types would have captured the strong semantic link in a more natural way.

We have also touched upon the interesting correlation between the typology of the Czech respondents and the group of adjectives, defined on the basis of their semantic and morphological transparency. For the Spanish data, which is clearly the most reliable dataset given the corpus size, we have demonstrated a direct correlation between the most transparent group T1 and the type-A translational respondents.

In the second instance, we addressed the iterative prefix re-/ri-, which lacks a direct analogical counterpart in Czech. We have defined three major types that might be viewed as too coarse-grained but turned out to be sufficient for the purpose of our study. These types capture three possible situations. First, the iterativity inherent in the prefix re-/ri- is explicitly coded by way of an adverb; second, the prefixed verb is translated by verbal respondents where iterativity is already – inherently or contextually – expressed; and third, the iterativity is not overtly expressed at all. Since this last type turned out to be the most frequent, a mention of this result is required. First, it is important to say that most verbs with the prefix re-/ri- that reach high frequencies and thus entered our lists are, in the overwhelming majority of cases, polysemous verbs with various intensifying nuances where the iterative meaning is confined to a couple of tokens. Second, when comparing the figures, one immediately notes too large a distance between the four languages under scrutiny. This is caused not only by the different behaviour of such verbs in one or the other language (a case in point is French where there is a large number of prefixed verbs with re-) but also by the classificatory difficulties. In fact, it is sometimes hard to tell whether the iterativity is present or not on the basis of a single segment. Therefore, it is important to take into account larger portions of text and also evaluate the contextual factors. Note that a similar inherent or contextually dependent presence of the analysed semantic notion in the Czech respondents is also observed by Čermák – Kratochvílová et al. (this volume) and Kratochvílová – Jindrová et al. (this volume).

We believe that despite all the difficulties that we have canvassed here, parallel-corpus based studies of word-formation processes might be a viable and promising area of research.

4. CAUSATIVE CONSTRUCTIONS IN ROMANCE AND THEIR CZECH RESPONDENTS

PETR ČERMÁK
DANA KRATOCHVÍLOVÁ
PETRA LAUFKOVÁ
PAVEL ŠTICHAUER

4.0 INTRODUCTION

This chapter focuses on the Romance construction *hacer/fare/faire/fazer* + infinitive, which is generally considered to represent the main tool for expressing causativity in Spanish, Italian, French and Portuguese. We consider causativity to be a universal category that can be found in languages across the whole world, despite the fact that its formal manifestations differ. The aim of this chapter is to compare this category in Romance and Czech. Using the parallel corpus InterCorp, we analyse all possible respondents of the *hacer/fare/faire/fazer* + infinitive construction, thus creating a typology of possible Czech expressions of causativity. Given the fact that Czech does not possess any direct counterpart for the Romance causatives and considering the inherently fusional character of this language (see Nádvorníková this volume), we move toward verifying whether Czech respondents of the analytic Romance construction will be predominantly fusional and whether it is possible to state that Czech causative prefixes are the best translation candidates for *hacer/fare/faire/fazer* + infinitive.

The chapter is organised as follows. In **Section 4.1**, we present a general definition of causativity. **Section 4.2** briefly resumes the main topics in causativity related to Romance languages. In **Sections 4.3** and **4.4**, we provide a detailed description of the expression of causativity in the Czech language. **Sections 4.5, 4.6** and **4.7** constitute the core of this chapter, presenting the results of the corpus analysis. **Section 4.8** presents the general conclusions regarding causativity in Romance and in Czech.

4.1 DEFINITION OF CAUSATIVITY AND ITS FORMS OF EXPRESSION

Following Comrie (1989), the construction we are interested in can be conceived as one of the main expressions of a very extensive category of causativity.[23] We understand

---

23 "We are concerned with various linguistic expressions of causation, and as a useful starting point is a characterization of the causative situation (event) as a whole. Any causative situation involves two component situations, the cause and its effect (result)" (Comrie 1989, 165).

causative constructions as grammatical means that describe the following situation: *the causer causes or initiates something that forces the causee to do something or to find himself in a state induced by the causer.*[24] This relationship between the causer and causee can have several formal manifestations. Comrie postulates three general types of causative expressions: analytic causatives, morphological causatives and lexical causatives, observing that "although, as with many typological distinctions, forms in languages do not always fit neatly into one or other of these three types, rather a number of intermediate types are found. The continuum as a whole ranges from analytic causatives through morphological causatives to lexical causatives" (Comrie 1989, 166–167).[25]

The analytic type is defined by the existence of "separate predicates expressing the notion of causation and the predicate of the effect, as in English examples like *I caused John to go*, or *I brought it about that John went…*" (Comrie 1989, 167). Morphological causativity is defined by a productive usage of affixes that express this notion. Finally, with lexical causatives "the relation between the expression of effect and the expression of causative macro-situation is so unsystematic as to be handled lexically, rather than by any productive process (*kill – die*)" (Comrie 1989, 168).

While this formal typology has been generally accepted in linguistics (see Kemmer – Verhagen 1994 and others), semantic and syntactic characteristics of the above-mentioned types have been widely discussed in current linguistics (see Kemmer – Verhagen 1994; Alsina 1992; Dixon 2000 and others). Throughout this chapter, we will discuss the general characteristics of Czech causativity with reference to the clearly analytic Romance type, postulating various questions regarding the very definition of this category, or rather the (im)possibility to identify it with the *hacer/fare/faire/fazer* + infinitive construction. When analysing the rather heterogeneous category of causativity in Czech, we will adopt Comrie's approach that permits us to analyse different kinds of causative expressions in terms of the gradual transition from the most fusional to the most analytic type.[26]

As previously mentioned, the result causativity is that the causee does something or finds himself in a certain kind of state. As we will discuss later, both Czech and Romance languages use different means for expressing these two situations. F. Čermák (2001, 253, 257) distinguishes *factitives* such as *usušit* 'to cause that X is dry' (i.e. the result is that the causee is in a certain state) and *causatives* such as *rozplakat* 'to cause that X is crying' (i.e. the result of the causer's activity is that the causee is doing something). Nevertheless, this differentiation is infrequent and most approaches do not make any distinction between these two terms (see Lázaro Carreter 1953, 72; Hernanz

---

24 Shibatani (1976) uses the terms 'causing event' and 'caused event'.
25 Although see the term 'causative continuum' in Shibatani – Pardeshi (2002a).
26 Thus, our aim has not been to explore the semantics of the relationship between forces constituting causativity, as we can see in Talmy (2000) and his successors (e.g., Soares Silva 2004). As is well known, Talmy considers force dynamics a semantic category, which has an important role in the language structure: "It is, first of all, a generalization over the traditional linguistic notion of 'causative': it analyzes 'causing' into finer primitives and sets it naturally within a framework that also includes 'letting', 'hindering', 'helping', and still further notions not normally considered in the same context" (409).

1999, 2247; Skytte – Salvi 2001, Salvi – Vanelli 2004). As has also been proven by our corpus analysis, the borderline between activity and state is sometimes unclear (the state being the result of previous activity, i.e., *zabít* 'to kill' means both 'to cause that somebody died' and 'to cause that somebody is dead').[27]

4.2 CAUSATIVITY IN ROMANCE LANGUAGES

Following Comrie's (1986) typology, systemic expressions of causativity in Romance languages can be divided into two large groups: analytic type (see **Section 4.2.1**) and synthetic type (see **Section 4.2.2**).

4.2.1 ANALYTIC TYPE

The analytic expression of causativity in all the Romance languages studied is primarily represented by a construction that combines a verb meaning 'to do', 'to make' (*hacer/ fare/faire/fazer*) and the infinitive. This construction does not display any significant syntactic or stylistic limitations and will be analysed in the following sections. Its formal and semantic properties are comparable to the English construction 'make sb do sth': *María me ha hecho reír / Maria mi ha fatto ridere / Marie m'a fait rire / A Maria fiz-me rir* = 'Mary made me laugh'.

When analysing the *hacer/fare/faire/fazer* + infinitive construction, we will refer to, for the sake of simplicity, the Romance causative construction, even though we are well aware that this generalisation is somewhat inadequate since we leave aside other Romance languages, especially Romanian, where causative constructions behave differently from the syntactic point of view and are construed with the subjunctive, see Pîrvu (2010) and Ciutescu (2013).

Apart from this clearly dominating structure, we can find other analytic expressions of causativity in the Romance languages. The usual form is a personal verbal form + infinitive, the most frequent being verbs corresponding to the English 'to let' (*dejar/lasciare/laisser/deixar*), which can combine with an infinitival completion and collaborate on the expression of causativity. In this construction, the causative meaning combines with other notions (especially the notion of 'permission'). The grade of causativity of this construction has been explored in numerous studies (see Hernanz 1999, 2258–2265; Grevisse – Goosse 2008, 987; Riegel – Pellat – Rioul 2008, 254 and 443; Gonçalves – Duarte 2001, 660; Enghels – Roegiest 2012 and 2013). Analyses originating in Talmy's force dynamics (Talmy 1985, 1988 and 2000) appear, along with others, in Soares da Silva (1998, 2001, 2004). As our main concern is the Czech respon-

---

27 In this study, we explore cases with the meaning 'to cause that somebody is doing something' only because the studied Romance construction does not have a factitive meaning.

dents of the Romance construction *hacer/fare/faire/fazer* + infinitive, constructions corresponding to the English 'let/have sb do smth' are not discussed here.

The expression of the causee's state (as a result of causer influence, see **Section 4.1**) can also be expressed by a semi-copulative verb followed by an adjective:

> Es. *Una máscara **me hacía invisible***. ('A mask made me invisible.')
> It. *Questo mi **rende nervoso***. ('This makes me nervous.')
> Fr. *Il me **rend fou***. ('He drives me crazy.')
> Pt. *O teu sorriso **faz-me feliz***. ('Your smile makes me happy.')

4.2.2 SYNTHETIC TYPE

Word-formatting processes creating causative verbs are rather limited in all studied languages. Causation resulting in the causee's state can be expressed by deadjectival verbs such as:

> Es. *triste* ('sad') > *entristecer* ('to make someone sad', 'to become sad')
> It. *pazzo* ('crazy') > *impazzire* ('to become crazy', 'to make someone crazy')
> Pt. *velho* ('old') > *envelhecer* ('to become old').

Nevertheless, in Romance languages (and also in Czech) the most frequent synthetic expression of causativity are unanimously *semantic verbs*, i.e. verbs that do not express causativity through morphological means (affixes):

> Es. *derribar* ('to push down')
> It. *uccidere* ('to kill')
> Fr. *abattre* ('to tear down')
> Pt. *tombar* ('to knock down').

This numerous group is formally very heterogeneous and its analysis in Romance languages will not be presented in this study.

4.2.3 CHARACTERISTICS OF THE ROMANCE CONSTRUCTION HACER/FARE/FAIRE/FAZER + INFINITIVE

Romance causative constructions have been widely studied from different perspectives, the most important ones being:

1) Syntactic features:
   - The definition, eventually the comparison with other infinitive constructions (Cano Aguilar 1977; Zubizarreta 1985; Hernanz 1999, 2247; Maldonado 2007;

Skytte – Salvi 2001, 499–509; Riegel – Pellat – Rioul 2008, 353; Arrais 1985; Soares da Silva 2005; Lopes – de Menezes 2018, Vesterinen 2012).

- The contrast between causative constructions with the infinitive and with finite verb: Es. *Sus palabras me hacen pensar* ('Their words make me think.') / *Sus palabras hacen que piense* (literally: 'Their words make that I am thinking'); (Dowling 1981; Vesterinen 2008a, 2008b).
- For Portuguese, the use of the personal (inflected) infinitive is also a topic (Cunha – Cintra 1987; Bechara 2009, 754; Araújo 2012, 11).
- Syntactic restrictions of causative constructions (Delbecque – Lamiroy 1999, 2012–2013; Riegel – Pellat – Rioul 2008, 231; Labelle 2017; Hu, 2018).
- Use of clitics and reflexive pronouns (Fernández Ordóñez 1999, 1326–1327; Hernanz 1999, 2249; Riegel – Pellat – Rioul 2008, 255; Wilmet 1997, 464; Grevisse – Goosse 2008, 1002; Gonçalves – Duarte 2001, 659; Araújo 2012, 11–14).

2) Semantic features (Campos 1999, 1534; Grevisse – Goosse 2008, 1047; Riegel – Pellat – Rioul 2008, 255 and 442; Vecchiato 2003).

3) Diachronic analyses (Davies 1995; Simone – Cerbasi 2001; Robustelli 2000).

4) Comparison with other languages (Katelhoen 2011; Gilquin 2015 and 2017; Heidinger 2015; Chen 2015).

We shall not discuss formal syntactic characteristics of the analysed constructions; the main concern is the comparison with Czech. Our approach to analysing causativity is the closest to Enghels – Roegiest (2012) and Enghels – Roegiest (2013), who also work with corpus data and compare several languages. However, from the point of view of content, their studies do not overlap with ours since their main concern is the causativity expressed through verbs *dejar* and *laisser*.

4.3 CAUSATIVITY IN CZECH

In Czech linguistics, causativity has been analysed within the framework of the broader category of semantic relationships that can be found in a sentence (see Daneš – Hlavsa 1981). This category is generally understood as a verbal one (Komárek – Kořenský et al. 1986; Čechová et al. 1996; Čermák 2001; Štícha et al. 2013), and while there have been attempts to approach it as an abstract and wide theoretical notion (see Štícha 1981), the attention has mostly been focused on its concrete formal expressions, i.e. causative verbs. The defining characteristics of Czech causative verbs can be resumed as 'to cause something to happen or someone to do something' (Karlík – Nekula – Pleskalová 2002, 413), thus corresponding to the basic characteristics of the *hacer/fare/faire/fazer* + infinitive construction.

While for the Romance languages it is relatively easy to postulate one dominant systemic expression of causativity, the formal organisation of this category in Czech is more dispersed and comprises all three of Comrie's types. Following the typology presented in Karlík – Nekula – Pleskalová (2002, 412–413), we can distinguish three large categories of causative expressions that are encoded in Czech:

1) Synthetic causativity – word-formatting causativity
2) Synthetic causativity – semantic causativity
3) Analytic causativity

A substantial feature of the majority of synthetic verbal causatives (i.e. types 1 and 2) is the incidence of pairs being made up of a non-reflexive, transitive, causative variant and a reflexive, intransitive and non-causative variant:

(1)

Pavel	*rozesmál*		*Marii.*
Paul	make.laugh-PST.3SG.NREFL		Mary-ACC

'Paul made Mary laugh.'

(2)

Marie	*se*	*rozesmála.*
Mary	REFL-ACC	start.laughing-PST.3SG

'Mary started to laugh.'

(3)

Pavel	*otočil*		*klíčem.*
Paul	turn.around-PST.3SG.NREFL		key-INS

'Paul turned the key around.'

(4)

Pavel	*se*	*otočil.*
Paul	REFL-ACC	turn.around-PST.3SG

'Paul turned around.'

The crucial fact is that the intransitive form is not conceived as causative, i.e. *rozesmát se* is not conceived as 'to make oneself laugh'.[28]

4.3.1 WORD-FORMATTING CAUSATIVITY

This causative type is derived by the affixes of non-causative verbs; the semantic feature of causativity is thus manifested in the morphological structure of the verb (see Comrie's 1986 morphological type, see also Perissutti 2017). There are several word-formatting processes that can be primarily associated with causativity, the crucial feature for their distinction being whether there is a change in the lexical basis

---

28   Exceptions are rare, for example, *zapálit něco* 'to set sth on fire', *zapálit se* 'to set oneself on fire'.

or not. There are causatives that do not have the same lexical basis as their non-causative counterparts; with other verbs, the lexical bases are identical and causativity is expressed only by prefixes (with these verbs, the word-formatting relationship is transparent and the causativity is obvious).

4.3.1.1 VERBS DERIVED FROM ANOTHER VERB

Change in the root (primarily -e- > -i-), generally also combined with a prefix such as po- or u-.

Sedět ('to be seated') > **po**sad**i**t ('to make someone sit somewhere'):

(5)
Pavel	sedí		na	židli.
Paul-NOM	sit-PRS.3SG.NCAUS	on	chair-LOC	

'Paul is sitting on a chair.'

(6)
Marie	posadila		medvídka	na	židli.
Mary-NOM	sit-PST.3SG.CAUS	teddy.bear-ACC	on	chair-ACC	

'Mary put the teddy bear on a chair.'

Ležet ('to be lying') > **po**lož**i**t ('to put something on a surface'):

(7)
Pavel	leží		v	posteli.
Paul-NOM	lie-PRS.3SG.NCAUS	in	bed-LOC	

'Paul is lying in the bed.'

(8)
Marie	položila		papíry	na	stůl.
Mary-NOM	lie-PST.3SG.CAUS	papers-ACC	on	table-ACC	

'Mary put the papers on the table.'

With the prefixed verbs (**po**sad**i**t, **po**lož**i**t), causativity is actually expressed through two formal features (prefix, root change). Therefore, these structures are transparent today for Czech speakers. However, with some old verbs without prefixes, the relationship with their original non-causative counterpart is not transparent anymore: vařit vodu ('to boil water') – vřít ('to be boiling'), mořit ('to bother') – mřít ('to be dying' – archaic), točit ('to spin') – téci ('to flow'), trápit ('to torment') – trpět ('to suffer') etc.

4.3.1.2 VERBS DERIVED FROM AN ADJECTIVE

These are frequent causative verbs formed from adjectives. Several Czech adjectives can be used to form a deadjectival verb that expresses a change of state:[29]

modrý ('blue') > **modřit** ('to make something blue', 'to paint something the colour of blue')
suchý ('dry') > **sušit** ('to dry something')

(9)
Látka	*je*	*modrá.*
fabric-NOM	be-PRS.3SG	blue-F

'The fabric is blue.'

(10)
Celý	*den*	*Marie*	*modřila*	*látku.*
whole-M	day-NOM	Mary-NOM	make.blue-PST.3SG	fabric-ACC

'Mary spent the whole day colouring the fabric blue.'

4.3.1.3 NO CHANGE IN THE LEXICAL BASIS, EXPRESSING CAUSATIVITY THROUGH A PREFIX ROZ-

The prefix *roz-* is considered to be a prototypical means for expressing morphological causativity in Czech. It is also one of the most productive and most polyfunctional prefixes in the Czech language, which complicates its analysis. Some of its meanings (e.g., spatial expansion *foukat* – 'to blow'/ *rozfoukat* – 'to disperse something through the air' or destruction *mixovat* – 'to mix something'/ *rozmixovat* – 'to liquidise something through mixing', see Štícha et al. 2013, 260–261) are not related to causativity. However, the meaning of ingressiveness (see Kratochvílová – Jindrová et al. this volume) is different: causativity and ingressiveness are closely related since, depending on the context, the same verb can bear both meanings:
- *roz* + intransitive reflexive verb → meaning 'sudden beginning of an action': *smát se* ('to laugh-REFL') – *rozesmát se* ('to start laughing')
- *roz* + transitive non-reflexive verb → causative meaning – *rozesmát někoho* 'to make sb laugh' (cf. **Section 4.3**).

As for the meaning 'gradual beginning of an action' (see Štícha 2018, 1060; Panevová – Karlík 2017), non-reflexive causative meaning is usually impossible (*rozhořet se* – 'to start burning', but *rozhořet něco – *'to put sth on fire'; exceptions are rare, *rozpovídat někoho* – 'to make sb talk', *roztančit někoho* – 'to make sb dance').

---

29 According to the above-mentioned Čermák's concept (Čermák 2001, 253 and 257), these constructions are facitives, not causatives.

Examples of the causative use of verbs with *roz-*:

smát se ('to laugh') > **roz**smát ('to make sb laugh')
plakat ('to cry') > **roz**plakat ('to make sb cry')

(11)

Marie	se	smála		jako	šílená.
Mary	REFL	laugh-PST.3SG.NCAUS		like	crazy-F

'Mary laughed like crazy.'

(12)

Ten	vtip	Marii	rozesmál.
that	joke-NOM	Mary-ACC	laugh-PST.3SG.CAUS

'The joke made Mary laugh.'

4.3.2 SEMANTIC CAUSATIVITY

Causativity might also be present in the very semantics of a verb, here we can distinguish two categories:

4.3.2.1 SUPPLETIVE TYPES

This group is mainly comprised of causative verbs that do not display any formal vicinity to their non-causative counterpart:

spadnout ('to fall down') > *shodit* ('to make something fall down').

Our data shows that this group is extremely heterogeneous, both for the contents and the form. Formally, verbs with prefixes prevail. However, with these verbs it is almost impossible to assign to the prefix a (purely) causative meaning, i.e. causativity is thus expressed by the verb as a whole:

přijít ('to come') > *povolat* ('to make somebody come').

In some cases, the base verb itself is causative, so the prefix can also express other meanings besides the causative (temporal, aspectual and others):

kroutit 'to twist-IPFV' – **za**kroutit 'to twist-PFV'
točit 'to spin-IPFV'– **o**točit, **poo**točit, **za**točit 'to turn-PFV'.

4.3.2.2 CAUSATIVE INTERPRETATION RESULTING FROM SYNTAX

This group is formed by verbs that can be interpreted either as causative or non-causative. This change is not reflected in any way in their form and results only from syntax. An example could be the verb *zblbnout* ('to become a fool', 'to make someone act like a fool'):

(13)
Pavel *zblbnul.*
Paul-NOM become.a.fool-PST.3SG
'Paul became a fool.'

(14)
Pavel *zblbnul* *Marii.*
Paul-NOM become.a.fool-PST.3SG Mary-ACC
'Paul made Mary act like a fool.'

4.3.3 ANALYTIC CAUSATIVITY

Analytic causativity, which is formally closest to the Romance type, is also present in the Czech system, its main manifestations being causative verbs followed by a subordinate clause or a nominal syntagma and semi-causative verbs followed by an infinitive.

4.3.3.1 CAUSATIVE VERBS FOLLOWED BY A SUBORDINATE CLAUSE

Partially synonymous verbs that could be translated as 'to cause something' (*způsobit, zapříčinit, vyvolat...*) can be combined with a subordinate clause:

(15)
Neobvykle *teplé* *počasí* *způsobilo,* *že* *tál* *led.*
unusually warm-N weather-NOM cause-PST.3SG that melt-PST.3SG ice-NOM
'The unusually warm weather caused the ice to melt.' (literally: 'The unusually warm weather caused that the ice melted.')[30]

4.3.3.2 CAUSATIVE VERBS FOLLOWED BY A NOMINAL SYNTAGMA

Partially synonymous verbs that could be translated as 'to cause something' (*způsobit, zapříčinit, vyvolat...*) can also be combined with a nominal syntagma:

---

30 For an extended discussion, see Macháčková (1982, 120).

(16)

Neobvykle	*teplé*	*počasí*	*způsobilo*	*tání*	*ledu.*
unusually	warm-N	weather-NOM	cause-PST.3SG	melting-ACC	ice-GEN

'The unusually warm weather caused the ice to melt.' (literally: 'The unusually warm weather caused the melting of the ice.')[31]

4.3.3.3 (SEMI-)CAUSATIVE VERBS FOLLOWED BY AN INFINITIVE

There are several verbs in Czech that can be considered semi-causative and enable completion by an infinitive (i.e. the type that is formally closest to the Romance construction). The most frequent are *nechat* (prevailing meaning being 'to leave'; the causative interpretation partially responds to the English 'to let'; cf. **Section 4.2.1**) and *dát* (prevailing meaning being 'to give'; the causative interpretation translates as 'to have something done'). For an extended discussion regarding this type and the semantic properties of the verbs *nechat* and *dát*, see Perissutti (2010; 2017) and Toops (1992; 2013).

(17)

Dal	*si*	*změřit*	*tlak.*
dát-PST.3SG	REFL.DAT	measure-INF	blood.pressure-ACC

'He had his blood pressure measured.'

(18)

Nechal	*si*	*změřit*	*tlak.*
nechat-PST.3SG	REFL.DAT	measure-INF	blood.pressure-ACC

'He had his blood pressure measured.' (literally: 'He let someone measure his blood pressure.')

(19)

Dal	*mu*	*vypít*	*lahvičku*	*jedu.*
dát-PST.3SG	he-DAT	drink-INF	bottle-ACC	poison-GEN

'He made him drink a bottle of poison.'

The choice of the verb influences the interpretation of the causative process. The causativity here can be conceived as a wide-scale with two poles: one of them being to leave, not to prevent from doing sth; the other expressing the notions of forcing someone to do something. The notion of forcing is also the main semantic characteristics of another Czech semi-causative verb *přimět* ('to move sb to sth', 'to force'):

---

31   For an extended discussion, see Macháčková (1982, 120).

(20)

Přiměl	*ho*	*vypít*	*lahvičku*	*jedu.*
force-PST.3SG	he-ACC	drink-INF	bottle-ACC	poison-GEN

'He forced him to drink a bottle of poison.'

4.4 OUR TYPOLOGY OF CZECH RESPONDENTS

In **Sections 4.3.1**, **4.3.2** and **4.3.3**, we presented all the types of Czech causative constructions that are generally considered in Czech grammars. For the data analysis, we decided to use a typology based on these types. Nevertheless, the corpus material has revealed causative expressions that did not fit either of the above-presented categories. Therefore, we adapted and enriched the original typology so as to cover as many expressions of causativity as possible. The typology we used for the data analysis can be resumed as follows:

Fusional types

Type 1: *rozplakat* type (cf. **Section 4.3.1.3**)
This type corresponds to the causativity expressed via the prefix *roz-*. Syntactic roles are maintained: 'X made Y cry' = 'X-NOM *rozplakat*-PST Y-ACC'.

Type 2: *posadit* type (cf. **Section 4.3.1.1**)
This type comprises morphologic causativity expressed by the root change *-e-* > *-i-* and, eventually, also by a prefix. Syntactic roles are maintained: 'X made Y sit down' = 'X-NOM *posadit*-PST Y-ACC'.

Type 3: *shodit* type (cf. **Section 4.3.2.1**)
All semantic causatives (in the broadest sense of this term), where no formal relationship between a non-causative verb and its causative counterpart can be found will be analysed as a *shodit* type. Syntactic roles are maintained: 'X made Y fall down' = 'X-NOM *shodit*-PST Y-ACC'.

Analytic types

Type 4: *dát vypít* type (cf. **Section 4.3.3.3**)
Analytic causatives that correspond to the pattern of semi-causative verb + infinitive (i.e. *dát, nechat, přimět* + infinitive) are analysed as a *dát vypít* type. Syntactic roles are maintained: 'X made Y drink something' = 'X-NOM *dát vypít*-PST Y-DAT something-ACC'.

Type 5: *dohnat k slzám* type
This kind of analytic causative was not mentioned in the general typology of Czech causativity, its inclusion into this set is based on the results of the corpus analyses. It is defined as an idiosyncratic union that is close to idioms. The notion of causativity results from the construction as a whole and the combinatorics is strongly limited with this being the main difference between this type and type 6. This group

also differs from type 8 since the syntactic roles are maintained. These "idiomatic causatives" are represented by Czech constructions such as:

(21)
Dohnat	*k*	*slzám*
drive-INF	to	tears-DAT

'Make cry.'

(22)
Dát	*na*	*srozuměnou*
give-INF	on	understanding-ACC

'Let know.'

(23)
Dát	*najevo*
give-INF	visibly

'Make clear to everyone.'

(24)
Vnuknout	*myšlenku*
input-INF	thought-ACC

'Inspire a thought.'

(25)
Dohánět	*k*	*šílenství*
drive-INF	to	craziness-DAT

'Drive someone crazy.'

Type 6: *způsobit tání* type (cf. **Section 4.3.3.2**)
This type comprises causativity expressed by causative verbs followed by a nominal, the nominal completion being a noun terminated by the suffix *-í*. The construction thus corresponds to a productive and stylistically unmarked expression of analytic causativity with verbs that translate as 'to cause' (*způsobit*) or 'to force' (*přimět*) followed by any deverbative noun (the change from the category of verbs to the category of nouns in Czech is formally represented by the suffix *-í*: *tát* – 'to melt' > *tání* – 'melting'). The resulting construction does not display any idiomatic characteristics.

Type 7: *způsobit, že tál* type (cf. **4.3.3.1**)
This type is represented by analytic causatives which have a clausal structure, i.e. a causative verb is followed by a subordinated clause containing a verb in finite form.

Other forms of expressing causativity

Type 8: *what makes you think that > proč myslíte?* ('why do you think that?')

This (rather heterogeneous) group was not mentioned in the general typology of Czech causativity. It is comprised of respondents that display a change in syntactic roles, i.e. a Romance construction corresponding to 'X made Y cried' is translated to Czech via the pattern 'Y cried'. The relationship between crying and X can be expressed in another way or can be omitted completely. This type is represented as follows:

Romance construction: *¿Qué te hace pensar que...? / Cosa ti fa pensare che...? / Qu'est--ce qui te fait penser que...? / O que é que te faz pensar que...?* ('What makes you think that?').

Czech respondent: *Proč myslíte?* ('Why do you think that?').

Other types

Type 9: translated differently

This group includes translations that while maintaining the original causative meaning, used resources different to those presented in types 1–8.

Type 10: no translation

When the original causative meaning misses any clear Czech respondent (either because the translator did not take it into account or due to a text-correspondence error in the corpus), we mark it as no translation.

4.5 METHODOLOGY

Following the general methodological procedure established for this monograph (see Nádvorníková this volume), we analysed the Romance causative construction in the corpus InterCorp. The basic queries had the following forms:

Es: *[lemma="hacer"] [tag="VLinf"]*
It: *[lemma="fare"] [tag="V.*inf.*"]*
Fr: *[lemma="faire"] [tag="VER:infi.*"]*
Pt: *[word="([Ff]aç.*|[Ff]az.*|[Ff]iz.*|[Ff]ez.*|[Ff]ar.*|[Ff]ê-.*|[Ff]á-.*|[Ff]i-.*|[Ff]eito)"]*
[]{0,5} [tag="VMN."] within <s id=".*" />*

For French, the initial concordance was completed by causatives that were found using a query that took in consideration the possible introduction of another syntactic element into the construction, especially the negative particle *pas*. This query had the following form:

[lemma="faire"] [tag="PRO."] []{0,5} [tag="VER:infi.*"], [lemma="faire"] [tag="ADV.*"]*
[]{0,5} [tag="VER:infi."].*

In the first stage, we created a list of the 20 most frequent infinitives that appeared in the construction in each language and compared them to seek the response to the question whether the causative construction displays similar combinatory preferences in all languages. Consequently, we manually analysed the Czech respondents of the Romance causative construction and attributed them to one of the types presented in **Section 4.4**. Our aim was to find the most frequent Czech respondents of Romance causativity. In the second plan, this analysis also enables us to determine whether these respondents differ somehow according to the source language (which would provide reasons to doubt the general correspondence of these constructions in Romance) and also to find out whether the Czech respondents reveal notions other than causativity (which might thus be attributed to the Romance constructions as secondary semantic features).

4.6 CAUSATIVE CONSTRUCTIONS IN ROMANCE – FORMAL COMPARISON

Table 4.1 resumes the 20 most frequent infinitive completions of the causative construction in all four analysed languages. We have underlined all the verbs that have a clear semantic respondent in at least two other languages.

Table 4.1 proves that the incidence and frequency of verbs used in the analysed construction do not correspond to the general incidence of verbs in the corpus, i.e., the Romance causative constructions present restrictions with respect to the infinitives with which they can combine.[32] At the same time, **Table 4.1** shows that the analysed causative construction has similar combinatory preferences in Spanish, Italian and French (we cannot consider Portuguese, due to the insufficient amount of data). Approximately half of the twenty most frequent infinitives have their semantic respondents in at least two of these three languages.

Despite the general correspondence, some interesting discrepancies can be found, especially when comparing the Italian and French data with the Spanish subcorpus, which is considerably larger. Corpus data proves that the Italian causative construction often enables completion with the verb *fare*, this infinitive being the seventh most frequent. In the Spanish subcorpus, this infinitive completion had a frequency of 5 (therefore, it is not listed in **Table 4.1**). The contrastive analysis suggests that while constructions such as *mi sono fatto fare un tatuaggio* ('I had a tattoo done') or *facciamo fare il bagno ai bambini* ('we make the children wash themselves') are relatively common in Italian, the Spanish causative construction allows similar completion only

---

32   As an example, in the Spanish corpus, the most frequent verbs are: 1. *ser*, 2. *haber*, 3. *estar*, 4. *decir*, 5. *tener*, 6. *hacer*, 7. *poder*, 8. *ir*, 9. *ver*, 10. *dar*, 11. *saber*, 12. *querer*, 13. *pasar*, 14. *parecer*, 15. *volver*, 16. *mirar*, 17. *pensar*, 18. *dejar*, 19. *poner*, 20. *hablar*. This means that only three of the 20 verbs used most frequently in our construction at the same time belong to the 20 most used verbs in general (*pasar*, *saber*, *ver*).

Tab. 4.1. The 20 most frequent infinitive completions of the Romance causative construction

Spanish	Total frequency	Italian	Total frequency	French	Total frequency	Portuguese	Total frequency
pasar	181	vedere	97	rire	44	sentir	13
sentir(se)	167	sapere	43	passer	33	tilintar	11
saber	141	venire	36	sauter	29	estremecer	10
pensar	135	sentire	35	venir	28	lembrar	10
ver	114	credere	33	comprendre	25	esperar	9
creer	99	capire	31	remarquer	25	esquecer	9
llegar	98	fare	25	tourner	25	perder	9
girar	93	passare	26	croire	23	rir	9
reír	89	portare	22	sortir	23	cair	8
perder	82	ridere	22	penser	22	girar	8
sonar	80	pensare	22	entendre	20	chorar	8
sufrir	65	entrare	22	entrer	20	bater	7
entrar	61	salire	20	voir	20	entrar	7
notar	56	dire	19	tuer	19	parecer	7
saltar	46	udire	18	souffrir	16	sair	7
llorar	46	tornare	16	oublier	14	saltar	7
venir	43	notare	18	savoir	14	sentar	7
llamar	43	morire	18	faire	13	sofrer	7
temblar	41	diventare	18	descendre	12	tremer	7
callar	40	impazzire	17	glisser	12	ver	7
caer	40	cadere	16	monter	12	vir	7
				mourir	12		
				taire	12		

rarely (data from the CORPES XXI corpus (RAE 2018) reveal its dialectal restriction and indicate that it is typical for the Río de la Plata area since 36% of all its appearances in this corpus come from this zone).[33]

The analysis also reveals that the French causative construction displays a clear tendency to combine with the verb *sauter* (the third most frequent completion). This construction lacks any direct respondent in Spanish (also in Italian and Portuguese)

---

33   Five examples from our Spanish corpus are by authors from Spain (Laforet), Mexico (Rulfo), Peru (Vargas Llosa), Argentina (Cortázar) and Chile (Zúñiga Pavlov).

due to the polyfunctionality of the verb *sauter*. The analysis of the respondents of *faire sauter* revealed a very large range of possible interpretations of this construction, which could be translated into English as 'prise', 'clatter down', 'break down', 'blow up', but also, expressively, as 'fuck'.

4.7 ANALYSIS OF CZECH RESPONDENTS

The analysis of Czech respondents of the Romance causative construction was divided into several stages:

1) Data restriction

   For Spanish, we reduced the basic concordance and analysed only those constructions that combined with the infinitive appearing at least 15 times in the corpus. The original data containing 4,533 appearances was thus reduced to a set consisting of 2,858 constructions in total, which contained 65 different infinitive completions. For Italian and French, the frequency limit was 10 appearances. This translated into a concordance consisting of 810 constructions (41 infinitives) for Italian and 621 constructions (37 infinitives) for French. For Portuguese, we worked with the complete concordance (due to the limited total amount of data), which contained 493 constructions with 212 different infinitive completions.

2) Analysis of Czech translation

   Consequently, we manually analysed all the Czech respondents of the Romance construction and assigned them to one of the 10 types described in **Section 4.4**. Since some of the above-presented types of expressing causativity in Czech display strong usage limitations, the analyses also focused on the number of verbs that were translated by each of them. The main objective was to pinpoint which expressions of causativity are frequent but tend to combine with a very small set of verbs, therefore displaying tendencies for lexicalisation. **Table 4.2** shows the frequency that each type was used for the translation. The three most frequent respondent types for each language are in bold.

As shown in **Table 4.2**, the most frequent respondent types are the same for all four languages, which confirms our observation from **Section 4.2**, that these constructions do not display any distinctive semantic differences throughout the four analysed languages and that it is possible (with certain limitations) to consider them as one unit. As can be observed, three types clearly prevail in all languages: one fusional (type 3), one analytic (type 4) and the type we called "change in syntactic roles" (type 8). **Table 4.3** resumes the number of verbs that were translated by each type in all four languages (three respondent types that combined with the largest set of verbs are again in bold).

Tab. 4.2. Type frequency

Type	Frequency in Spanish		Frequency in Italian		Frequency in French		Frequency in Portuguese	
	Ranking	%	Ranking	%	Ranking	%	Ranking	%
1	6	4	8	1	6	4	7	3
2	9	1	9–10	0	8	1	8	1
3	1	40	1	41	1	46	1	33
4	3	13	3	15	3	14	3	13
5	4	10	5	5	4	9	5–6	6
6	10	0	9–10	0	10	0	10	0
7	7	3	6	5	7	1	5–6	6
8	2	21	2	21	2	19	2	29
9	5	7	4	8	5	5	4	8
10	8	1	7	4	9	1	9	1

Tab. 4.3. Number of verbs in which the particular types occur

Type	1	2	3	4	5	6	7	8	9	10	Total amount of verbs
Number of Spanish verbs	11	2	53	52	44	1	41	60	49	18	65
In %	17	3	82	80	68	2	63	92	75	28	
Number of Italian verbs	2	1	40	32	13	0	19	40	27	18	41
In %	5	2	98	78	32	0	46	98	66	44	
Number of French verbs	3	2	33	27	28	0	8	35	16	4	37
In %	8	5	89	73	76	0	22	95	43	11	
Number of Portuguese verbs	9	3	81	47	24	1	24	82	35	3	212
In %	4	1	38	22	11	0	11	39	17	1	

When analysing **Table 4.3**, two observations can be made:

a) The three most frequent respondent types (3, 4, 8) do not display any clear tendency to combine with concrete verbs. Therefore, these types can be considered central. The remaining types – we might call them peripheral – display stronger preferences for the concrete verbs (or types of verbs) they usually combine with.

b) The final results are strongly influenced by the corpus size: the data from the Portuguese subcorpus differs from those obtained from the other subcorpora since –

as has been explained above – we worked with the whole corpus, also including into our analysis the infinitives with one incidence.

Given the differences in the size of the different subcorpora we worked with, we will present a more detailed commentary only with regard to Spanish, which offers the largest dataset.

When analysing the Czech respondents with respect to the infinitive completion of the Spanish construction, we can postulate a scale ranging from the verbs that are generally translated by one single type to those that have very heterogeneous typological respondents:

- *Matar* 'to kill' (96% of respondents corresponded to type 4); *constar* 'to state' (95% of respondents corresponded to type 3 and the rest to type 10), *brillar* 'to shine' (90% of respondents corresponded to type 8)
- *Hablar* 'to speak' (6 typological respondents, the most frequent ones appeared in only 23% of cases), *decir* 'to tell' (the most frequent respondents appeared in only 29% of cases).

There are other verbs between these two poles. The data shows that the most frequent typological respondent appears in 60% with 26 verbs, in 50% with 10 verbs, in 40% with 15 verbs, in 30% with 12 verbs and in 20% with 2 verbs. The most frequent number of typological respondents is 5 (for example, *caer* 'to fall', *cambiar* 'to change'), 4 (e.g., *dormir* 'to sleep') and 3 (e.g., *abrir* 'to open'). The verb displaying the largest scale of typological respondents (7) in our material is the verb *girar* 'to turn'.

This short commentary on the Spanish data enables us to draw several partial conclusions: 1) with most verbs, Czech typological respondents are significantly heterogeneous; 2) there are just a few verbs with one unanimous respondent, i.e. the tendency to lexicalisation is not very frequent.

4.7.1 PRIMARY CZECH RESPONDENTS

The three most frequent Czech respondents of the Romance causative construction, which altogether constituted approximately 70% of all respondents, proved to be types 3, 8 and 4. We will analyse each one of them in greater detail in the following sections.

4.7.1.1 TYPE 3 – *SHODIT* TYPE (*HACER CAER / FAR CADERE / FAIRE TOMBER / FAZER CAIR*)

In approximately 40% of cases, the Romance construction is translated by an inherently causative verb that does not possess any structurally related non-causative counterpart. The dominance of this type for expressing causativity in Czech is also proven by the fact that it was used for the translation of a large set of infinitives in all four languages (see **Table 4.3**). It is also worth observing that among the Czech respondents, there were many verbs which are usually not analysed as causatives in Czech grammars. This is a strong reason to consider the Czech causativity in the widest possible sense and to approach it as a highly abstract category, which is connected to the semantics of concrete verbs and to the Aktionsart in the narrowest sense of the meaning, see (26), (27), (28), (29). For an extended discussion regarding Aktionsart in Czech and Romance, see Kratochvílová – Jindrová (this volume).

(26) Es.
Me pareció distinguir la cabellera plateada del Maestro en el Segundo palco de mi lado, pero en ese instante mismo desapareció como si lo **hubieran hecho caer** de rodillas. → Měl jsem dojem, že v druhé lóži od sebe vidím Mistrovu stříbrnou hřívu, ale vzápětí zmizela, <u>jako **by ho srazili** na kolena</u>.
Literally: <u>*as if they **had brought** him to his knees*</u>.
Julio Cortázar, *Konec hry* (*Final del juego*), transl. Mariana Housková, Brno: Julius Zirkus, 2002.

(27) It.
Ancora anni dopo, a Bad Hollen, raccontavano che era stato come se qualcuno, dal campanile, **avesse fatto cadere** un pianoforte dritto su un deposito di lampadari di cristallo. → Ještě léta potom v Bad Hollenu vyprávěli, že to bylo <u>jako kdyby někdo</u> **shodil** <u>ze zvonice klavír</u> přímo na skladiště křišťálových lustrů.
Literally: <u>*as if someone **had thrown** a piano from the belfry*</u>.
Alessandro Baricco, *Oceán moře* (*Oceano mare*), transl. Alice Flemrová, Prague: Eminent, 2001.

(28) Fr.
Il s'agissait juste de faire couler un peu d'encre pour rappeler que d'autres **avaient fait couler** un peu de sang. → Vždyť šlo pouze o to vyplýtvat trochu inkoust, aby se druhým připomnělo, <u>že oni **vyplýtvali** trochu krve</u>.
Literally: <u>*that had **wasted** some blood*</u>.
Pierre Assouline, *Zákaznice* (*La Cliente*), transl. Lubomír Martínek, Prague: Prostor, 2000.

(29) Pt.
Como se tudo fosse muito simples e a memória o **fizesse perder** tempo. → Jako by všechno bylo velice prosté a <u>paměť ho jenom **zdržovala**</u>.
Literally: <u>*and memory only **slowed** him **down***</u>.
Hélia Correia, *Ďáblova hora* (*Montedemo*), transl. Vlasta Dufková, Prague: Odeon, 1986.

The aim of this study is not to analyse in detail the factors influencing the choice of Czech respondents (this being a desideratum for future studies). Nevertheless, it can be indicated that these factors are numerous and two of these appear to be particularly important: the meaning of the fully semantic verb and the presence/absence of a verb complement (and its meaning). Both these factors are closely related as the following example shows.

Our data shows that with the Spanish construction *hacer caer* 'make fall', one-seventh of all appearances correspond to the locution *hacer caer en la cuenta*, where *caer en la cuenta* means 'to realise'. In these cases, Czech respondents are the verbs *vysvětlit*, *upozornit*, *připomenout*, *oznámit*, all of which have the approximate meaning of 'to make realise', 'to announce', see (30):

(30) Es.
El sirio Moisés le **hizo caer** en la cuenta de una novedad: llegaba un circo. → Syřan Moisés **mu** však **oznámil** novinku: přijel cirkus.
Literally: *he **told him** the news*.
Gabriel García Márquez, *Zlá hodina* (*La mala hora*), transl. Vladimír Medek, Prague: Odeon, 2006.

In other cases – where no complement is present – the Czech respondents of *hacer caer* are, for example, *srazit, porazit, spustit, shodit, povalit, upustit*, all of which have the approximate meaning 'to make fall':

(31) Es.
—Venga el que **ha hecho caer** ese fusil —gritó.
„Kdo **upustil** pušku, ať vystoupí," zvolal.
Literally: *who **dropped** the rifle*.
Mario Vargas Llosa, *Město a psi* (*La ciudad y los perros*), transl. Miloš Veselý, Prague: Mladá fronta, 2004.

Therefore, the possible combination of a verb with a complement influences the selection of the Czech respondent. A similar situation can be observed with the vast majority of verbs. The choice of a specific verb is also influenced by other factors (style, language variant etc.).

4.7.1.2 TYPE 8 – *WHAT MAKES YOU THINK THAT* > *PROČ MYSLÍTE?* ('WHY DO YOU THINK THAT?')

The second most frequent respondent type is characterised by the change of syntactic roles. This type also appeared with the widest range of verbs (see **Table 4.3**). Its most frequent realisations can be summarised as follows:

1) The Czech respondent contains two main clauses with causation generally being expressed by conjunctions such as *a tak* ('and so') or *a proto* ('and because of that'):

(32) Fr.
Elle ne parlait pas, ne semblait pas avoir le sens commun et ne cessait de sourire, ce qui la **faisait prendre** communément pour une arriérée. → Nemluvila a vypadala trochu tak, jako by ani neměla všech pět pohromadě, jen se usmívala, **a** snad **proto ji** sousedé **považovali** za zaostalou.
Literally: ***and** maybe **because of that**, the neighbours **considered** her retarded.*
Frédéric Tristan, *Hrdinné útrapy Baltazara Kobera* (*Les Tribulations héroïques de Balthasar Kober*), transl. Oldřich Kalfiřt, Prague: DharmaGaia – Dauphin, 2003.

2) The Czech respondent contains a subordinated clause, usually with a temporal or consequential meaning:

(33) Es.
—¡Basta! —interrumpió el capitán dando un puñetazo sobre la mesa que **hizo bailar** los platos y las copas. → „Tak dost!" přerušil je kapitán ranou pěstí do stolu, **až se** talíře a sklenky **roztančily**.
Literally: ***so that** plates and glasses **started to dance**.*
Isabel Allende, *Dcera štěstěny* (*La hija de la fortuna*), transl. Monika Baďurová, Prague: BB art, 2004.

3) In the Czech respondent the causer is expressed in different ways, usually by an adverbial (34) or by the modal verb *muset* ('have to') (35):

(34) Es.
Es el género de calamidades que un día te **harán caer** los brazos con desaliento o gritar con indignación. → To je přesně typ pohromy, **kvůli níž** ti malomyslně **klesnou** ruce a nejradši bys křičel vzteky.
Literally: ***because of which** your arms **will decline** helplessly.*
Ernesto Sábato, *Abbadón zhoubce* (*Abbadón el exterminador*), transl. Anežka Charvátová, Brno: Host, 2002.

(35) Pt.
Não queria ser visitada assim, tão acabada, **fizera** a amiga **jurar** nada dizer a ninguém. → Nepřála si, aby ji někdo navštěvoval tak zničenou, přítelkyně **musila přísahat**, že nikomu nic neřekne.
Literally: *the friend **had to swear**.*
Jorge Amado, *Pastýři noci* (*Os Pastores da Noite*), transl. Pavla Lidmilová, Prague: Odeon, 1983.

As can be observed, Czech respondents maintain causativity to different extents and while the causer is also expressed by different means, in some cases causativity is not overtly expressed at all.

4.7.1.3 TYPE 4 – DÁT VYPÍT TYPE

The most frequent analytic expression of causativity was represented by type 4, i.e. a combination of a semi-causative verb with the infinitive. Although this respondent type formally corresponds to the original Romance construction, we must bear in mind that this correspondence is only partial. The Czech verb *udělat*, which would be the best candidate for the translation of *hacer/fare/faire/fazer* cannot appear in this kind of construction and all Czech verbs that allow completion with an infinitive, thus forming a causative construction, are only semi-causatives, which also have other non-causative interpretations.

The corpus analysis reveals that beside the traditionally mentioned semi-causative verbs such as *dát, nechat, přimět* (see **Section 4.3.3.3**) and *donutit* ('to force'), there are also others that can gain a causative interpretation when followed by an infinitive form, such as: *pomoci* ('to help'), *poručit* ('to order'), *přikázat* ('to command'), *mínit* ('to have in mind'), *dovolit* ('to allow'), *dokázat* ('to manage'), *umožnit* ('to enable'), *poslat* ('to send sb somewhere'), *naučit* ('to teach'). Given the frequency the Romance construction was translated by a semi-causative Czech respondent, it is possible to state that the contrastive analysis reveals a wide range of semantic notions associated with *hacer/fare/faire/fazer* + infinitive that can be considered only partially causative and that this construction clearly displays secondary meanings that cannot be attributed solely to the category of causativity.

(36) It.
Il Comandante, che **si faceva chiamare** re di Roma, era un mangione e beone coatto; e l'alcool serviva come eccitante e narcotico usuale agli occupanti sia nel quartier generale come alla base. → Velitel, který **si nechal říkat** římský král, byl velký jedlík a pijan, alkohol sloužil okupantům jako nejobvyklejší dráždidlo a droga jak v hlavním štábu, tak dole v základních složkách armády.
Literally: *who **had others call him** Roman king*.
Elsa Morante, *Příběh v historii* (*La storia*), transl. Zdeněk Frýbort, Prague: Odeon, 1990.

(37) Fr.
Quant à Bruno, le jugement se poursuivrait jusqu' à épuisement du dossier – ce qui signifiait, que le Saint-Office tenterait de **faire avouer** au malheureux tous les secrets qu'il avait juré sur son âme de ne jamais révéler. → Bruna zamýšleli vyšetřovat tak dlouho, dokud soud nedospěje k úplnému vyčerpání spisu – jinými slovy dokud svatá inkvizice nebožáka **nedonutí přiznat** veškerá tajemství, včetně těch, o nichž by přísahal při své nesmrtelné duši, že je nikdy neodhalí.

Literally: ***force to confess***.
Frédéric Tristan, *Hrdinné útrapy Baltazara Kobera* (*Les Tribulations héroïques de Balthasar Kober*), transl. Oldřich Kalfiřt, Prague: DharmaGaia – Dauphin, 2003.

(38) Pt.
É novo… Parece que o éter desenvolve, **faz aflorar** a alma de as frutas… → To je úplná novinka… Éter prý **pomáhá odhalit** duši ovoce…
Literally: ***helps to reveal*** the soul of fruits.
José Maria Eça de Queirós, *Kráčej a čti* (*A Cidade e as Serras*), transl. Marie Havlíková, Prague: Academia, 2001.

4.7.2 SECONDARY CZECH RESPONDENTS

Types 1–2, 5–7 and 9–10 constituted in total less than one-third of all Czech respondents of the Romance causative construction. The most frequent representatives of this group proved to be rather heterogeneous respondents subsumed under type 5 (*dohnat k slzám* type, i. e. idiomatic expressions of causativity) and respondents marked as type 9, where causativity is expressed by means others than those described in types 1–8. This can be seen as yet further proof that Czech causativity is a highly complex category, which cannot be identified by one or two dominant forms of expression.

4.7.2.1 TYPE 5 – *DOHNAT K SLZÁM* TYPE

The above-mentioned inherent complexity of Czech causativity and the heterogeneity of its formal manifestations can be observed even within the very category of the idiomatic expressions of causativity. As described in **Section 4.4**, these constructions are lexical idiosyncratic units bordering with phraseological units and collocations (combinations of verbs and complements are not free; there are important restrictions).

(39) Es.
Vaciló, sin saber qué hacer, hasta que las señas insistentes de Borobá le **hicieron dudar** de que su amiga se encontrara allí. → Zaváhal, nevěda co dělat, až mu Borobiny naléhavé posunky **vnukly pochybnost**, jestli tam jeho přítelkyně vůbec je.
Literally: *Borobá's insisting gestures **inspired doubts** in him*.
Isabel Allende, *Království Zlatého draka* (*El Reino del Dragón de Oro*), transl. Monika Baďurová, Prague: BB-art, 2004.

(40) It.
Se c'è una cosa capace di **farti impazzire** è l'elastico delle calze troppo stretto. → Pokud existuje něco, co tě může **dohnat k šílenství**, je to příliš úzká gumička u ponožek.

Literally: **_drive_ _you_ _crazy_**.
Alessandro Baricco, *City* (*City*), transl. Alice Flemrová, Prague: Volvox Globator, 2000.

(41) Fr.
Je suis sûr que ça la **fait jouir**, de mariner un obèse sans défense, nu et imberbe. → Určitě jí to **dělá potěšení** máčet bezbranného obézního chlapa, nahého a bez jediného chlupu na těle.
Literally: *it certainly **gives** her **pleasure***.
Amélie Nothomb, *Vrahova hygiena* (*Hygiène de l'assassin*), transl. Jarmila Fialová, Prague – Liberec: Paseka, 2001.

(42) Pt.
Mas o que a torturava, a **fazia chorar** todos os dias era a idade de ele ser um enjeita-dinho. → Denně ji však **pohnula k pláči** trýznivá myšlenka, že dítě bude sebranec.
Literally: *every day, the tormenting thought that the child would be a bastard **moved her to tears***.
José Maria Eça de Queiroz, *Zločin pátera Amara* (*O Crime do Padre Amaro*), transl. Zdeněk Hampl, Prague: Státní nakladatelství krásné literatury a umění (SNKLU), 1961.

The corpus analyses reveal that respondents forming this category can differ even when analysing the respondents of constructions with the same infinitive completion, see (42) and (43).

(43) Es.
Cada animalito que se echaba a la boca venciendo la repugnancia, lo **hacía sonreír** pensando en su maestro, a quien tampoco le gustaban los cangrejos. → Každé to zvířátko, které s přemáhaným odporem pojídal, **u něj vzbuzovalo úsměv**, když pomyslil na svého učitele, který raky také neměl rád.
Literally: ***arose** his **smile***.
Isabel Allende, *Dcera štěstěny* (*Hija de la fortuna*), transl. Monika Baďurová, Prague: BB Art, 2004.

(44) It.
(...) e subito ricostruivate la grande catena dell' essere, in love and joy, perché tutto quel che nell' universo si squaderna nella vostra mente si era già riunito in un volume, e Proust vi avrebbe **fatto sorridere**. → (...) hned jste se pustily do ve-likánského řetězce bytí podle vzoru love and joy, protože všechno, co ve vesmíru jsou jen pouhé listy, ve vaší mysli je už svázáno do jednoho svazku, a Proust by vám pouze **vyloudil úsměv** na rtech.
Literally: ***wheedled a smile** on the lips*.
Umberto Eco, *Foucaultovo kyvadlo* (*Il pendolo di Focault*), transl. Zdeněk Frýbort, Prague: Český klub, 2001.

4.7.2.2 TYPE 9 – OTHER TRANSLATION

Analyses of the respondents attributed to this type revealed several different possibilities of expressing notions included in the *hacer/fare/faire/fazer* + infinitive construction. The most common type can be defined in terms of using a deverbative noun/adjective to substitute the Romance infinitive, the general pattern is: 'wind makes leaves fall' > 'leaves fallen by the wind', see (44):

(45) Pt.
(...) uma linda capela branca que as freiras **fizeram construir** em a frente de o colégio e que dominava a cidade desde o morro (...). → Tato deska byla zasazena v pěkné bílé kapli **zbudované** jeptiškami naproti ústavní škole a shlížející na město se svého pahorku (...).
Literally: **built** *by nuns*.
Jorge Amado, *Země zlatých plodů* (*São Jorge dos Ilhéus*), transl. Jaroslav Rosendorfský, Prague: Československý spisovatel, 1950.

Other respondents attributed to this category could be defined by the missing respondent of the verb *hacer/fare/faire/fazer*:

(46) It.
Soprattutto però era una città istruita: è sempre il Villani a **farci sapere** che gli 8–10.000 bambini fiorentini sapevano tutti leggere e scrivere (...). → Především však byla městem vzdělaným: **podle Villaniho** umělo 8–10 tisíc florentských dětí číst a psát (...).
Literally: **according to Villani**.
Giuliano Proccaci, *Dějiny Itálie* (*Storia degli italiani*), transl. Bohumír Klípa – Drahoslava Janderová – Kateřina Vinšová, Prague: Nakladatelství Lidové noviny, 2007.

4.7.2.3 TYPE 7 – ZPŮSOBIT, ŽE TÁL TYPE

The most analytic type of expressing causativity (i.e. a verb corresponding to 'to cause something' followed by a subordinate clause) was the sixth or seventh most frequent type (depending on the concrete Romance language). Given the wide range of its possible completions (see **Table 4.3**), this type proved to be productive, but also a rather marginal means of expressing causativity in Czech. Nevertheless, the scale of Czech verbs that correspond to the Romance verb *hacer/fare/faire/fazer* is very wide and underlines notions other than the pure causativity that can be attributed to the Romance construction. Apart from the verbs *způsobit* ('to cause-PFV') and *způsobovat* ('to cause-IPFV'), this respondent type included verbs expressing:

1) The subject's consent or permission: *svolit* ('to consent'):

(47) Es.
Lepprince le **hizo pasar** y me rogó que me quedase. → <u>Lepprince **svolil, ať vstoupí**</u>, a poprosil mě, abych zůstal.
Literally: <u>Lepprince **permitted that he entered**</u>.
Eduardo Mendoza, *Pravda o případu Savolta* (*La verdad sobre el caso Savolta*), transl. Petr Koutný, Prague: Odeon, 1983.

2) The subject's will: *přikázat* ('to order'), *požadovat* ('to demand'), *nařídit* ('to command'), *chtít* ('to want'), *říct* ('to tell'), *přimět* ('to force'):

(48) It.
Il giovane ufficiale con secchi ordini li **fece portare** via. → Mladý důstojník stroze **přikázal, aby** je **odnesli**.
Literally: **commanded that they were taken away**.
Italo Calvino, *Naši předkové* (*I nostri antenati*), transl. Zdeněk Digrin – Vladimír Mikeš, Prague: Odeon, 1970.

3) The subject's effort to create or finish something: *zařídit* ('to make arrangements'), *postarat se* ('to make sure'), *dát si práci* ('to make an effort'), *dělat* ('to make'), *přispět k* ('to contribute to'):

(49) Fr.
Maître Flinker, reprit-il, je vais vous **faire prêter** deux apprentis par quelque autre imprimeur de la ville (...). → Mistře Flingere, **zařídím, aby** vám někdo z tiskařů ve městě **půjčil** dva učně (...).
Literally: <u>I will **make arrangements so that** someone **lent** to you</u>.
Frédéric Tristan, *Hrdinné útrapy Baltazara Kobera* (*Les Tribulations héroïques de Balthasar Kober*), transl. Oldřich Kalfiřt, Prague: DharmaGaia – Dauphin, 2003.

4) The logical or unintentional consequence of a previous state or action: *vést k* ('to lead to'), *dohánět k* ('to drive sb to smth'):

(50) Pt.
E sentira a, porventura, essa felicidade, que dão os amores ilegítimos, de que tanto se fala nos romances e em as óperas; que **faz esquecer** tudo em a vida, afrontar a morte, quase fazê-la amar? → A prožívala snad takové štěstí, které člověk cítí z nedovolených milostných vztahů, o nichž se tolik mluví v románech a operách a <u>které člověka **dohánějí k tomu, aby zapomněl**</u> na život, a smrti nejen čelil, nýbrž po ní i téměř toužil?
Literally: <u>that **drive** a person **to forget**</u>.

Eça de Queirós, *Bratranec Basilio* (*O Primo Basílio*), transl. Zdeněk Hampl, Prague: Odeon, 1989.

4.7.2.4 TYPE 1 – ROZPLAKAT TYPE

Despite the fact that the Czech prefix *roz-* is often mentioned as a significant means of expressing causativity, it did not appear very frequently in our data. While this could be attributed to the fact that type 1 is defined in a much more precise way than the other types (i.e. it is defined by one single prefix; therefore, it does not admit formal variability as the other types do), we claim that the main reason for its low frequency lies in its strong combinatory limitations (see Section. **4.3.1.3**). The *roz-* prefix proved to be a productive causative prefix, that, nevertheless, combined mostly with verbs expressing an emotional reaction such as *brečet* ('to cry'), *smát se* ('to laugh'), *slzet* ('to shed tears'), *lkát* ('to wail'); movement such as *tančit* ('to dance'), *chvět se* ('to tremble'), *točit* ('to spin around'), *houpat* ('to swing'), *třást* ('to shake'), *kmitat* ('to wiggle'); or sound such as *zvučet* ('to make sounds'), *znít* ('to resonate').

4.7.2.5 TYPE 2 – POSADIT TYPE AND TYPE 6 – ZPŮSOBIT TÁNÍ TYPE

These types appeared the least frequently in our data, which is caused by their narrow definition: they are defined in terms of a rather infrequent derivational change (type 2), or in terms of the presence of one particular verbal form, i.e., verbal noun (type 6). Thus, type 2 includes a very limited group of verbs. The low frequency of type 6 can also be influenced by the corpus we used (noun phrases composed of a verbal noun are typical for specialist or administrative language rather than for narrative).

4.7.2.6 TYPE 10 – NO TRANSLATION

As it follows from the definition, in this type, the causative meaning completely disappeared in the Czech respondent, which gave us no reason to address it in our study.

4.8 CONCLUSIONS

When analysing the Czech respondents of the Romance causative construction, we can observe that it is difficult to precisely determine the proportion of analytic and fusional resources. With reference to Czech causativity, it is better to mention a continuum. If we conceive the analysed Romance construction as an expression of "pure" causativity, we can also present the respondents as a typological means of expressing this category in Czech. The scale of Czech causative expressions, starting with the most fusional and ending with the most analytic, can be represented as follows:

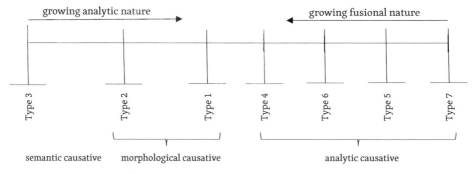

Fig. 4.1. *Scale of analytical/fusional Czech respondents of the Romance causative construction*

From our understanding, the most fusional expression is represented by semantic causatives (type 3) where the notion of causativity cannot be attributed to any formal constituent and as a result, is not overtly coded in any way. The analyses have revealed this type of expressing causativity to be the most frequent.

The fusional morphological causative expression can have two formal representations. We consider the *posadit* type (type 2) to be the most fusional since the infix, which is the bearer of causative interpretation, can be considered to be non-transparent in present-day Czech and most native speakers do not feel it as causative at all. The *roz-* prefix (type 1) can be considered to be the purest representation of morphological causativity in Czech (nevertheless, it is not used very often, as proven by the corpus analysis).

The rest of the schema can be considered analytic. We analyse the *dát napít* type (type 4) as the least analytic, given the limited set of finite verbs that can appear in the construction and the fact that it can only combine with an infinitive. The *způsobit tání* type (type 6) also allows only one kind of completion (a deverbative noun); the first part of the construction can be formed by different causative verbs although this list is also limited to a certain extent. The *dohnat k slzám* type (type 5) displays clear idiomatic characteristics and we consider it less fusional given the different kind of constituents that can form the causative construction (causative meaning is expressed by the construction as a whole; the parts of the construction can have different forms but cannot be combined freely and we cannot mention predictability and productiveness). Finally, the most analytic kind of expression (*způsobit, že tál*, type 7) has the form of a sentence. Analyses have revealed that this kind of construction can be considered marginal when analysing Czech causativity.

While being one of the most frequent, it is impossible to include the *why do you think that?* type (type 8) into the schema, due to the largest heterogeneity of its possible realisations and, most importantly, due to the fact that it does not fulfil the definition criteria of a causative construction (see **Section 4.1**). As can be observed, the causative scheme where the causer causes the causee to do something is not complete here: in an explicit way, only the fact that the causee is doing something or that he/she is in a state is expressed. The role of the causer has disappeared or is present only implicitly. While this type formally differs from the others, they share a common feature that can be resumed in terms of depicting causativity in the widest possible sense (including expressions of consequences and effects). Therefore, we can conclude that the Romance causative constructions are a means of expressing a highly abstract causal relationship between two entities. Since the Czech respondents that were attributed to this type generally displayed not only notions of cause but also of effect or consequence, we can observe that these semantic features are also inherently present in the Romance *hacer/fare/faire/fazer* + infinitive construction and that the label of pure causativity that has been traditionally associated with it proves to be insufficient.

When analysing all fusional and all analytic expressions of causativity as one unit, we realised that the traditional supposition that Romance analytic causatives are generally translated with a fusional resource in Czech cannot be considered truthful. When modifying **Table 4.2** with regard to the analytic/fusional nature of the respondent types (fusional: types 1, 2, 3; analytic: types 4, 5, 6, 7; type with another form of expressing causativity), we obtain **Table 4.4** and **Graph 4.1**:

Tab. 4.4. Fusional and analytic types in our data (types 9 and 10 not included)

Type	Fusional (%)	Analytic (%)	Other form of expressing causativity (%)
Spanish	45	26	21
Italian	42	25	21
French	51	24	19
Portuguese	37	25	29

We can notice that although there are more analytic than fusional types (4 vs 3), the fusional type prevails in our data set (mostly in French, less in Spanish and Italian and the least in Portuguese).[34] If we reflect this data on the scale presented in **Figure 4.1**, this produces the following **Graph 4.2**:

Several conclusions can be drawn from **Graph 4.2**:
1) The dominance of the most fusional type (type 3) – only type 8, which remains out of our typological continuum, displays a similar frequency.
2) While with the fusional expressions it is possible to clearly determine one prevailing respondent type (type 3), with the analytic types, the prevalence of the *dát napít* type (type 4) is considerably less distinct.

---

34   However, the differences cannot be considered significant because the respective language subcorpora do not have the same parameters.

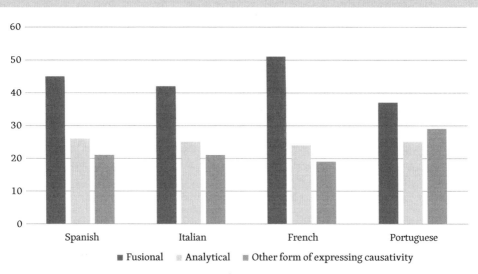

Graph 4.1. Fusional and analytical types in our data (types 9 and 10 not included)

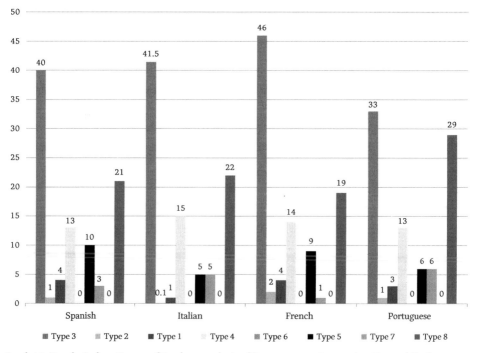

Graph 4.2. Typological continuum of Czech respondents of Romance causative construction and the frequency of concrete types[35]

---

35   The graph reflects % with regard to the whole; however, the last column in each language – i.e. changes in syntactic roles – does not actually belong to the scheme and is only included for comparison.

3) Transparent fusional morphological expressions of causativity (types 1, 2) are rather marginal.
4) Our type 8 (changes in syntactic roles), which does not figure among the expressions of causativity generally presented by Czech grammar, was a very frequent respondent of the examined Romance construction. This proves our wide conception of causativity to be justified: instead of a traditional causative expression, the speaker often prefers to display the causee as the subject of an action while the causer is expressed in another way (for example, by adverbials of cause).

We conclude by emphasising that even if we have presented a specific form of a typological scale of respondents to the examined construction, the data analysis shows that some specific Czech constructions are difficult to assign to one concrete type and there are many transitive stages (also, the definition of analytic types is by itself a generalisation: the scale does not consist of discrete units). This can be considered as confirmation of Comrie's (1989) conception of causative expressions in terms of a continuum.

In light of the above-presented analyses, we can formulate two general observations:

1) The analysed constructions display similar combinatory preferences in all four languages and the Czech respondents do not differ according to the source language.
2) The Czech respondents of the Romance causative construction tend to be heterogeneous and reveal an inherently different organisation of this category in Czech.

Contrastive analyses proved to be a useful tool not only for comparing Romance languages with a typologically different language but also for presenting the category of causative in Czech from a new perspective. Our analyses clearly reveal its inherently heterogeneous character, which oscillates between fusional and analytic forms of expression. The Czech respondents of the Romance constructions also reveal that the basic definition of causativity as "someone causes something that forces someone to do something" (for an extended discussion, refer to **Section 4.1**) is often insufficient for explaining the complex semantics of the *hacer/fare/faire/fazer* + infinitive construction, thus presenting possibilities for future research.

5. INGRESSIVE PERIPHRASES IN ROMANCE AND THEIR CZECH RESPONDENTS

DANA KRATOCHVÍLOVÁ
JAROSLAVA JINDROVÁ
PAVEL ŠTICHAUER
ELIŠKA TŘÍSKOVÁ

5.0 INTRODUCTION

The goal of this chapter is to present the most frequent Romance verbal periphrases that express the beginning of a process and their Czech respondents, thus aiming to adopt a new perspective on the abstract notion of ingressivity and presenting its possible realisations in the Czech language. The chapter is organised as follows. In **Section 5.1**, we present some general remarks regarding verbal periphrases in Romance languages. Since our contrastive perspective points out the necessity to analyse the semantic features they express with respect to aspect and Aktionsart, **Section 5.2** introduces how these categories are represented in Romance languages and in Czech. Further on, we concentrate on ingressivity and its relationship with these categories. In **Section 5.3**, we present the results of a series of corpus analyses that concentrated on Romance ingressive periphrastic constructions and their Czech respondents. **Section 5.4** highlights the most important conclusions that can be based on these analyses.

5.1 VERBAL PERIPHRASES IN ROMANCE

Verbal periphrases constitute an important element of the verbal system of all four of the Romance languages studied. In general terms, their main function consists of focusing on a specific stage of a process, presenting it from the perspective of its beginning, its progress or its end.[36] From this point of view, these constructions are closely related to aspect and Aktionsart. In the Czech tradition, the notions they express are rather treated within a more specific category called *způsob/povaha slovesného děje*, which could be translated as *the character of verbal action* (see Dušková 2012). These categories and their respective position in the Romance and Czech verbal systems will be discussed in **Section 5.2**.

---

36 The combinations of modal verbs and the infinitive and even the construction *hacer/fare/faire/fazer* + infinitive are sometimes also treated as verbal periphrases, see Drzazgowska (2011). However, we will consider as proper verbal periphrases only those constructions that are directly related to the phases of a process. For an extended discussion related to *hacer/fare/faire/fazer* + infinitive, see Čermák – Kratochvílová et al. (this volume).

Typically, Romance verbal periphrases display the following structure: semi-auxiliary verb (+ preposition) + non-finite verbal form.[37] The resulting constructions can express several tempo-aspectual meanings that can be attributed to one of these six basic types:

1) Imminent future – *It is about to rain*
   Es. *Está para llover* / It. *Sta per piovere* / Pt. *Está para chover*
2) Beginning of a process – *It starts to rain*
   Es. *Empieza a llover* / It. *Comincia a piovere* / Fr. *Il commence à pleuvoir* / Pt. *Começa a chover*
3) Process in progress – *It is raining*
   Es. *Está lloviendo* / It. *Sta piovendo* / Fr. *Il est en train de pleuvoir* / Pt. *Está a chover*[38]
4) The end of a process – *It stopped raining*
   Es. *Ha dejado de llover* / It. *Ha smesso di piovere* / Fr. *Il a cessé de pleuvoir* / Pt. *Deixou de chover*
5) The repetition of a process – *It started to rain again*
   Es. *Ha vuelto a llover* / It. *È tornato a piovere* / Pt. *Tornou a chover*
6) Habituality – *It usually rains here a lot*
   Es. *Aquí suele llover mucho* / It. *Qui suole piovere molto* / Pt. *Aqui costuma chover muito*

5.1.1 APPROACHES TO VERBAL PERIPHRASES AND THE GOAL OF OUR STUDY

Verbal periphrases have been largely discussed in linguistic literature. There are three main approaches which the different authors adopt:

1) The very definition of periphrastic constructions, their distinction from idioms, the combinatory possibilities, the semantics of periphrastic constructions and their inventory. See Drzazgowska (2011), Fente Gómez – Fernández Álvarez – Feijó (1994), Fogsgaard (2002), García Fernández (2006), Gómez Torrego (1988; 1999), Jindrová (2016), Olbertz (1998), Verroens (2011).
2) The position of verbal periphrases within the verbal system, their relationship to aspect and Aktionsart. See Barroso (1994; 1999; 2000), Begioni (2012), Camus Bergareche (2004), Dietrich (1983), Gosseline (2011), Laca (2002), Pešková (2005).
3) Contrastive analyses of verbal periphrases across different Romance languages or the expression of notions expressed by Romance periphrastic constructions in

---

37   The commonly used French progressive construction corresponding to the English *be* + *-ing* form displays a more complex structure constituted by the verb *être* ('to be') followed by *en train de* ('in the process of') + infinitive. In Romanian, a completion by the subjunctive is also possible, for verbal periphrases in Romanian and their comparison to Spanish, see Topor – Fernández – Vásquez (2006; 2007; 2008).
38   The construction with infinitive is typical for European Portuguese; in the Brazilian variant, the construction *Está chovendo* with gerund is used.

typologically different languages. See Kratochvílová – Jindrová (2017), Głowicka (2013), Luque (2008), Pešková (2018), Sánchez Montero (1993), Topor – Fernández – Vázquez (2006; 2007; 2008), Zieliński (2017).

Our approach to the study of Romance verbal periphrases aims to complement the discussion represented by works cited as types b) and c). Leaving aside problems regarding the formal aspects of verbal periphrases and following the general aim of this monograph, we adopt a purely synchronic and contrastive perspective. Our goal is to analyse the most frequently used ingressive Romance periphrases and their Czech translations. Since the Czech language does not possess any clear structural respondent for Romance ingressive constructions, we opt for analysing them within the general categories of aspect, Aktionsart and manner of action, thus defining the relationship between ingressivity and these categories.

5.2 ASPECT AND AKTIONSART

While there is no general agreement regarding the linguistic category that verbal periphrases express, it is commonly assumed that the notions expressed by these constructions are related to the category of aspect and/or Aktionsart. Therefore, a contrastive analysis must bear in mind the inherent differences in the way these categories are expressed in the Romance languages and in Czech. Taking the traditional Comrie's (1976) approach to aspect as a starting point, we can postulate several key structural differences.

5.2.1 ASPECT AND AKTIONSART IN ROMANCE LANGUAGES

When cross-linguistically analysing the category of aspect, Comrie (1976) distinguishes the basic opposition *perfective/imperfective* (with respective subclasses, such as *habitual* or *progressive*). In the studied Romance languages, this opposition is systematically encoded solely in the morphology of past tenses, which differentiate between the processes conceived as a whole (Es. *hablé* / It. *ho parlato (parlai)* / Fr. *j'ai parlé (je parlai)* / Pt. *falei*)[39] and those representing a certain circumstance and conceived as lasting for a longer time with no attention to the beginning or end (Es. *hablaba* / It. *parlavo* / Fr. *je parlais* / Pt. *falava*).

While the category of aspect, in the narrower sense of the term, is expressed morphologically, the category of *Aktionsart* (*inherent/internal/lexical aspect, manner of ac-*

---

39 Spanish (and, to a lesser extent, also Portuguese) also maintain the distinction between the perfective (Es. *hablé* / Pt. *falei*) and the perfect (Es. *he hablado* / Pt. *tenho falado*); in Italian and French the original perfect (compound) forms tend to substitute the perfective ones in the spoken language, thus neutralising this opposition.

tion) has been traditionally conceived in terms of tempo-qualitative meanings result-ing from the semantics of a verb. This category is thus related to notions such as *telic/atelic, punctual/durative, state/process* (see Comrie 1976; Smith 1997; Albertuz 1995). However, in Romance linguistics, Aktionsart is usually understood in a broader sense and is also related to the phrasal characteristics of a process, thus including the *in-choativity, progressivity* (*durativity*), *intromission, termination* or *iterativity* (see Pawlak 2008; Begioni 2012).

Given the close relationship between aspectual and Aktionsart-related notions and the limited representation of the category of aspect in Romance languages (in com-parison to Slavic languages, see **Section 5.2.2**), some authors argue against separat-ing these two categories and point out their inherent interconnection (see Fernández Pérez 1993; Gosselin 2011).

5.2.2 ASPECT AND AKTIONSART IN CZECH

The Czech category of aspect is largely comparable to the widely studied Russian one (see Comrie 1976, 125; Smith 1997, 227–259; Croft 2012, 110–114). The Czech verbal sys-tem presents a systemic opposition between perfectivity and imperfectivity in all tenses and moods. Perfectivity in Czech is generally expressed through prefixes:

Psát ('to be writing-IPFV')
Napsat ('to write something-PFV')
Dopsat ('to finish writing-PFV')
Přepsat ('to rewrite something-PFV')
Zapsat ('to take a note-PFV')
Rozepsat ('to start writing something-PFV')
Připsat ('to add something in written-PFV')

As can be observed, the Czech perfective prefixes are often polyfunctional and, to-gether with perfectivity, also express other notions related to the tempo-qualitative characteristics of a process.[40] These characteristics are studied within the category of *manner of action* (*způsob slovesného děje*), a term corresponding to Aktionsart which is, however, used more often in Czech linguistics (see Komárek – Kořenský et al. 1986, 185–187; Karlík – Nekula – Rusínová 1995, 209-213; Karlík – Nekula – Pleskalová 2002, 567-569; Chromý 2018). Nübler (2017) distinguishes the following groups of a manner of action: *ingressive, evolutive, delimitative, resultative, terminative, perdurative, finitive, exhaustive, total, saturative, extensive, cumulative, intensive, excessive, semelfactives, mo-mentary, iterative, diminutive, comitative, frequentative, stative, decursive* and *mutative.*

---

40   For an extended discussion regarding Czech affixes, see Štichauer et al. (this volume).

5.2.3 VERBAL PERIPHRASES AND THE RELATIONSHIP
TO ASPECT AND AKTIONSART

As can be observed, notions expressed by verbal periphrases, such as the beginning of a process, the duration of a process or its repetition, correspond to types of Aktionsart / manner of action, as conceived both by the Romance and Czech tradition. However, identifying periphrases entirely with this category is not possible since, when expressed through a periphrastic construction, these notions are external and subjective, i.e. they do not result naturally from the semantics of a verb. Analysing periphrases within the framework of aspect is equally problematic given the possibility to combine, for example, progressivity and perfectivity (Es. **Estuvo lloviendo** *una hora* – 'It rained for an hour') or termination and imperfectivity (It. *Giorno dopo giorno si ripeteva lo stesso:* **smetteva di piovere** *e poi tutto cominciava di nuovo* – 'Every day, the same thing used to happen: it used to stop raining and then it all used to start again').

The problematic nature of verbal periphrases generally leads the authors to apprehend the category of aspect in a much broader sense than it is customary in Czech linguistics and to analyse these constructions as forms of expression of this category, see Barroso (1988; 1994; 2000), Olbertz (1998), Fogsgaard (2002), Camus Bergareche (2004), RAE (2009). Given the inherent structural differences between aspect in Czech and in Romance, we opt for a different approach. Following Pawlak (2008) and Zavadil – Čermák (2010), we associate the notion of aspect solely with the perfective/imperfective opposition. Our claim here is that ingressivity, durativity, iterativity etc. are more closely related to manners of action, extending, however, the definition of this category and conceiving its formal manifestations in terms of a continuum that includes both internal notions resulting from the very semantics of a verb, both the external and explicit expression of these notions. While adopting the traditional definition of the manner of action (henceforth referred to as MoA) in terms of a complex and heterogeneous category related to the qualitative characteristics of a process that allows their division into groups (see Zavadil – Čermák 2010, 314; Nübler 2017), we choose to approach it in highly abstract terms, distinguishing three main levels of its expression:

1) Internal MoA
   The internal manner of action corresponds with the narrowest understanding of Aktionsart, i.e. with the inherent semantic properties of the processes allowing their classification.
2) Derivative MoA
   The expression of the tempo-qualitative characteristics through an affix and/or through reflectivity.
3) Analytical MoA
   The expression of the tempo-qualitative characteristics of a process through a productive verbal or verbo-nominal construction.

Further on, we shall concentrate only on one particular type of MoA and will analyse the expression of ingressivity.

5.2.4 INGRESSIVE MOA

Ingressivity (sometimes the terms *inchoativity* or *inceptivity* are used in the same sense, see, for example, Barroso 1999; Fogsgaard 2002; Luque 2015) can be defined as the presentation of a process from the perspective of its beginning or its initial stage (see Zavadil – Čermák 2010, 316). Comrie (1976, 19–20) analyses ingressivity within the framework of the perfective aspect. Further on, Zavadil – Čermák (2010, 316–319) distinguish four subtypes of ingressivity:

1) imminent ingressivity, i.e. imminently expected process (*It's about to rain*),
2) dispositional ingressivity, i.e. imminently planned process (*I am about to leave*),
3) initial ingressivity, i.e. the proper beginning of a process (*It starts to rain*),
4) inceptive ingressivity, i.e. the initial process in a sequence of actions (*He started by saying his name*).

We focus solely on type 4), i.e. initial ingressivity, in this chapter.

5.2.4.1 INITIAL INGRESSIVITY IN ROMANCE LANGUAGES

5.2.4.1.1 DERIVATIVE INGRESSIVE MOA IN ROMANCE

Verbal pairs corresponding to opposition ingressive (perfective) / progressive (imperfective) are rather infrequent in Romance languages (especially in comparison to Czech). Begioni (2010, 34) mentions the French prefix *en-* and the Italian prefix *ad-*, which (when combined with a reflexive pronoun) form pairs such as It. *dormire*, Fr. *dormir* ('to sleep') / It. *addormentarsi*, Fr. *s'endormir* ('to fall asleep'). In Spanish, a similar pair is created when using the reflexive pronoun: *dormir* ('to sleep') / *dormirse* ('to fall asleep'). In Portuguese, a combination of a prefix and a suffix is used: *dormir* ('to sleep') / *adormecer* ('to fall asleep'). Given the marginal status of this form of expressing ingressivity, these pairs will not be discussed in this monograph.

5.2.4.1.2 ANALYTICAL INGRESSIVE MOA IN ROMANCE

In Romance, the main tool for expressing ingressivity are verbal periphrases. All four Romance languages studied here dispose of a set of partially synonymous constructions that emphasise the beginning of a process. Their common semantic feature can be defined as [+ingressive]; however, they differ with regard to their frequency of use, the type of infinitives they typically combine with and the (non-)presence of secondary semantic notions such as [+effort], [+unexpectancy], [+inappropriateness] etc. In general terms, ingressive periphrases in Spanish, Italian, French and Portuguese can be divided into three groups:

1) Ingressive constructions expressing the mere beginning of a process

These periphrases correspond to the neutral English construction *start + -ing*. They do not add any specific secondary semantic notion to the representation of a process in its initial phase and do not display any considerable combinatory limitations. In all four languages, these periphrases contain a semi-auxiliar that corresponds to the English verbs *to start* or *to begin*:

> Es. *Empezar a* + infinitive, *comenzar a* + infinitive[41]
> It. *Cominciare a* + infinitive, *iniziare a* + infinitive
> Fr. *Commencer à* + infinitive, *commencer de* + infinitive
> Pt. *Começar a* + infinitive[42]

2) Ingressive constructions expressing the beginning of a process and the notion of effort on the part of the subject

In all the languages studied, there is one commonly used ingressive construction that does not display any significant combinatory limitations although it modifies the basic ingressive notion by adding the semes of [+effort] [+subject's interest] [+motivation] [+intentionality], thus making it comparable to the English construction *to get down to sth*:[43]

> Es. *Ponerse a* + infinitive (see García Fernández et al. 2006, 218–223; Zavadil – Čermák 2010, 318; Kratochvílová – Jindrová 2017)
> It. *Mettersi a* + infinitive (see Sánchez Montero 1993, 28; Luque 2008)
> Fr. *Se mettre à* + infinitive (see Haton 2005; Pauly 2005; Verroens 2011)
> Pt. *Pôr-se a* + infinitive (see Barroso 2016; Kratochvílová – Jindrová 2017)

3) Highly stylistically marked ingressive constructions

In all four languages studied, there is a group of periphrastic constructions that can be described in terms of the lower overall frequency of use and a specific semantic feature added to the notion of ingressivity. Sometimes, a clear tendency to prefer

---

41   In Spanish, there are two more constructions, *principiar a* + infinitive and *iniciar a* + infinitive, which would fit the description of this group. However, in present-day language, these periphrases are seldom used (see Kratochvílová – Jindrová 2017) and, due to their limited presence in the corpus we work with, will not be analysed here.

42   The Portuguese construction *principiar a* + infinitive is similar to its Spanish counterpart (i.e. its use is very limited in present-day language) and it is not analysed here, see Kratochvílová – Jindrová 2017.

43   In general, the notion of [+suddenness] is also present although it is less distinct than with periphrases forming the third group.

a concrete type of infinitive completion can also be observed. Given the huge number of these constructions (that can especially be found in Spanish and in Portuguese) and the limited frequency of their usage, not all stylistically marked periphrastic construction could be studied in this monograph. For the corpus analysis, we chose the following seven constructions that do not display any considerable diatopic restrictions, had a frequency ≥ 15 in our respective subcorpora and are largely discussed in the literature. These constructions were further divided into three subgroups based on the semantic features associated with them. These notions are marked in square brackets; considerable combinatory limitations are specified in curly brackets.

[+suddenness] [+unexpectancy]
Es. *Echarse a* + infinitive {+verbs of emotional reaction} (see Gómez Torrego 1999, 3374)
Es. *Echar a* + infinitive {+verbs of movement} (see Gómez Torrego 1999, 3347)

[+suddenness] [+abruptness] [+previous retention]
Es. *Romper a* + infinitive {+verbs of emotional reaction} {+verbs of physical activity} {+ verbs of interpretation} {+verbs expressing a change of state} {+verbs associated with meteorological phenomena} (see García Fernández et al. 2006, 230–232)
Es. *Largarse a* + infinitive (see García Fernández et al. 2006, 183)
It. *Scoppiare a* + infinitive {+verbs of emotional reaction} (see Bertinetto 2001, 155; Sánchez Montero 1993, 32)
Pt. *Romper a* + infinitive (see Barroso 1994, 124–125; Kratochvílová – Jindrová 2017)

[+suddenness] [+abruptness] [+vehemence]
Es. *Lanzarse a* + infinitive (see Zavadil – Čermák 2010, 319)

As can be observed, the number of periphrases analysed in each language is not the same, we analyse eight Spanish ingressive constructions, four Italian and only three French and Portuguese ingressive periphrases. This discrepancy is given by two factors:

1) The overall number of ingressive periphrastic constructions and their productivity in present-day language differs distinctively according to the specific language. The widest set of constructions, which are also highly productive, can be found in Spanish and Portuguese (see Barroso 1994; 1999, 337; Zavadil – Čermák 2010; Drzazgowska 2011; Jindrová 2016; Kratochvílová – Jindrová 2017). Slightly more limited is the list of Italian verbal periphrases (see Sánchez Montero 1993; Hamplová 1994; Bertinetto 2001) while the most limited set of ingressive constructions can be found in French (see Haton 2005).
2) The lowest number of Portuguese ingressive constructions that could be analysed is given by the limited extension of the Portuguese subcorpus.

5.2.4.2 INITIAL INGRESSIVITY IN CZECH

5.2.4.2.1 DERIVATIVE INGRESSIVE MOA IN CZECH

There are several prefixes in the Czech language that can be attributed to an ingressive function. Nevertheless, these prefixes are always polyfunctional and ingressivity is not their unique function. Ingressivity can also inherently combine with other notions (such as a very short duration of a process or spatial interpretation in terms of moving somewhere) while the separation of these two notions proves to be impossible. In her extensive study of ingressive prefixes in Czech, Reichzieglová (2010) works with the following set of prefixes that (based on the data provided by three dictionaries) express ingressivity: *na-, pro-, roz-, vy-, vz-* and *za-*. In the newly published academic grammar of Czech, Štícha et al. (2018), also mention the ingressive interpretation of the prefixes *u-* and *po-*; on the other hand, they do not consider the prefix *na-* as clearly ingressive. By combining these two classifications, we obtain the following set of Czech prefixes with a possible ingressive interpretation:

Prefix *roz-*
The most frequent ingressive suffix in Czech; in Riechzieglová's corpus-based analysis, it constitutes almost half of all the tokens (cf. 2010, 103). Its usage does not present any considerable combinatory limitation. However, a tendency to combine with verbs expressing emotional reaction is clearly observable (cf. Reichzieglová 2010, 103). The ingressive meaning is generally accompanied by reflexivity; non-reflexive predicates with *roz-* often acquire a causative interpretation (see Čermák – Kratochvílová et al. this volume):

(1)
Pavel   *se*   *smál.*
Paul   REFL   laugh-PST.3SG.IPFV
'Paul was laughing.'

(2)
Pavel   *se*   *roze-smál.*
Paul   REFL   INGR-laugh-PST.3SG.PFV
'Paul started to laugh.'

(3)
Pavel   *roze-smál*   *Marii.*
Paul   INGR-laugh-PST.3SG.PFV   Mary-ACC
'Paul made Mary laugh.'

Štícha et al. (2018, 1060) also mention the notion of high intensity that can be associated with this prefix in its ingressive interpretation:

hořet ('to be in flames')
rozhořet *se* ('to start burning' – in a given context, the optional interpretation of progressive growing stronger of the flames is possible).

Prefix *vy-*

Štícha et al. consider this prefix to be one of the most polysemantic (cf. 2018, 1067). The ingressive interpretation is associated with its directional function, which relates to moving from one place to another or to leaving a place. This naturally translates into the frequent combination with verbs of movement:

(4)
Pavel	*šel*	*pomalu.*
Paul	go-PST.3SG.IPFV	slowly

'Paul went slowly.'

(5)
Pavel	*vy-šel*	*z*	*domu.*
Paul	INGR-go-PST.3SG.PFV	from	house-GEN

'Paul went out of the house.'

This prefix can also accentuate the initial phase of an already very short process. Reichzieglová (2010, 108) also mentions the notion of unintentionality from part of the subject:

křičet ('to yell-IPFV')
křiknout ('to yell-PFV', i.e. 'to yell only once and shortly')
vykřiknout ('to produce a short yell-PFV')

In our corpus analysis, this prefix was the second most frequent (after the prefix *roz-*).

Prefix *za-*

While this prefix is relatively frequent (in Reichzieglová's (2010) corpus it is in the second position), it cannot express the sole notion of ingressivity, Reichzieglová (2010, 110) mentions a "semantic microstructure" combining the beginning of a process with other features. The most frequent notion here is that of a very short duration of the process:

smát se ('to laugh-IPFV')
rozesmát *se* ('to start laughing-PFV' – the laughing took a while, maybe even progressively became stronger)
zasmát *se* ('to give a short laugh-PFV')

Prefix *na-*

This prefix combines ingressivity with semantic features related to the low intensity of the process or its low impact:

(6)

Pavel	kousl		do	jablka.
Paul	bite-PST.3SG.PFV		in	apple-GEN

'Paul gave one bite in an apple.'

(7)

Pavel	na-kousl	jablko.
Paul	INGR-bite-PST.3SG.PFV	apple-ACC

'Paul started eating an apple by giving one bite.' (Frequently, the implication that the subject did not finish eating the apple is present.)

Prefix *u-*

In its ingressive interpretation, it expresses a sudden beginning of the process (cf. Štícha et al. 2018, 1064):

cítit ('to feel', 'to smell')

ucítit ('to start feeling', 'to start smelling')

Prefix *vz-*

In its ingressive interpretation, this prefix combines with a very limited set of verbs, giving rise to rather archaic forms such as:

plát ('to be in flames' – only used in literary language)

vzplát ('to start burning' – only used in literary language)

Prefix *po-*

Ingressive interpretations of this prefix are rather marginal and are associated with a short duration of a process:

myslet si ('to think something', 'to have an opinion about something')

pomyslet si ('to imagine something for a short period of time' – with a subtle emphasis on the initial stage of the process)[44]

Prefix *pro-*

The ingressive interpretation of this prefix is also very limited, Štícha et al. (2018, 1050) mention only the pair:

mluvit ('to speak-IPFV')

promluvit ('to speak-PFV' – with the emphasis on the beginning of the process)

Reichzieglová (2010, 102–103) presents a list of 45 verbs with this prefix that could be considered ingressive. Nevertheless, this ingressivity is always combined with other notions and is present only marginally.

---

44 Štícha et al. (2018, 1046) also mention its possible ingressive interpretation in combination with verbs related to a change of position: *kleknout si* ('to get on knees') / *pokleknout* ('to get on knees' – with a subtle emphasis on the beginning of the process). However, we consider the presence of the semantic notion of ingressivity inconclusive here.

5.2.4.2.2 ANALYTICAL INGRESSIVE MOA IN CZECH

Given the nature of the Czech tempo-aspectual system, the MoA is generally studied within the category of word-formation and is identified with the analysis of verbal prefixes and their function (or with the combination "prefix + reflexive pronoun"), see Karlík – Nekula – Rusínová (1995, 209–216), Komárek – Kořenský et al. (1986, 185). However, the beginning of a process can also be expressed in an analytic way. In our corpus analysis, we found six constructions that were used systematically for the translation of Romance ingressive periphrases.

1) Verbal constructions

Neutral ingressivity can be expressed through the combination of the verb *začít* ('to begin') and an infinitive. The resulting construction does not display any combinatory limitations and expresses the mere beginning of a process, thus being comparable to the neutral Romance constructions Es. *empezar a* / Es. *comenzar a* / It. *cominciare a* / It. *iniziare a* / Fr. *commencer* à / Fr. *commencer de* / Pt. *começar a* + infinitive:

(8)
Pavel	*začal*	*zpívat.*
Paul	start-PST.3SG.PFV	sing-INF

'Paul started to sing.'

An analogical construction might also be formed with the verbs *jmout se* ('to set about doing something' – archaic) and *počít* ('to begin' – archaic). However, both verbs are rather obsolete in present-day language and ingressivity is not often expressed in this way (as was also proven by the corpus analysis).

2) Verbo-nominal constructions

When analysing Czech translations of Romance ingressive constructions, we found four productive verbo-nominal constructions that express the beginning of a process. Unlike the neutral *začít* + infinitive, they cumulate several aspectual-qualitative features in their semantic matrix with some of them corresponding to those expressed by stylistically marked Romance ingressive periphrases:

a) *Dát se do* + noun

This construction is formed by the verb *dát* ('to give') in the reflexive form and the preposition *do* ('in', 'into') followed by a noun in genitive. The literal meaning would be 'to give oneself into something'. It is a highly productive ingressive construction that emphasises the subject's involvement or effort, thus being comparable to the Romance periphrases Es. *ponerse a* / It. *mettersi a* / Fr. *se mettre* à / Pt. *pôr-se a* + infinitive. It does not present any considerable combinatory limitations, and when analysed in the SYN2015 corpus[45] the five most frequent noun completions were: *pohyb* ('movement', f = 390), *práce* ('work', f = 204), *řeč* ('talking', f = 187), *smích* ('laughter', f = 154), *pláč* ('crying', f = 104).

(9)

Pavel	*se*	*dal*	*do*	*zpěvu.*
Paul	REFL	give-PST.3SG.PFV	into	singing-GEN

'Paul started to sing.' (The notions of singing with pleasure and joy are perceptible here.)

b) *Pustit se do* + noun

This construction is formally similar to *dát se do* + noun. It is formed by the verb *pustit* ('to release') in the reflexive form, also followed by the preposition *do* ('in', 'into') and a noun completion in the genitive. The literal translation would be 'to release oneself into doing something'.

The semantic difference between *dát* and *pustit se do* + noun is rather subtle, being the notions of the subject's effort and personal involvement stronger in the case of *pustit se do* + noun. The seme of intentionality is also more perceptible, which translates into the fact that this construction generally does not combine with nouns describing an emotional reaction, such as *laughter* or *crying*. When analysed in SYN2015,[46] the five most frequent nominal completion were: *práce* ('work', f = 330), *boj* ('fight', f = 98), *jídlo* ('food', 'meal', f = 81), *čtení* ('reading', f = 51), *psaní* ('writing', f = 51).

(10)

Pavel	*se*	*pustil*	*do*	*práce.*
Paul	REFL	release-PST.3SG.PFV	into	work-GEN

'Paul put himself to work.'

c) *Propuknout v* + noun

This ingressive construction is comparable to the Romance periphrases Es. *romper a* / Es. *largarse a* / It. *scoppiare a* / Pt. *romper a* + infinitive. It is formed by the verb *propuknout* ('to break out', 'to erupt', 'to burst out'), the preposition *v* ('in', 'into') and a nominal completion in the accusative. It expresses a sudden beginning of a process with the notion of previous retention (which results from the semantics of the verb *propuknout*).

It differs from *dát/pustit se do* not only in the semantics but also in its strongly limited combinatorics and presents a strong preference for nouns expressing emotional reactions. The five most frequent completions found in SYN2015[47] were

---

45 A representative corpus of contemporary written Czech, see Cvrček – Čermáková – Křen (2016) and Křen – Cvrček – Čapka et al. (2016). The query had the following form: *[lemma="dát"][word="se"]?[word="do"][tag="N.*"]*.

46 The query had the following form: *[lemma="pustit"][word="se"]?[word="do"][tag="N.*"]*.

47 The query had the following form: *[lemma="propuknout"][word="v"][tag="N.*"]*.

pláč ('crying', f = 102), *smích* ('laughter', f = 26), *jásot* ('exultation', f = 12), nadšení ('enthusiasm', f = 3), *slzy* ('tears', f = 3).

(11)

Pavel	*propukl*	*v*	*pláč.*
Paul	erupt-PST.3SG.PFV	into	crying-ACC

'Paul burst into tears.'

d) *Vrhnout se do/na* + noun

When used to express the beginning of a process, this construction is highly stylistically marked and expresses notions of the subject's involvement and interest, but also suddenness, rashness and often imprudence. These semantic features result from the meaning of the verb *vrhnout se* ('to through/fling oneself at something'), which in this construction combines with the prepositions *do* ('in', 'into') or *na* ('on', 'onto') and a nominal completion in the genitive or accusative (depending on the preposition). Thus, the semantics of this construction are largely comparable to those attributed to the Spanish periphrasis *lanzarse a* + infinitive. Nevertheless, the ingressive usage of this construction is limited in present-day language and sometimes it is difficult to differentiate its ingressive meaning from a locative one (literally or metaphorically 'to throw oneself on something' or 'to dive into something'). When analysing this construction in SYN2015,[48] we found the following five most frequent nominal completions: *práce* ('work', f = 50), *boj* ('fight', f = 30), *akce* ('action', f = 13), *útok* ('attack', f = 12), *příprava* ('preparation', f = 5).

(12)

Pavel	*se*	*vrhl*	*do*	*práce.*
Paul	REFL	throw-PST.3SG.PFV	into	work-GEN

'Paul put himself to work.' (With great enthusiasm, but also too rashly.)

5.3 CORPUS ANALYSIS

5.3.1 METHODOLOGY

In order to find ingressive Romance periphrases, we used the following analogical queries:

Es.
[lemma="poner."][word="a"][tag="VLinf"]*
[lemma="poner."][]{1,1}[word="a"][tag="VLinf"]*

---

48   The query had the following form: *[lemma="vrhnout"][word="se"]?[word="do"][tag="N.*"]*.

It.
[lemma="mettere"] [word="a"] [tag="V.*inf.*"]

Fr.
[lemma="commencer"][word="à"][tag="VER:infi"]
[lemma="commencer"][word="de|d'"][tag="VER:infi"]
[word="me|m'|te|t'|se|s'|nous|vous"][]{0,3}[lemma="mettre"][word="à"][tag="VER:infi"]

Pt.
[lemma="pôr"][word="a"][tag="V.*"]
[lemma="pôr"][tag="PP."][]{0,2}[word="a"][tag="V.N"]
[tag="PP. "][lemma="pôr"][word="a"][tag="V.N"]

Progressively, we manually analysed the Czech respondents of the analysed periphrases and attributed them to one of the following types:

1) Verb + infinitive
   a) *Začít* + infinitive
   b) Other verb + infinitive
2) Verbonominal construction
   a) *Dát se do* + noun
   b) *Pustit se do* + noun
   c) *Propuknout v* + noun[49]
   d) *Vrhnout se do/na* + noun[50]
3) Prefix
   a) *Roz-*
   b) Other prefix[51]
4) Other construction[52]
5) No translation[53]

---

49 In the tables containing the results, this type is mentioned only when it appeared at least once in the corpus.
50 In the tables containing the results, this type is mentioned only when it appeared at least once in the corpus.
51 This kind of translation was attributed to the use of any of the prefixes mentioned in **Section 5.2.4.2.1** that expressed ingressivity in the given context (often together with other semantic features).
52 Translations labelled as *other translation* did not correspond to any of the above-mentioned expressions of ingressivity. However, the notion of the beginning of the process was clearly present (for example, it was expressed lexically or through an idiomatic construction).
53 The type *no translation* corresponded to those cases where the notion of ingressivity was not present at all in the Czech respondent.

5.3.2 RESULTS OF THE CORPUS ANALYSES

5.3.2.1 INGRESSIVE CONSTRUCTIONS EXPRESSING THE MERE BEGINNING
OF A PROCESS

In the respective subcorpora, we found the following stylistically neutral ingressive constructions that had a frequency ≥ 15:

Es. *Empezar a* + infinitive, *comenzar a* + infinitive

It. *Cominciare a* + infinitive, *iniziare a* + infinitive

Fr. *Commencer à* + infinitive, *commencer de* + infinitive

Pt. *Começar a* + infinitive

Tab. 5.1. Czech translations of ingressive constructions expressing the mere beginning of a process

	Verb + infinitive		Verbonominal construction		Prefix		Other construction	No translation
	Začít	Other verb	*Dát se do*	*Pustit se do*	*Roz-*	Other prefix		
Es. *Empezar a* (3,562)	2,827	27	49	19	90	90	117	343
Es. *Comenzar a* (1,467)	1,155	7	18	10	38	41	66	132
It. *Cominciare a* (113)	69	1	3	0	4	4	6	26
It. *Iniziare a* (30)	21	0	1	2	0	3	1	2
Fr. *Commencer à* (152)	129	0	2	2	1	4	13	1
Fr. *Commencer de* (29)	19	0	0	0	0	4	6	0
Pt. *Começar a* (549)	330	24	14	6	23	16	43	93
Total (5,902)	4,550	59	87	39	156	162	252	597
%	77.1	1.3	1.5	0.7	2.6	2.7	4.3	10.1

The analysis clearly reveals that the stylistically neutral character of Romance constructions is best reflected in Czech through the *začít* + infinitive construction, which was used in 77.1% of cases, see for example, (13):

(13) Pt.
O mendigo deu boa-noite à negra, se arrastou até debaixo da lâmpada da casa fronteira e **começou a ler** o jornal. → Žebrák se dal dobrou noc černošce, dovlekl se pod lampu sousedního domu a **začal číst** noviny.

Literally: *he **started to read** the newspaper*.
Jorge Amado, *Pot* (*Suor*), transl. Otokar Fischer, Prague: Lidové noviny, 1949.

In approximately 10.1% of cases, the ingressivity of the original Romance construction was not overtly expressed in the Czech translation. As this is the second most frequent type, the question arises of whether ingressivity is completely absent in the Czech translation or whether it is inherently present in the internal MoA of the verb corresponding to the Romance infinitive, see (14), (15) and (16):

(14) Es.
Cuando la mujer **empezó a volver** en sí, Mendibj le tapó la boca y le entregó el papel. → Když žena zase **přišla** k sobě, Mendíbž jí zacpal ústa a podal jí ten lístek.
Literally: *when the woman **regained** consciousness again*.
Julia Navarro, *Bratrstvo turínského plátna* (*La Hermandad de la Sábana Santa*), transl. Vladimír Medek, Prague: Mladá fronta, 2006.

(15) It.
Mio fratello era nell' età in cui si **comincia a prendere** piacere alle letture più sostanziose (...). → Bratr byl ve věku, kdy **přicházíme** na chuť hutnější četbě (...).
Literally: *when we **develop** the taste for more solid reading*.
Italo Calvino, *Naši předkové* (*I nostri antenati*), transl. Zdeněk Digrin – Vladimír Mikeš, Prague: Odeon, 1970.

(16) Pt.
Estava **começando a escurecer** quando chegou com seu rebanho diante uma velha igreja abandonada. → **Už se stmívalo**, když přivedl své stádo ke starému opuštěnéu kostelu.
Literally: ***it was already getting dark***.
Paulo Coelho, *Alchymista* (*O Alquimista*), transl. Pavla Lidmilová, Brno: Jota, 1995.

While ingressivity is not explicitly present in either of the examples presented above, the verbs used in the Czech respondents imply a change of state, which is naturally connected to the notion of the beginning of a new process. The verbal periphrases used in the Romance originals accentuate the notion of ingressivity which, nevertheless, is to a certain extent present in the semantics of the auxiliated verb. The Czech respondents do not entirely lack the notion of ingressivity; they solely omit its emphasising.

5.3.2.2 INGRESSIVE CONSTRUCTIONS EXPRESSING THE BEGINNING OF A PROCESS AND THE NOTION OF EFFORT BY PART OF THE SUBJECT

In this section, we analyse the following set of verbal periphrases:
Es. *Ponerse a* + infinitive
It. *Mettersi a* + infinitive

Fr. *Se mettre à* + infinitive
Pt. *Pôr-se a* + infinitive

Our goal is to determine whether (or how) the semantic notions of [+effort] [+subject's interest] [+motivation] that combine with [+ingressivity] are reflected in the Czech translations. The results are resumed in **Table 5.2**.

Tab. 5.2. Czech translations of ingressive constructions expressing the beginning of a process and the notion of effort by part of the subject

	Verb + infinitive		Ingressive construction + noun		Prefix		Other construction	No translation
	Začít	**Other verb**	**Dát se do**	**Pustit se do**	**Roz-**	**Other prefix**		
Es. *Ponerse a* (1,232)	587	27	125	48	103	78	63	201
It. *Mettersi a* (168)	41	0	23	11	21	4	15	53
Fr. *Se mettre à* (207)	124	0	16	4	29	15	16	3
Pt. *Pôr-se a* (123)	37	14	4	6	9	14	5	34
Total (1,730)	789	41	168	69	162	111	99	291
%	45.6	2.4	9.7	3.9	9.3	6.4	5.7	16.8

As can be observed, the dominance of the neutral translation type *začít* + infinitive is less distinctive. While this type of translation does not explicitly reflect the notion of effort from the part of the subject that is associated with these periphrases, its presence can be often found in the very semantics of the infinitive appearing in the construction, which inherently implies the subject's involvement and interest, see (17), (18), (19).

(17) Es.
En fin, la divergencia se hace superlativa cuando se **ponen a pensar** en los medios que exige una instauración de la paz sobre este pugnacísimo globo terráqueo. →
K svrchovaným neshodám dochází, **začnou**-li **uvažovat** o prostředcích nastolení míru na naší velmi svárlivé zeměkouli.
Literally: *if they **start to think** about*.
José Ortega y Gasset, *Vzpoura davů* (*La rebelión de las masas*), transl. Václav Černý – Josef Forbelský, Prague: Naše vojsko, 1993.

(18) It.
All'inizio aveva accumulato idee, poi si era **messa a riempire** quaderni d'appunti. → Na začátku nahromadila nápady a pak **začala zaplňovat** sešity poznámkami.
Literally: *she **started to fill** the notebooks with notes*.
Alessandro Baricco, *City (City)*, transl. Alice Flemrová, Prague: Volvox Globator, 2000.

(19) Fr.
De temps en temps, il s'approchait de notre groupe, nous écoutait et quand je **me mettais à raconter** mes histoires françaises, il me fixait d'un air méfiant. → Občas se k našemu hloučku přiblížil, chvíli nás poslouchal, a když jsem **začal vykládat** svoje francouzské historky, upřel na mě podezíravý pohled.
Literally: *when I **started to narrate** my French tales*.
Andrei Makine, *Francouzský testament (Le Testament français)*, transl. Vlasta Dufková, Prague – Liberec: Paseka, 2002.

Once again, the type labelled as *no translation* was the second most frequent. As in the case of the neutral constructions analysed in **Section 5.3.2.1**, the absence of any explicit expression of ingressivity was often associated with verbs expressing a change of state or a momentary action, i.e. verbs containing inherent ingressivity (20):

(20) Pt.
Ah, porque não me disse? – e **pôs-se a limpar** as mãos ao avental. → "Proč jste to neřekl hned?" – a **otřela si** ruce do zástěry.
Literally: *she **wiped** her hands on the apron*.
Fernando Namora, *Muž s maskou (O Homem Disfarçado)*, transl. Pavla Lidmilová, Prague: Svoboda, 1979.

Nevertheless, the missing explicit notion of ingressivity in many cases also resulted from the strengthening of the secondary semantic notions of effort expressed by these periphrases. This kind of translation is represented by (21) and (22):

(21) Es.
Después se **pusieron a fumar** hombro contra hombro, satisfechos. → Pak se opřeli jeden druhému o rameno a spokojeně **pokuřovali**.
Literally: *they were happily **puffing away***.
Julio Cortázar, *Nebe, peklo, ráj (Rayuela)*, transl. Vladimír Medek, Prague: Mladá fronta, 2001.

(22) It.
Mi sono messa a correre verso la foresta come non avevo mai corso prima d'allora, e ho continuato finché sono crollata perterra; (...). → **Hnala jsem se** k lesu jako ještě nikdy v životě a pak jsem běžela dál, dokud jsem nepadla; (...).

Literally: *I **rushed** towards the wood*.
Sebastiano Vassalli, *Nespočet* (*Un infinito numero*), transl. Kateřina Vinšová, Prague – Litomyšl: Paseka, 2003.

The Czech respondent of the neutral Spanish verb *fumar* ('to smoke') in (21) contains a higher level of expressiveness since the verb *pokuřovat* (in contrast to the neutral *kouřit* – 'to smoke') also implies certain pleasure and involvement in the action of smoking, thus roughly corresponding to the English verb 'to puff'. In (22), the neutral Italian verb *correre* ('to run') is translated by the Czech verb *hnát se* ('to rush', 'to dash'), which in its semantics contains the notion of [+effort] [+subject's interest] [+motivation].

5.3.2.3 INGRESSIVE CONSTRUCTIONS EXPRESSING THE BEGINNING OF A PROCESS AND THE NOTIONS OF SUDDENNESS AND UNEXPECTEDNESS

In this section, we analyse the Spanish constructions *echarse a* + infinitive and *echar a* + infinitive. While the additional semantic notions expressed by these periphrases are the same (see García Fernández et al. 2006, 121–126), they differ in the combinatorics since *echarse a* combines mostly with verbs of emotional reaction while *echar a* combines with verbs of movement (cf. Gómez Torrego 1999, 3374). The infinitive completions with f ≥ 10 that were found in our corpus are resumed in **Tables 5.3** and **5.4**.

Tab. 5.3. Infinitive completions of echarse a.

Echarse a +	Frequency
reír ('to laugh')	212 (60.6%)
llorar ('to cry')	96 (27.4%)
temblar ('to tremble')	11 (3.1%)
andar ('to walk')	11 (3.1%)
correr ('to run')	10 (2.9%)

Tab. 5.4. Infinitive completions of echar a.

Echar a +	Frequency
correr ('to run')	124 (48.0%)
andar ('to walk')	118 (39.9%)
caminar ('to walk')	16 (5.4%)
volar ('to fly')	12 (4.0%)

The limited combinatorics of these constructions also influenced the Czech translations resumed in **Table 5.5**.

Tab. 5.5. Czech translations of ingressive constructions expressing the beginning of a process and the notions of suddenness and unxepectancy

	Verb + infinitive		Ingressive construction + noun			Prefix		Other construction	No translation
	Začít	Other verb	Dát se do	Pustit se do	Propuknout v	Roz-	Other prefix		
Es. *Echarse a* (350)	24	0	78	4	3	188	23	21	9
Es. *Echar a* (296)	2	0	26	0	0	76	118	51	23
Total (646)	26	0	104	4	3	264	141	72	32
%	4	0	16.1	0.6	0.5	40.9	21.8	11.1	4.9

The dominant type of translation was the prefix *roz-* followed by the translation type marked as other prefix (generally corresponding to the prefix *vy-* here). With the construction *echarse a* + infinitive, the analytic type *dát se do* + noun was also frequently used (approximately 22.3% of all respondents). The strong dominance of these respondent types is not surprising since they correspond extremely accurately to all notional and combinatory characteristics of the analysed constructions. All three types imply a sudden beginning of a process. *Roz-* and *dát se do* prefer the combination with verbs or nouns corresponding to emotional reaction (*plakat* 'to cry', *brečet* 'to cry', *smát se* 'to laugh' / *pláč* 'crying', *brek* 'crying', *smích* 'laughter'), in its ingressive interpretation the prefix *vy-* generally combines with verbs of movement (see **Section 5.2.4.2**). Therefore, the prototypical respondents found in the analysed concordance can be represented by (23), (24) and (25):

(23) Es.
Se revelaba sólo a medias, fugazmente, en un juego exasperante de sombras chinescas, pero al despedirse, cuando ella estaba a punto de **echarse a llorar** por hambre de amor, le entregaba una de sus prodigiosas cartas.
Objevoval se jen napůl, prchavě, v nesnesitelné stínohře, která ji přiváděla k zoufalství, ale při loučení, kdy <u>se</u> z hladu po lásce <u>už už chtěla</u> **rozplakat**, předal jí jeden ze svých úžasných dopisů.
Literally: <u>*she was about to* **start crying**</u> (*plakat* = 'to cry', *rozplakat se* = 'to start crying').
Isabel Allende, *Dcera štěstěny* (*Hija de la fortuna*), transl. Monika Baďurová, Prague: BB Art, 2004.

(24) Es.
Ruibérriz **se echó a reír** ahora, el labio vuelto y la dentadura relampagueante como si le estallara.
Ruibérriz **se dal do smíchu**, horní ret se mu ohrnul a zuby se blýskaly, jako by metaly blesky.

Literally: **_he gave himself into laughter_** (he started to laugh).
Javier Marías, _Vzpomínej na mě zítra při bitvě_ (_Mañana en la batalla piensa en mí_),
transl. Marie Jungmannová, Prague: Argo, 1999.

(25) Es.
La muchacha **echó a andar**.
Dívka **vykročila**.
Literally: _the girl **made first steps**_ (she started to walk towards somewhere).
Camilo José Cela, _Úl_ (_La colmena_), transl. Alena Ondrušková, Prague: Odeon, 1968.

5.3.2.4 INGRESSIVE CONSTRUCTIONS EXPRESSING THE BEGINNING OF A PROCESS AND THE NOTIONS OF SUDDENNESS, ABRUPTNESS AND PREVIOUS RETENTION

In this section, the following set of periphrases will be analysed:

Es. _Romper a_ + infinitive
Es. _Largarse a_ + infinitive
It. _Scoppiare a_ + infinitive
Pt. _Romper a_ + infinitive

All these constructions are highly stylistically marked and, consequently, less frequently used than the periphrases analysed in previous sections. The semantic notions

Tab. 5.6. Czech translations of ingressive constructions expressing the beginning of a process and the notions of suddenness, abruptness and previous retention

	Verb + infinitive		Ingressive construction + noun			Prefix		Other construction	No translation
	Začít	Other verb	Dát se do	Pustit se do	Propuknout v	Roz-	Other prefix		
Es. _Romper a_ (58)	5	0	10	0	6	27	3	6	1
Es. _Largarse a_ (36)	5	0	7	3	0	15	1	3	2
It. _Scoppiare a_ (16)	0	0	6	0	2	3	2	3	0
Pt. _Romper a_ (15)	0	0	11	0	2	2	0	0	0
Total (125)	10	0	34	3	10	47	6	12	3
%	8	0	27.2	2.4	8	37.6	4.8	9.6	2.4

associated with these constructions naturally result in their frequent combination with verbs of emotional reaction, thus expressing the subject's intention to suppress or slow down the manifestation of his feelings and the abrupt outbreak. While in English, similar notions can be attributed to the idiom 'to burst into tears', Czech offers a semi-productive ingressive construction *propuknout v* + noun, which also combines with verbs of emotional reaction and displays the same semantics as the Romance constructions analysed here (see **Section 5.2.4.2.2**). However, despite the existence of this apparently ideal Czech respondent, the Czech respondents, as resumed in **Table 5.6**, display great variability.

As in the case of *echarse a* + infinitive, the most frequent respondent type was the prefix *roz-*and the construction *dát se do* + noun. The construction *propuknout v* + noun appeared more frequently than with *echarse a* + infinitive although its overall frequency proved to be relatively low.

5.3.2.5 INGRESSIVE CONSTRUCTIONS EXPRESSING THE BEGINNING OF A PROCESS AND THE NOTIONS OF SUDDENNESS, ABRUPTNESS AND VEHEMENCE

While the Spanish ingressive periphrases *lanzarse a* + infinitive points out notions similar to those presented in **Section 5.3.2.4**, such as suddenness and abruptness, we analyse it separately to find out whether the substitution of the seme [+previous retention] with the seme [+vehemence] has any consequences on the Czech respondents. The results are summarised in **Table 5.7**.

Tab. 5.7. Czech translations of ingressive constructions expressing the beginning of a process and the notions of suddenness, abruptness and vehemence

	Verb + infinitive		Ingressive construction + noun			Prefix		Other construction	No translation
	Začít	Other verb	*Dát se do*	*Pustit se do*	*Vrhnout se do/na*	*Roz-*	Other prefix		
Es. *Lanzarse a* (27)	8	3	0	3	2	1	3	3	4
%	29.6	11.1	0	11.1	7.4	3.7	11.1	11.1	14.8

The analysis reveals that the presence of [+vehemence] has strong consequences on Czech respondent types. While the notions of sudden beginning and abruptness (potentially accompanied by the previous retention) expressed by the periphrases analysed in **Sections 5.3.2.3** and **5.3.2.4** found their prevailing respondents in the prefix *roz-* (eventually the prefix *vy-* in the case of verbs of movement) and the construction *dát se do* + noun, *lanzarse a* + infinitive lacks any clearly dominant Czech respondent.

The notion of vehemence and an abrupt or sudden beginning expressed by the Spanish construction finds its theoretical respondent in the Czech constructions *vrhnout se do/na*. Nevertheless, this type of translation was found only twice in our corpus. The remaining respondents oscillated between the complete omission of any notions apart from the mere beginning of a process (26) and an explicit expression of vehemence which also supposed the lack of [+ingressivity] (27):

(26) Es.
Casi temí que de entre la jungla de la habitación pudiera surgir un borzog y se **lanzara a morderme** las pantorrillas .
Skoro jsem dostal strach, že z té džungle vyskočí borzog a **začne** mě **hryzat** do lýtek.
Literally: ***he starts to bite*** *my calves*.
Pablo Tusset, *Nejlepší loupákův zážitek* (*Lo mejor que le puede pasar a un cruasán*), transl. Ondřej Nekola, Prague: Garamond, 2007.

(27) Es.
Es como si de pronto se hubiera **lanzado a recobrar** el tiempo perdido conmigo.
Jako by si **honem chtěla vynahradit** čas, který se mnou ztratila.
Literally: *as if **she quickly wanted to compensate** for the time*.
Arturo Pérez Reverte, *Kůže na buben* (*Piel del tambor*), transl. Vladimír Medek, Prague: Euromedia Group, 2004.

5.4 CONCLUDING REMARKS

The analyses presented in this chapter revealed two systemic similarities between Romance languages and Czech.

1) The tendency to combine ingressivity with other qualitative features referring to the beginning of a process

Both in Romance languages and in Czech, a clear tendency to combine [+ingressivity] with other semes can be observed. In Romance, the secondary notions result from the original semantics of the semi-auxiliary verb (for an extended discussion, see Kratochvílová – Jindrová 2017) and are expressed through the periphrastic construction. In Czech, the accumulation of several aspectual-qualitative characteristics is typical for prefixes; nevertheless, the analyses proved that the verbo-nominal constructions *dát se do / pustit se do* + noun are also highly productive in the present-day language.

2) Combinatory tendencies/limitations

Both Czech prefixes and verbo-nominal ingressive constructions display certain combinatory preferences. It is interesting to observe that these limitations are often comparable to those found with Romance periphrastic constructions. In Romance languages, there is a set of ingressive expressions that often combine with verbs of emotional reaction (Es. *echarse a* / Es. *romper a* / It. *scoppiare a* + infinitive).[54] In Czech, the tendency to combine with similar verbs can be observed with the prefix *roz-* and the verbo-nominal constructions *dát se do* and *propuknout v* + noun. A tendency to combine with verbs of motion can also be found both in Spanish (*echar a* + infinitive) and in Czech (the prefix *vy-*).

The key structural differences can be summarised in three points:

1) Formal expression of ingressivity

While in the Czech language ingressivity and the category of MoA, in general, is typically associated with prefixes, the analyses prove that this category has, in fact, three major forms of expression: the neutral construction *začít* + infinitive, verbal prefixes (especially *roz-*) and the verbo-nominal constructions *dát se do* and *pustit se do* + noun. The heterogeneity of Czech respondents presents the category of ingressivity in a new light. We conclude that the notion of beginning a process is distributed through the whole Czech verbal system and is systemically expressed both analytically (verbal and verbo-nominal constructions) and synthetically (prefixes). These observations could lead to a general question of whether identifying the category of MoA solely with prefixes in Czech is appropriate and whether notions such as ingressivity, iterativity and frequentativity should not be comprehended rather as abstract and polyfacetic categories that display a larger scale of systemic expressions. An analysis of the concurrence of word-formatting and analytical (lexical) resources could provide new insights into the category of MoA in Czech.

2) Productivity of highly stylistically marked constructions

The analyses have also revealed that both in Romance languages and in Czech, the beginning of a process is a commonly expressed semantic feature that has, in all the analysed languages, its preferred means of expression. Nevertheless, their set differs notably not only according to the specific Romance language but also when contrasting the highly stylistically marked Romance constructions and their Czech respondents. Despite the fact that the Czech language offers a theoretically ideal counterpart for the constructions Es. *romper a* / Es. *largarse a* / It. *scoppiare a* / Pt. *romper a* + infinitive (i.e. the verbo-nominal construction *propuknout v* + noun) and for the Spanish periphrasis *lanzarse a* + infinitive (i. e. *vrhnout se do/na* + noun), the frequency of these translations was very limited, and the Romance constructions were generally translated with a construction displaying a lower degree of stylistic markedness. When analysing ingressivity in Czech as a whole and considering all its above-mentioned systemic expressions (*začít* + infinitive, verbo-nominal constructions, prefixes) as respondents of

---

54   The Portuguese periphrasis *desatar a* + infinitive displays similar combinatory preferences; however, it was not analysed here due to its low frequency in the corpus. In French, there is a frequently used expression *éclater de rire* ('to burst into laughter'), which, nevertheless, combines solely with *rire*. Therefore, we consider it to be an idiom and not a proper verbal periphrasis.

Romance ingressive periphrases, we conclude that their set and their usage is more comparable to Italian or French than to Spanish or Portuguese.

3) Inherent MoA and its explicit emphasising

The high frequency of cases where the Czech respondents of Romance ingressive constructions did not express ingressivity at all or lacked any explicit expression of secondary semantic notions attributed to the original periphrasis, suggests that Czech displays a greater sensitivity to meanings related to MoA that are, nevertheless, inherent and are contained solely in the semantics of a verb. This observation supports our original claim that Aktionsart in the narrowest sense of the term is inherently connected to other expressions of MoA and that the category of the manner of action should be analysed in a broader sense and should not be identified with one single expression tool.

6. THE ROMANCE GERUND AND ITS CZECH RESPONDENTS

OLGA NÁDVORNÍKOVÁ
LEONTÝNA BRATÁNKOVÁ
ŠTĚPÁNKA ČERNIKOVSKÁ
JAN HRICSINA

6.0 INTRODUCTION

The aim of the chapter is to analyse one of the non-finite verbal forms in Romance – the gerund – and its Czech respondents. Given the differences of the *valeur* of the gerund in the four Romance languages under scrutiny, the comparison is based on the cross-linguistic term *converb* (Haspelmath – König 1995 and **Section 6.2**). This approach allows us to involve in the comparison the Czech converb, transgressive as well (see Nedjalkov 1995), and to investigate to what extent it may be considered a systemic respondent of the Romance gerund.

The chapter is organised as follows: in the first **Sections** (**6.1** and **6.2**), we briefly resume the main morphological, syntactic and semantic properties of the Romance gerund (and the Czech transgressive), using the notion of converb as *tertium comparationis* (for the importance of this notion in contrastive linguistics, see e.g. Goddard – Wierzbicka 2008 or Barlow 2008). **Section 6.3** puts forward the typology of the Czech respondents of the Romance gerund and defines the basic properties of the transgressive. The corpus analysis, representing the core of the study, first introduces the data and the general frequency of the gerund in the four Romance languages under investigation (**6.4**). The main research, presented in **Section 6.5**, focuses on correspondences between the semantic types of the (adverbial) Romance gerund and its Czech respondents. In the final part of the study (**6.6**), we summarise the main outcomes of the research, particularly those related to the similarities and dissimilarities between the converbs in the five languages under analysis, and we suggest some open questions for future research.

6.1 MORPHOLOGY OF THE ROMANCE GERUND

The Romance gerund has its origins in the late Latin ablativus gerundii (CANTANDŌ, see also Kortmann 1991, 220 or Haspelmath 1995, 45) although its evolution in the four Romance languages was different (see e.g. Bourciez 1946, 81, 216, 432 and 508) – and so is its present position in the system of non-finite verb forms. In Italian, Portuguese and Spanish, the gerund is formed using the suffix *–ndo*, adhering to the verbal root with thematic vowels varying according to the verbal group (-a-ndo / -e-ndo, e.g. in Italian *am-ando, vend-endo, sal-endo*, in Portuguese *falar* > *fal-a-ndo* or in Spanish *hervir>hirviendo*). In French, on the contrary, only the form with the thematic vowel -a- was retained (-a-ndo), giving in contemporary French [ã]. Since the form of the present participle (-*antem*) resulted in the same suffix ([ã]), the two forms are nowadays distinguished only by the preposition *en* preceding V-ant and forming the gerund in French (en *parl*-ant)[55]. In contemporary French linguistics (Halmøy 1982, 50; Kleiber 2007a or a detailed summary in Nádvorníková 2012, 1–8), *en* is no more considered a preposition, but a part of a discontinuous morpheme (*en ...-ant*). Haspelmath puts forward the hypothesis of *en* as a prefix, employed as a *converb marker* (Haspelmath 1995, 9).

In French linguistics, the original prepositional meaning of *en* is sometimes regarded as the reason for the constraints concerning the temporal relationship of the process conveyed by the gerund with the main verb: in fact, only simultaneity or immediate anteriority are accepted in the gerund in French (see Gettrup 1977; Kleiber 2007b, etc.). However, in Portuguese and in Spanish, the preposition (*en* in Spanish and *em* in Portuguese) assigns different meanings to the gerund: (immediate) anteriority in Spanish. and in Portuguese (cf. Carvalho 2003, 108)[56] or durativity (in Portuguese).[57] Moreover, in the four Romance languages under analysis, the gerund may convey the anteriority explicitly by the compound form (e.g. in Spanish *hablando* and *habiendo hablando*).

Morphologically, all four gerunds are invariable forms; although in Italian, Spanish and Portuguese, clitics are added after the suffix –*ndo* (in French, clitics – and the negative morpheme – are placed between the two parts of the discontinuous morpheme, e.g. *en **ne le lui** disant pas*).[58] As non-finite forms, gerunds are not able to convey the categories of tense, mode and person. Therefore, their syntactic and semantic interpretation is mostly based on the context. For this reason, Haspelmath (1995) considers the Romance gerund a *contextual converb*.

6.2 ROMANCE GERUND AS A CONVERB

Haspelmath (1995, 3; highlight O. N. et al.) defines the cross-linguistic category of converb as "a **nonfinite verb form** whose **main** function is to mark **adverbial** subordi-

---

55   In Old French, other prepositions were also used to form the gerund – especially *à, de, par* and *sans*. Moreover, the gerund was sometimes used without any preposition at all (see Grevisse – Goosse 2008, 1152), merging formally with the form of the present participle. The systematic use of *en* in the form of the gerund only settled during the 18th century.

56   Alarcos Llorach (1994, 183) points out that the presence/absence of *en* may change the meaning of the gerund in Spanish: cf. **Leyendo** *el periódico se durmió* (simultaneity) 'He fell asleep reading the newspaper' and **En leyendo** *el periódico se durmió* (immediate anteriority) 'He fell asleep immeadiately after reading the newspaper'.

57   E.g. **Em sendo** *novos, tudo se faz facilmente* 'When we are young, everything is easy' (Cuesta – Luz 1980, 535).

58   In Spanish, the deminutive suffix –*ito* may be added to the gerund: *callar>callando>callandito: Debíamos acercarnos* **callandito** 'We had to approach very quietly-DEMIN'.

nation". In other words, the converb is typically a nonfinite verb form subordinated to the main verb in the function of *adverbial modifier* (Haspelmath 1995, 4).

The converb category includes not only the English participial adjunct in -*ing* but also the Romance *gerund*,[59] the Russian *деепричастие* and the Czech *transgressive* (Nedjalkov, 1995). At first glance, the classification of the (invariable, non-congruent) Romance gerund and the congruent Czech transgressive in the same category may seem incoherent. However, Nedjalkov explicitly states that although the zero agreement is the most frequent in the category of converbs, it is not the only one possible (Nedjalkov 1995, 117–118). Moreover, the Czech transgressive has displayed a strong tendency to the zero agreement since the 16th century (see Dvořák 1970, 89–90) although this evolution was disrupted by a normative intervention during the national revival movement.[60]

From the semantic point of view, König (1995, 58) and Nedjalkov (1995, 106–110) distinguish three main types of converbs:

a) specialised converbs – "are associated with only one or two circumstantial ('adverbial') interpretations regardless of the context" (op. cit., 107) and there are several converbal markers (affixes), e.g. in Korean or in Japanese;
b) contextual converbs – these convey a large number of adverbial meanings, depending on the context (this being the case of the Romance and Slavic converbs as well as English or Latin);
c) narrative converbs, present, for example, in Turkic languages, merely express a coordinative connection, typically in chains of several converbs in narratives.

According to König (1995, 58) and Nedjalkov (1995, 108), the Romance gerund and the Slavic converbs belong to the "contextual converbs" type, because as already mentioned, their semantic interpretation is mostly based on context. The factors involved in the semantic interpretation of the Romance gerund (and the Czech transgressive) will be introduced in **Sections 6.2.2 and 6.5.1**. First, it is necessary to resume the syntactic functions assumed by the Romance gerund, pointing out their non-adverbial (i.e. non-converbal) uses, which will not be taken into account in this study.

6.2.1 SYNTACTIC FUNCTIONS OF THE ROMANCE GERUND

In the four Romance languages analysed in this study, the gerund assumes the function of an adverbial modifier, given by Haspelmath (1995) as one of the main properties of the converb (see above). However, in Portuguese, Spanish and Italian, the gerund also has other functions.

---

59 "The Romance gerund is a rather typical converb" (Haspelmath 1995, 45).
60 The result of the natural development of the transgressive may be observed in Czech dialects not affected by the normative intervention (see Michálková 1962; Dvořák 1978, 55–57 or the comparison with the French gerund in Nádvorníková 2013b).

First, we must mention the periphrastic use of the gerund, conveying various aspectual meanings (durative, terminative, etc., see e.g. Bourciez 1946, 466) in combination with the finite verb. Thus, the periphrastic gerund is not subordinated to the main verb in the function of an adverbial modifier but forms with it one complex predicate. Periphrastic constructions are particularly frequent in Spanish and in Portuguese; in Italian and in French, we can find only a progressive periphrase (*stare* + gerund in Italian; *aller (en) -ant* in French). However, in French, this construction is extremely rare and displays strong lexical constraints (see Nádvorníková 2012, 222–224)[61]. The contrastive analysis of Romance gerundival periphrases and their Czech respondents may provide new insights into the expression of aspect and Aktionsart in these languages, but in this study, focused on the converbal uses of gerunds, it will not be addressed. For an extensive discussion regarding the Romance verbal periphrases, see Kratochvílová – Jindrová et al. (this volume).

The main difference between Spanish and Portuguese on the one hand, and Italian and French on the other, consists of the fact that in the latter, the gerund is not only an adverbial modifier but also fulfils the functions associated in the former ones with the present participle or the adjective in general. Henceforth, the gerund in Italian and in French may be considered to be a "monofunctional, canonical converb" (as well as the Russian деепричастие and the Czech transgressive), while in Spanish and in Portuguese, the gerund would belong more to the category of polyfunctional, potential quasi-converbs (see Nedjalkov 1995, 104sq.). In fact, Portuguese and Spanish gerunds are predicative, especially after verbs of perception (e.g. Es. *Las vi* **alejándose** – 'I saw them **going away**' and Pt. *Via-a* **passeando** *no jardim* – 'I used to see her **walking** in the garden'). Moreover, in both languages the gerund is attested in an attributive position, although this use is condemned by the norm (with the exception of lexicalised forms, such as Es. *agua hirviendo* or Pt. *água fervendo* – literally: 'water boiling').[62]

Gerunds in absolute constructions are used in Portuguese and in Spanish, and partially in Italian. In these constructions, the controller of the gerund is not coreferential with the subject of the main clause; thus, the gerund may have its own "subject" (in Spanish and in Portuguese it is usually placed after the gerund – Es. *Rosario no se opondrá tampoco*, **queriéndolo yo**, 'Rosario will not oppose either **if I want it**' or Pt. *Não* **podendo** *ajudá-los* **eu**, *veio o meu irmão*, '**Not being able** to help them **myself**, my brother came'). The French gerund does not enter into these types of absolute constructions, unlike the present participle. Moreover, the norm requires the strict coreference of the controller of the French gerund with the subject of the main clause, even though numerous studies demonstrate that the violation of this rule is not infrequent and usually does not render the sentence ambiguous (Halmøy 1994; Nádvorníková 2012, 36–44 and 386–400; Reichler-Béguelin 1995).[63] In this study, absolute uses of Romance

---

61 As pointed out by Gougenheim (1929, 3), Veenstra (1946, 51) and Arnavielle (1997, 69), the progressive periphrase *aller (en) -ant* used to be very frequent in Old French.

62 Spanish and Portuguese gerunds may also be used as predicates, without the main verb, and express the injunctive meaning. However, this use is quite specific, and – in Portuguese – depreciative (Pt. *Andando!* – 'Walk!').

63 The same rule of coreference is stipulated for the Czech transgressive (see Havránek – Jedlička, 1981, 260 or

gerunds are taken into account, since they convey the "adverbial subordination" typical for converbs.

6.2.2 SEMANTIC INTERPRETATION OF THE (ADVERBIAL) ROMANCE GERUND

The scale of meanings conveyed by the Romance adverbial gerund (and the Czech transgressive) is very large (König – Auwera 1990, 342; Halmøy 2003a etc.), ranging from the accompanying circumstance to the manner, means, cause, temporal meaning (*repère temporel*, see Gettrup 1977), concession and condition. Moreover, these meanings often overlap (e.g. manner/means, cause and temporal meaning of anteriority, etc.) and the overall meaning of the gerund may remain vague.[64]

Halmøy (1982, 2003a) suggested to systematise the gerundial meanings in two groups: on the one hand, the "Type A", based on the (chrono)-logical relationship between the gerund and the main clause and including the temporal meaning, the cause, the condition and the concession; on the other hand, "Type B", conveying pure accompanying circumstance (*circonstance concomitante*). Kleiber (2007b, 117 or 2009, 19) later stated that the French *gérondif* does not convey any of these meanings and he reduced the meaning of the French *gérondif* on the interpretative instruction, which is very close to Haspelmath's definition of the converb given above: "associer sur un mode subordonné ou circonstanciel le procès du SG [syntagme gérondif] *à la prédication principale*".

Factors influencing the interpretation of the gerund are grammatical, syntactic, semantic and pragmatic (König 1995, König – Auwera 1990, 337 or Nádvorníková 2012) and involve not only the gerund but also the main verb.[65] For example, at the morphological level, the compound form of the gerund conveys the meaning of anteriority, often triggering causal interpretation (the cause preceding the consequence). Similarly, the conditional interpretation of the gerund is often based on the conditional form of the main verb. One of the main syntactic factors involved in the semantic interpretation of the gerund is its position vis-à-vis the main verb: in Portuguese, for example, gerunds in the anteposition often convey the temporal meaning of anteriority, whereas the postposed forms are more related to the posteriority. In French, the anteposition may have the same effect as in Portuguese although the French gerund, even in the postposition, never conveys posteriority (see the constraint of *en* in 6.1) – this meaning is expressed by the other V-ant form, the present participle.

König (1995, 69) illustrates the complexity of the interpretation of contextual converbs in the example of concession, which is based on inferences, i.e. on pragmatic

---

Karlík, Nekula – Rusínová 1995, 336-337). However, Dvořák (1970, 37-45), in his diachronic study points out that 30% of transgressives in the 17th century, i.e. before the normative intervention, were non-coreferential.

64   Moortgat (1978, 157) considers the French gerund a "semantic chameleon" (see also Halmøy 2003a).

65   Kleiber (2009) points out that the semantic interpretation of the gerund is based on the lexical and aspectual meanings of the gerund and the main verb.

factors (*p & q, if p then not-q*). Due to the complexity of its interpretation, the conces-sive meaning of the gerund is signalled by lexical means (in French the adverb *tout* preceding the gerund,[66] in Portuguese *mesmo/embora* or in Spanish by *aun* and in Ital-ian by *pur*). Nevertheless, the causal relationship also involved in the concessive mean-ing, is not indicated lexically, but is deduced on the basis of shared knowledge (cf. the meaning of manner in Fr. *il est parti* **en claquant la porte** / Es. *se fue* **cerrando la puerta** / 'he left **slamming the door**' and causal meaning in Fr. *il a réveillé son petit frère* **en claquant la porte** / Es. *Despertó a su hermanito* **cerrando la puerta** 'he woke his little brother **by slamming the door**', see Halmøy 2003a, 88 or Nádvorníková 2013a).[67] The shared knowledge is also necessary for the interpretation of the meaning of manner and of the specific meaning of "equivalence" (Type A', Halmøy 2003a, 100), e.g. Fr. *il a commis une erreur* **en se mariant** 'he made a mistake **in getting married**' (the main clause is a re-interpretation of the gerund; similarly in Es. *Esta mañana ha caído estrep-itosamente el mercado americano,* **confirmándose así los pronósticos de la prensa** – 'This morning, the American market fell spectacularly, **thus confirming the prognostics of the press**'). Dvořák (1978, 29–30) identified a similar meaning of the Czech trans-gressive.

Finally, the meaning of the gerund may be indicated by a close lexical relationship between the main verb and the gerund: in this very specific case, the gerund conveys the manner of the realisation of the main process, e.g. Fr. *dire* ('to say') – *chuchoter* ('to whisper') (*dit-elle* **en chuchotant** – 'she said **whispering**', Cs. **zašeptala**), Fr. *arriver* ('to arrive') – *courir* ('to run') (*il est arrivé* **en courant** – 'he came **running**', Cs. **přiběhl**; Es. *salir* ('to leave') – *correr* ('to run') (*salir* **corriendo** – 'run away', literally: 'leave **run-ning**', Cs. **utéct**) etc. Halmøy (2003a, 104) identified this type (Type B') for the verbs of speech and the verbs of movement in French. In the case of verbs of movement, this type of gerund illustrates the typological characteristics of Romance languages point-ed out by Talmy (2000, 102), based on the means of expressing the *Manner* and the *Path* of the movement. In fact, all four Romance languages under scrutiny in this study are *verb-framed languages*, conveying the *Path* of the movement by the finite verb (*ar-river, salir* etc.) and the *Manner* by the gerund (*en courant, corriendo* etc., op. cit., 222 or 114). Czech (and English), on the contrary, belong to the *satellite-framed languages*, con-veying the *Path* by the satellite (particles in English – *away, off, out*, etc. and prefixes in Czech – *při-, od-, vy-* etc.) and the manner of movement of the finite verb (English) or the verb root (in Czech). We expect that the analysis of the Czech respondents of the Romance gerund will reflect this typological difference.

---

66   The adverb *tout* preceding the gerund in French emphasises the simultaneity of both processes; if they are incompatible, the resulting meaning may be adversative or concessive (Nádvorníková 2007 and 2012).

67   Since the meanings of *manner* and *means* are closely interconnected (see Nádvorníková 2013a), we put them in our analyses in one group (*Manner*), see **Section 6.5.1**.

6.3 TYPOLOGY OF CZECH RESPONDENTS OF THE ROMANCE GERUND

As non-finite verb forms, converbs are an important means of syntactic condensation: they convey the meaning corresponding to a finite clause in fewer words and make the sentence structure more compact (see Mathesius 1961, 146). Thus, converbs may be placed in the middle of the scale of syntactic condensation (Vachek 1955 or Nosek 1964): between the finite clauses in a subordinate or a coordinate structure on the one hand, and the nominalisations, such as NPs or PPs, on the other.

However, as suggested above, the Czech converb, transgressive, almost disappeared from contemporary use and is considered bookish (the present transgressive) or even archaic (the past transgressive). In other words, the potential systemic respondent of the Romance gerund is no more available in Czech. Consequently, we expect that most of the respondents of Romance converbs will belong to the other parts of the scale of syntactic condensation conveying the same meaning. In both cases, the implicit meaning of the Romance gerund may be rendered more explicit (by a conjunction introducing the finite clause or a preposition in PPs).

The classification of the Czech respondents of the Romance gerunds takes into account in the first place their position on the scale of syntactic condensation: finite verbs (in coordinate or subordinate structures), non-finite verb forms, and nominalisations. The syntactic and semantic specification of finite clauses is then given by the conjunctions introducing these structures (*protože* – 'because'; *když* – 'when';[68] *a* – 'and';[69] *tak* – 'so', *že* – 'that' etc.); juxtaposition (JUXT), i.e. asyndetic coordination, was classified as a special category. We considered a special category also for the change in the hierarchy of clauses (the original subordinate non-finite clause becomes the main clause, and the original main clause is rendered as a subordinate one).[70]

The semantic specification of nominalisations is especially given by the preposition (in the case of PPs, e.g. *při příchodu* – 'upon arrival') or by the case (the instrumental). The translation respondents reflecting the typological difference between Czech and Romance related to the way of expression of the *Manner* and *Path* of the movement (see **Section 6.2.2**) were put in a special category (see the analysis in 6.5.2.3).

Finally, particular attention was focused on the potential systemic respondent of the Romance gerund, the transgressive (see **Section 6.5.2.3**). The analysis of Czech transgressives as respondents of Romance gerunds was completed by a backward analysis, focused on the Romance respondents of the transgressive (in translated as

---

68   We are aware of the fact that the conjunction *když* 'when' is semantically vague (polysemous), as it introduces subordinate clauses conveying not only temporal meaning but also condition or cause. In fact, this property corresponds perfectly to the semantic vagueness of the Romance gerund (see above).

69   We also took into account the adverbs specifying the relationship between the two clauses coordinated by *a/ and*, especially the adverbs *přitom* or *zároveň* (meaning 'at the same time').

70   In some cases, the original main clause is rendered completely implicit, especially in introductory clauses to direct speech, e.g. Fr. *fis-je **en baissant la tête*** 'I said, **hanging my head**' > Cs. **sklonil jsem hlavu** – 'I hung my head' (see Nádvorníková, forthcoming b).

well as non-translated texts, see Chlumská 2017). In this way, it is possible to find out whether the Romance gerund represents the dominant respondent of the Czech transgressive or whether other types of respondents prevail.

6.4 DATA ELABORATION AND QUANTITATIVE ANALYSIS OF THE ROMANCE GERUND

The analysis of Romance gerund carried out on the InterCorp parallel corpus was focused on the adverbial (converbal) use of this form and on the typology of its Czech respondents (see **Section 6.5**). Nevertheless, the data extracted from the corpus provided some interesting findings concerning the comparison of the frequency of the gerund in the four Romance languages.

Regular expressions used in the corpus took into account the potential variants of gerunds: clitics (postposed in Italian, Portuguese and Spanish and placed between the preposition and V-ant in French, see **Section 6.1**; and in **Table 6.1** for the queries) and potential extraction noises (non-gerundival expressions in -*ndo*, such as Es. *cuando* – 'when'). From this overall number of occurrences (see line 2 in **Table 6.1**), a sample for

Tab. 6.1. Occurrences of the Romance gerund in the InterCorp parallel corpus

	Frequency of gerund	Fr.	Es.	It.	Pt.
1	Size of the subcorpus (tokens)	1,533,451	9,326,150	1,631,204	1,485,541
2	Total N° of concordance lines	2,641[71]	68,526[72]	8,914[73]	12,924[74]
3	Size of the sample analysed manually – with noises	2,641	3,000	2,534	2,539
4	N° of gerunds (including periphrases) – without noises	2,363	2,971	2,322	2,422
5	N° of gerunds (without periphrases)	2,362	1,965	1,857	1,991
6	N° of adverbial gerunds	2,362	1,561	1,857	1,448

71   [word="(E|e)n"] [word=".*ant"]; [word="(E|e)n"] []{1,2} [word=".*ant"] – the results obtained with this query contained 20% of noises. No occurrence of gerund including three positions between the preposition and the V-ant was found.

72   [word=".*ndo(me|te|le|lo|la|se|nos|os|les|los|las(lo|la|le(s)?)?)?)?" & tag!= "NP" &tag!= "NC" &tag!= "ADJ" & tag!= "ORD" &tag!="NMEA" & tag!="ADV" & word!="(.|!)?[Cc]u[aa]ndo" & word!= "ando|entiendo|extiendo|comprendo"]

73   [word=".*ando|.*endo" & !word="(q|Q)uando"]; [word=".*(a|e)ndo(ce|ci|gli|glie|la|le|li|lo|me|mi|ne|se|si|te|ti|ve|vi)"]; [word=".*(a|e)ndo((ce|ci|gli|glie|la|le|li|lo|me|mi|ne|se|si|te|ti|ve|vi)(ce|ci|gli|glie|la|le|li|lo|me|mi|ne|se|si|te|ti|ve|-vi)"]

74   [word=".*ando|.*endo|.*indo|.*ondo" & word!="[Qq]uando"]

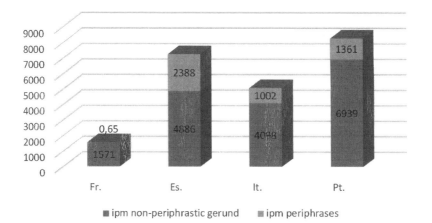

Graph 6.1. Relative frequency of the periphrastic and non-periphrastic gerund in French, Spanish, Italian and Portuguese

manual analysis was extracted, in which we observed syntactic and semantic types of Romance gerunds and the corresponding Czech respondents (see line 3 v **Table 6.1**).

The samples extracted for manual analysis contain from 2,500 to 3,000 occurrences (see line 3 in Table 3.1); in French, all the occurrences were analysed (compare lines 2 and 3 in Table 6.1). After the elimination of extraction noises, the resulting samples for manual analysis are slightly smaller (see line 4 in **Table 6.1**). For our study, focused on the adverbial uses of the gerund, we eliminated periphrastic gerunds (see Line 5 in **Table 6.1** and **Graph 6.1** above) and the non-adverbial uses of this form (see Line 6 in **Table 6.1** and **Section 6.4.2** below).

Given the differences in the size of the four subcorpora (see the introductory chapter in this volume and line 1 in **Table 6.1**), the absolute frequency of the gerund in our corpus is the highest in Spanish. Nevertheless, a better overview is obviously provided by relative frequencies (ipm – see **Graph 6.1**): their comparison reveals that the frequency of the gerund is the highest in Portuguese, followed by Spanish and Italian.

Graph 6.1 shows the comparison of the relative frequencies of the Romance gerund in its periphrastic and non-periphrastic uses. It demonstrates that in Spanish and Portuguese, the general relative frequencies of the gerund are comparable. Nevertheless, the relative frequency of the periphrastic uses of the gerund is higher in Spanish than in Portuguese.[75] This may be caused by the fact that since the 18th century, the gerund has been progressively replaced in European Portuguese by prepositional use of infinitive (*a* + Infinitive) in some functions, namely in periphrastic constructions, e.g. Pt. *estar fazendo / estar a fazer* ('to be doing'). In future research, a contrastive analysis

---

75 The most frequent periphrases in the Spanish subcorpus involve the verbs *estar* (439 occurrences of 1,006) and *seguir* (202 occurrences). We also include among the periphrastic uses of the Spanish gerund in Spanish the semi-periphrastic constructions, such as *empezar/comenzar* 'start' + gerund – 'start/begin by doing sth'.

of the periphrastic gerund in Spanish, Portuguese (and Czech) may be of interest, but in this study, we restrict ourselves to non-periphrastic uses of the gerund to allow for the comparison with the cross-linguistic category of the converb.

In Italian, the total relative frequency of the gerund is lower than in Spanish and Portuguese although the periphrastic uses of the gerund still represent 20% of this number (in Spanish, this proportion is 33% and in Portuguese only 18%). In French, the periphrastic use of the gerund is attested by only one occurrence of 2,363,[76] which basically means that the French gerund is limited to non-periphrastic use. **Graph 6.1** also shows that the frequency of the gerund is three times lower in French than in the other three Romance languages, which may be caused both by the quasi-absence of the periphrastic use of this form in contemporary French as well as by the concurrence of the present participle and the absence of non-adverbial uses of the gerund (see below).[77] Thus, among the four Romance languages under investigation in this study, French appears to be the most specific in terms of frequency and use of the gerund.

Nevertheless, the global figures provided in **Graph 6.1** have to be specified in two aspects: first, related to the composition and size of the corpus used in this research (see **Section 6.4.1**), and second, regarding the syntactic functions of the non-periphrastic gerund (see **Section 6.4.2** and **Table 6.2**).

6.4.1 FACTORS INFLUENCING THE FREQUENCY OF THE ROMANCE GERUND

The relative frequency of the gerund shown in **Graph 6.1** may be particularly influenced by the fiction text type that prevails in our corpus. For example, a detailed analysis of the relative frequency of the gerund in the different texts of the Italian subcorpus reveals the lowest relative frequency of the gerund in two non-fiction texts (Giorgio Agamben – *Mezzi senza fine*, 3,453 ipm and Giuliano Procacci – *Storia degli Italiani*, 2,945 ipm; cf. 5,100 ipm in the whole Italian subcorpus in **Graph 6.1**). In the French subcorpus, we observed a lower frequency of the gerund not only in non-fiction[78] but also in fiction emulating spoken language (five of Asterix's adventures, on average 539 ipm, and a novel by Ferdinand Céline – *D'un château à l'autre*, only 346 ipm; cf. 1,571 ipm in the whole French subcorpus in **Graph 6.1**).[79] This tendency is corrobo-

---

76 The progressive periphrase *aller (en) V-ant* (see 6.2.1): La chair du requin aspirait les épices, des odeurs de coquillages **allaient en montant**. → Žraločí maso vsakovalo koření, <u>vůně škeblí</u> **byla stále výraznější.** Patrick Chamoiseau, *Solibo Ohromný* (*Solibo le Magnifique*), transl. Růžena Ostrá, Brno: Atlantis, 1993. Literally: <u>the mussel odour</u> **was still stronger**.

77 For this reason, all the occurrences of the French gerund available in the corpus were analysed (in the other three Romance languages, only samples were used).

78 Georges Duby – *Dames du XIIᵉ siècle* (1,057 ipm) and Albert Camus – *Carnets II* (essays), 846 ipm and Antoine de Saint-Exupéry, *Lettre à un otage*, 610 ipm.

79 Moreover, as shown in Nádvorníková (2012), the text type influences not only the frequency of the gerund but also the proportions of its semantic types (in fiction, the meaning of accompanying circumstance prevails, whereas in non-fiction, the meaning of manner/means is the most frequent), see below for more details.

rated by recent research conducted on a spoken corpus (the gerund in spoken French is rare and often non-coreferential, see Escoubas-Benveniste 2013). In consequence, future research into gerunds should also investigate the frequency and use of this form in other text types.

In Spanish and in Portuguese, another factor comes into play: the variety of the language. In non-European varieties of these languages, the relative frequency of the gerund is higher than in the European ones. In Spanish, for example, the first five ranks in the frequency list are occupied by texts written by Juan Carlos Onetti (Uruguay, 13,095 ipm), Alejo Carpentier (Cuba, 11,913 ipm), Juan Rulfo (Mexico, 11,857 ipm), Luis Sepúlveda (Chile, 11,657 ipm) and Jorge Zúñiga Pavlov (Chile, 10,667 ipm); cf. 7,274 ipm in the whole Spanish subcorpus in **Graph 6.1**. In Portuguese, the gerund is frequent not only in texts written by Brazilian authors (such as Jorge Amado) but also in novels by one European author (Eça de Queiroz), writing in the 19th century, when the Portuguese gerund was not yet so much affected by the competition with the construction *a* + infinitive (see above and also Kratochvílová – Jindrová et al. this volume).

Finally, it is also necessary to point out that in fiction, special idiolects of authors may considerably modify the frequency of the gerund. For example, in Spanish and in Portuguese, a very high frequency of the gerund in texts whose authors prefer writing in long, complex sentences (e.g. Teolinda Gersão in Portuguese, 14,576 ipm, cf. 8,300 ipm for the whole Portuguese subcorpus in **Graph 6.1**)[80] can be observed. Moreover, two texts written by the same author may display considerable differences in the frequency of the use of the gerund, depending on the specific style of the text (e.g. the frequency of the gerund is 8,362 ipm in the novel *Sogni di sogni* by Tabucchi, but only 4,343 ipm in another novel by the same author – *Il gioco del rovescio*). For this reason, we systematically indicate the name of the author and the title of the text in the examples provided in the main part of our study (see 6.5).[81]

6.4.2 SYNTACTIC FUNCTIONS OF THE ROMANCE NON-PERIPHRASTIC GERUND

As mentioned in **Section 6.2.1**, the Romance gerund in its non-periphrastic use can fulfil not only the function of an adverbial modifier, typical for the converb but also other syntactic functions. However, in the samples manually analysed in our research (see line 5 in **Table 6.1**), the adverbial modifier represents the dominant function of the gerund in the four Romance languages under scrutiny:

---

80 In the French subcorpus, we observed a potential effect of the interference of the mother tongue of the author: the highest relative frequency of the gerund was identified in the novel *Le Testament français* written by Andreï Makine (5,184 ipm), whose mother tongue is Russian, where the converb деепричастие is very frequent.

81 Despite the specificities given by the composition of the corpus, the data appears to be sufficiently reliable. For example, in the subcorpus of the French corpus FRANTEXT limited to novels published after 1950 (24 million tokens), the relative frequency of the gerund is 1,640 ipm; in the InterCorp French subcorpus, this number is comparable – 1,571 ipm (see **Graph 6.1**).

Tab. 6.2. Syntactic functions of the non-periphrastic Romance gerund

Syntactic function of the non-periphrastic gerund		Pt.		Es.		It.		Fr.	
Converbal	Adverbial modifier	1,448	72.73%	1,561	79.44%	1,822	98.12%	2,297	97.21%
Converbal	Absolute construction	169	8.49%	24	1.22%	20	1.08%	–	–
Non-converbal	Attributive	228	11.45%	133	6.77%	–	–	–	–
Non-converbal	Independent predicate	95	4.77%	88	4.48%	–	–	–	–
Non-converbal	Predicative	35	1.76%	153	7.79%	–	–	–	–
Non-converbal	Other	16	0.80%	6	0.31%	15	0.81%	65	2.75%
	Total	1,991	100%	1,965	100%	1,857	100%	2,362	100%

The functions of the Romance gerund resumed in **Table 6.2** can be divided into converbal and non-converbal. Apart from the typical and dominant function of the adverbial modifier (more than 70% in Portuguese and in Spanish, and more than 90% in Italian and in French), we can also consider as converbal the use of gerund in an absolute construction (see the same approach in Haspelmath 1995, 87) since it corresponds to the category of adverbial subordination (with semantic vagueness), see the following example in Italian:

(1) It.
Cominciavano i duelli, ma già il suolo **essendo** ingombro di carcasse e cadaveri, ci si muoveva a fatica, (...). → Došlo na souboje, ale <u>země už **byla**</u> tak posetá harampádím a mrtvolami, že byl každý pohyb těžký, (...).
Literally: <u>*the ground **was** already*</u>.
Italo Calvino, *Naši předkové* (*I nostri antenati*), transl. Zdeněk Digrin – Vladimír Mikeš, Prague: Odeon, 1970.

The gerund in an absolute construction can also be used as pragmatic marker conveying comments upon the main clause, e.g. in the so-called *incisos* in Spanish:

(2) Es.
Durante algunos minutos, que me parecieron eternos y que después, **recordando** todo el asunto, advertí de que efectivamente lo fueron, pensé en cuál debía ser mi comportamiento. → Pár minut, které mi připadaly nekonečné a vlastně takové i byly, <u>**když si** to teď **vybavuju**</u>, jsem přemýšlel, jak bych se měl zachovat.
Literally: <u>***when I** now **recall** it*</u>.
Jorge Zúñiga Pavlov, *La Casa Blů* (*La Casa Blů*), transl. Dita Grubnerová, Prague: Garamond, 2006.

In our corpus, the use of the gerund in an absolute construction is more frequent in Portuguese than in Spanish and in Italian (8% and 1% respectively)[82] although this result may be influenced by the difference in size and composition of the subcorpora and is to be verified in further research.

Unlike the gerund in an absolute construction, the category of "independent predicate" does not correspond to converbal use any more: although the gerund retains its (vague) adverbial meaning, it is not subordinated to a finite verb and is characterised by a strong narrative dynamism. Typically, there are several gerunds cumulated in one (complex) sentence. The non-subordinate character of this use of the gerund is reflected by its most typical respondent in Czech: independent finite clauses:

(3) It.
Saltandogli d'intorno, e **correndogli** sotto le zampe, e **volandogli** al di sopra, e **pungendolo** da tutte le parti; e non **lasciandogli** posa, e **guizzandogli** davanti, e **riapparendogli** da due lati quasi contemporaneamente fino a moltiplicarsi alle sue pupille e farlo impazzire, come se non un solo Nino gli fosse contro, ma cento. → **Běhal by** kolem něho, **podlézal** pod ním a **přelétal** nad ním, **bodal** ho ze všech stran a **nepopřál** mu oddechu, tu by **stál čelem** k němu a pak zas na jedné a v tu ránu na druhé straně, až by se v jeho zřítelnicích zmnožil a pilot by začal šílet v domnění, že proti sobě nemá jednoho, ale sto Ninu.
Literally: *he would run around him, he would slip under him and fly over, he would bite him and he would not give him a moment of peace, suddenly, he would appear in front of him.*
Elsa Morante, *Příběh v historii* (*La storia*), transl. Zdeněk Frýbort, Prague: Odeon, 1990.

This use of the gerund is close to the "narrative converb" defined by Haspelmath – Nedjalkov (Haspelmath 1995, 58; Nedjalkov 1995, 106–110 and 6.2 in this chapter) and similar to the narrative use of the present participle in French.

Typically, non-converbal uses of the gerund are attributive and predicative. Although previously condemned by the norm (see **Section 6.2.1**), these functions are quite well attested to in our data in Portuguese and in Spanish – see **Table 6.2** and the following example for Spanish:

(4) Es.
El ejemplo de las esposas de los militares **actuando** en vez de sus maridos fue rápidamente imitado. → Příklad manželek **jednajících** za své důstojnické chotě se brzy rozšířil.
Literally: *wives acting-*ADJ.
Isabel Allende, *Paula* (*Paula*), transl. Anežka Charvátová, Prague: Slovart, 1998.

---

82   In Italian, absolute constructions are considered formal and are restricted to written language.

Czech respondents of these uses of the gerund reflect their adjectival character: active participles in *-ící* (as in (4)), or subordinate attributive or predicative clauses.

Finally, the category "other" in **Table 6.2** especially includes the lexicalised forms of the gerund (e.g. *en attendant* – 'in the meanwhile' or *en passant* – 'by the way').[83]

The results presented in **Table 6.2** confirm the difference between Spanish and Portuguese on the one hand, and Italian and especially French on the other. Typically, non-converbal, adjectival uses (attributive or predicative) are attested only in the former; the use of the gerund as independent predicate and in absolute constructions are attested in Spanish, Portuguese and Italian, but not in French.

In French and in Italian, an adverbial modifier (including absolute constructions) represents the overwhelming majority of the occurrences of the gerund. Therefore, the gerund in Italian and in French may be considered as representing the category of the monofunctional, canonical converb (see the classification in Nedjalkov 1995, 104sq.), whereas in Portuguese and Spanish, the gerund is closer to the category of bi-functional, potential quasi-converb (ibid.). However, in the four Romance languages, the dominant use of the gerund is adverbial (in absolute or non-absolute construction), which will be investigated in the next section.

6.5 THE ADVERBIAL ROMANCE GERUND AND ITS CZECH RESPONDENTS

This section, representing the core of our research, presents the semantic types of the adverbial Romance gerund – in absolute as well as non-absolute constructions (**Section 6.5.1**) and puts them in correspondence with their respondent types in Czech (**Section 6.5.2**).

6.5.1 SEMANTIC TYPES OF THE ROMANCE ADVERBIAL GERUND AND THE CZECH TRANSGRESSIVE

As suggested in **Section 6.2**, the Romance gerund belongs to the category of the *contextual converb*, i.e. its semantic interpretation depends on the grammatical, syntactic, semantic and pragmatic factors given by the context. For this reason, the quantification of the semantic types of the Romance gerund is very difficult – not only the meaning usually remains vague but the semantic types often overlap (especially the categories of CIR-accompanying circumstance and Manner, or TEMP-temporal and CAUSE).[84]

---

83   For the lexicalization of the gerund *en passant*, see Stosic 2012.

84   In our analyses, we distinguished the categories of X (representing the pure case of the meaning, e.g. CIR) and X+ (representing the meaning overlapping with another one, e.g. CIR+, combining the meaning of accompanying circumstance with the Manner). For the sake of simplicity, we did not include these categories in **Table 6.3**.

Thus, the quantification given in **Table 6.3** shows more tendencies than the strictly separated categories:

Tab. 6.3. Semantic types of Romance gerund and Czech transgressive[85]

Meaning	Pt.		Es		It.		Fr.		Cs.
CIR	1,364	84.35%	652	41.14%	897	48.70%	1,105	46.78%	62.70%
Manner	97	6.00%	471	29.72%	429	23.29%	556	23.54%	11.00%
TEMP	87	5.38%	324	20.44%	215	11.67%	557	23.58%	9.50%
CAUSE	30	1.86%	47	2.97%	233	12.65%	19	0.80%	10.40%
CONCESS	18	1.11%	11	0.69%	22	1.19%	21	0.89%	0.00%
COND	16	0.99%	19	1.20%	41	2.23%	39	1.65%	0.50%
Other	5	0.31%	61	3.85%	5	0.27%	65	2.75%	5.90%
Total	1,617		1,585		1,842		2,362		100.00%

Table 6.3 shows that despite the differences in the proportions of the semantic types of Romance gerunds and the Czech transgressive, the results reveal striking similarities between the five converbs. In fact, although the exact proportions are different, the *order* of the semantic types is identical in the five languages with the most frequent type being the accompanying circumstance (CIR), followed by the Manner and the TEMPoral meaning. The specific meanings of CAUSE, CONCESSion and CONDition are rare. In what follows, we will introduce these semantic types in order of frequency, pointing out the contextual factors allowing for their identification.

Converbs conveying the meaning of **accompanying circumstance** are important (and frequent) in narrative texts because they express, in a condensed way, a process concomitant with another one, without a logical (causal) relationship between them (e.g. Fr. *regarder – boire* in (5) or Pt. *correr – berrar* in (6)). In the four Romance languages as well as in the Czech transgressive, this meaning represents more than 40% of the occurrences of the converb.

(5) Fr.
Il était un peu plus de cinq heures du matin, et nous buvions des capuccinos sous l'auvent de bois d'une échoppe d'artisan, **en regardant** la neige tomber devant nous dans la ruelle. → Bylo něco po páté hodině ráno a my jsme pili kapucino pod dřevěnou stříškou stánku nějakého řemeslníka, **dívali se**, jak před námi v uličce padá sníh.
Literally: *they **watched**-IPFV*.
Jean-Philippe Toussaint, *Milovat se (Faire l'amour)*, transl. Jovanka Šotolová, Prague: Garamond, 2004.

---

85   Data for the Czech transgressive is taken from the research conducted by Dvořák (1978, 33).

(6) Pt.

Corremos pela beira do comboio, **berrando** com desespero : (...). → Rozběhli jsme se podél vlaku a zoufale **řvali**: (...).

Literally: _they **yelled in dispair**-IPFV_.

José Maria Eça de Queiroz, _Kráčej a čti_ (_A Cidade e as Serras_), transl. Marie Havlíková, Prague: Academia, 2001.

In French, the simultaneity of both processes may be emphasised by the adverb _tout_ placed before the gerund:

(7) Fr.

(...) l'écrivain psychédélique Carlos Castaneda (environ 61 ans) bouffe son peyotl avec Jean Eustache (63 ans), **tout en consultant** les plus-values boursières du capital de Ghost Island. → (...) psychedelický spisovatel Carlos Castaneda (kolem 61 let) konzumuje svůj peyotl s Jeanem Eustachem (63 let), **a přitom konzultuje** burzovní přírůstky hodnoty kapitálu Ghost Islandu.

Literally: _**and at the same time, he consults**_.

Frédéric Beigbeder, _99 franků_ (_99 francs_), transl. Markéta Demlová, Prague: Motto, 2003.

In our corpus, the construction _tout_ + gerund represents 4% of all the occurrences (93 of 2,362); most of them (73%) convey the meaning of accompanying circumstance with the others expressing the concession (see below).

In non-fiction, the frequency of the converb conveying the meaning of accompanying circumstance may be much less frequent than in fiction, since, in non-fiction, logical (causal) relations between facts and events are often displayed. This hypothesis is corroborated on the one hand by the results obtained from the non-fiction subcorpus of the French corpus FRANTEXT, where the most frequent meaning of the French gerund is not accompanying circumstance, but the means (Nádvorníková 2012). On the other hand, the research conducted by Dvořák (1978, 33) on the Czech transgressive, shows a comparable frequency of accompanying circumstance and Manner/Means (23.4% and 19.5% respectively). Therefore, any future research into the semantic types of converbs should also include a non-fiction subcorpus.

The meaning of accompanying circumstance in fiction is particularly frequent in introductory clauses to direct speech, i.e. a context typical for fiction.[86] In this case, the converbs specify the various circumstances of direct speech, such as mimics, gestures, bodily movements, eye contact, etc. (see Nádvorníková 2009; Šustrová 2010 or Nádvorníková, forthcoming b). In the four Romance languages, one of the most frequent gerunds in this context is _smiling_ (Fr. _en souriant_, It. _sorridendo_ etc.):[87]

---

86   E.g. in French, converbs used in this context represent almost one-third (27%) of all the occurrences of the meaning of accompanying circumstance while 12% of all the occurrences of gerund.

87   Other verbs frequent in this context are e.g. 'sighing' (Pt. _suspirando_, (32)) or 'laughing' (It. _ridendo_, see note 46).

(8) It.

"Andiamo a Mudabiri", disse lui **sorridendo**, "al tempio di Chandranath". →
„Jedeme do Múdabidri", <u>odpověděl</u> **s úsměvem**, „do Čandranáthova chrámu."
Literally: *(he) answered **with a smile***.

Antonio Tabucchi, *Indické nokturno* (*Notturno indiano*), transl. Kateřina Vinšová,
Prague: Argo, 2002.

The meaning of the gerund in this use often overlaps with the meaning of **Manner**,
since the circumstances conveyed by the converb trigger inferential processes related
to the intentions or emotions of the speaker (e.g. (8)). The way of speaking can also
be conveyed by a close lexical relationship between the gerundival verb and the main
verb (cf. **Section 6.2.2** and "Type B" identified by Halmøy 1982, 2003a):

(9) Fr.

Puis, penchée vers l'écran qu'elle touchait presque des lèvres, elle a ajouté **en
chuchotant** d'un air entendu : (...). → Pak se nachýlila k obrazovce, až se jí skoro
dotýkala rty, a **<u>šeptem</u>** dodala jakoby spiklenecky: (...).
Literally: ***in whisper***.

Camille Laurens, *Láska, román* (*L'Amour, roman*), transl. Alexandra Pfimpflová,
Prague: Euromedia Group – Odeon, 2004.

Unlike the examples introduced so far, the **Means**, representing a sub-type of
Manner, is based on the causal relationship between both processes:

(10) Es.

Después de la derrota de Accio, se ganó el favor de Augusto **traicionando** a Antonio y
revelando el posible paradero secreto de Cleopatra, (...). → Po porážce u Actia <u>získal</u>
Augustovu přízeň **zradou** Antonia a **odhalením** tajného úkrytu Kleopatry, (...).
Literally: *he insinuated himself into August's favour **by the treason** on Antonio and **by
the exposure** of Cleopatra's secret shelter*.

Eduardo Mendoza, *Podivuhodná cesta Pomponia Flata* (*El asombroso viaje de Pomponio
Flato*), transl. Jana Novotná, Prague: Garamond, 2009.

(11) It.

Se verrai con me, Pamela, imparerai a soffrire dei mali di ciascuno e a curare i tuoi
curando i loro. → Jestliže půjdeš se mnou, Pamelo, naučíš se trpět neduhy ostat-
ních a léčit svoje **tím, že budeš léčit** cizí.
Literally: ***by that that you will cure***.

Italo Calvino, *Naši předkové* (*I nostri antenati*), transl. Zdeněk Digrin, Vladimír
Mikeš, Prague: Odeon, 1970.

The third most frequent semantic type of converb, after the accompanying circumstance and the Manner, is **TEMPoral**. It is similar to the meaning of accompanying

circumstance by the fact that it may convey a process simultaneous with the main verb without a logical (causal) relationship between them (see (12)). Nevertheless, unlike the accompanying circumstance, its main function is to convey the time frame (*cadre temporel*, see Gettrup 1977 and Halmøy 2003a) of the main process. For this reason, the gerund conveying the meaning of TEMPoral is often placed in the anteposition.

Comparing e.g. (5) and (12), we can see that in (5), the gerund conveys a process simply juxtaposed to the main process, whereas in (12) and (13), it serves as the anchor point of the main process:

(12) Fr.
Un soir, **en me promenant** à travers les ruelles du grand marché, je vis un homme mettre le feu à un liquide contenu dans un bol: (...). → **Když jsem se** jednou večer **procházel** uličkami velkého města, uviděl jsem muže, jak zapaluje jakousi tekutinu nalitou do nádoby: (...).
Literally: ***when** one evening **I walked**-IPFV through the streets*.
Sandrine Mirza, *Po stopách Marka Pola* (*Sur les traces de Marco Polo*), transl. Vladimír Čadský, Prague: Knižní klub, 2005.

(13) Es.
Una vez, **hablándome** de la más pequeña, se puso a llorar y finalmente dijo que no entendía nada. → **Když** mi jednou **vyprávěl** o mladší dcerce, dal se do pláče a prohlásil, že ničemu nerozumí.
Literally: ***when** once **he told**-IPFV me*.
Roberto Bolaño, *Divocí detektivové* (*Los detectives salvajes*), transl. Anežka Charvátová, Prague: Argo, 2008.

Temporal relationship conveyed by the gerund is usually simultaneity or anteriority with an overlap of both processes, or at least temporal contiguity (Gettrup 1977). The meaning of immediate anteriority may be signalled in Spanish by the preposition *en* and in Portuguese *em* placed before the gerund (see **Section 6.1**):

(14) Pt.
(...) mas **em** ele **subindo** um pouco mais inventa-se-lhe logo toda a espécie de vilanias. → (...) můžeme ho dokonce postrčit, ale **jakmile** trochu **povystoupí**, hned se na něj nakydá kdejaká špína.
Literally: ***as soon as he rises** a bit*.
Fernando Namora, *Muž s maskou* (*O Homem Disfarçado*), transl. Pavla Lidmilová, Prague: Svoboda, 1979.

The relationship with posteriority is not possible in the French gerund; in Italian, it is considered exceptional (see Renzi – Salvi – Cardinaletti 2002, 575); in Spanish and in Portuguese, it is condemned by the norm (see e.g. Gómez Torrego 2006, 500 for Spanish) although especially in journalistic texts, it is attested (see Králová 2012, 43).

In French, the meaning of posteriority is possible in the other V-ant form, the present participle (see Havu – Pierrand 2008). In the following example, the Spanish gerund clearly expresses a process posterior to the main verb:

(15) Es.
(…) apretábase un corrillo de borrachos en torno a un ciego que acababa de rajarse la garganta **perfilando** melismas por soleares. → (…) hlouček opilců se tlačil kolem slepce, který si právě odkašlal **a spustil** trylky andaluské písničky.
Literally: ***and he started*** to sing.
Alejo Carpentier, *Výbuch v katedrále* (*El siglo de las luces*), transl. Eduard Hodoušek, Prague: Odeon, 1969.

Examples (13) and (14) illustrate the close interconnection between the TEMPoral meaning and the first of the three less frequent meanings of the converb – **the CAUSE**. In fact, the causal relationship is usually superposed to the TEMPoral one. Similar to the above-mentioned meaning of Manner-Means, the interpretation of the three last meanings of a converb (cause, condition and concession) is based on shared knowledge of the causal relationships between events and inferences, i. e. on pragmatic factors (cf. for example *il est parti **en claquant** la porte* – Manner vs *il a réveillé son petit frère **en claquant** la porte* – CAUSE, Halmøy 2003a). Only the concession may also be signalled by lexical means (*tout* or *même* in French, *mesmo* or *embora* in Pt, *aun* in Spanish and *pur* in Italian, see below).

The causal interpretation of gerunds is frequent when the meaning of the gerund conveys anteriority (usually in anteposition to the main verb) and is expressed by verbs of perception. In this case, the complements of the verb of perception in the gerund encode the stimulus of the perception, and the main verb encodes the reaction of the perceptor – usually emotions or bodily movements, mimics, speech, etc. potentially considered as manifestations of emotions (see Nádvorníková, forthcoming a).

(16) Fr.
En voyant le corps supplicié de son chien, Nicolas fondit en larmes. → **Když si Nicolas všiml** zmučeného těla svého psa, propukl v pláč.
Literally: ***when Nicolas noticed***.
Bernard Werber, *Mravenci* (*Les Fourmis*), transl. Richard Podaný, Prague: Euromedia Group – Knižní klub, 2005.[88]

As shown in the next example, the reaction may be not only overtly emotional but also verbal:

---

88 The emotion may be conveyed explicitely as well – see (30).

(17) It.
Infine Malachia, **vedendo** che il mio maestro pareva seriamente intenzionato a oc-
cuparsi delle cose di Venanzio, gli aveva detto chiaro e tondo che forse, prima di
frugare tra le carte del morto, era meglio ottenere l'autorizzazione dell'Abate; (...).
→ **Když** Malachiáš nakonec **viděl**, že můj mistr má vážně v úmyslu zabývat se Ve-
nantiovými knihami, řekl mu na rovinu, že než se začne v pergamenech zesnulého
přehrabovat, měl by si snad vyžádat svolení opatovo.
Literally: *when Malachiáš finally saw*.
Umberto Eco, *Jméno růže* (*Nome della rosa*), transl. Zdeněk Frýbort, Prague: Odeon,
1988.

The relationship with anteriority and the anteposition of the gerund are frequent
in CAUSE because the cause naturally precedes the consequence given by the main
clause. However, the anteriority is rarely expressed explicitly by the compound form
of the gerund, since the lexical and aspectual meanings of the gerundival verb and the
main verb are able to also convey anteriority (see e.g. the inchoative verbs of perception in (16) and (17) and the punctual main verbs).

The two last meanings of the gerund are even less frequent than CAUSE (only 1%
or 2%). This very low frequency may be the consequence of the high cognitive effort
necessary for their interpretation. In both cases, it is first necessary to interpret the
inferences relating the two processes, and then to consider the result as potential
(conditional), or non-effective (concession).

As mentioned above, the conditional meaning is usually triggered by the conditional mode of the main verb. Nevertheless, the future tense or modal verb *pouvoir*
('can') may have the same effect – see König – Auwera 1990). The two following examples show that the conditional meaning can also be caused/triggered by the imperative
(18) or by the form of the pluperfect subjunctive, corresponding in French to the past
conditional (19):

(18) Pt.
Depois, quinta de-manhã-cedo, o senhor **querendo** ir, então vai, mesmo me deixa
sentindo sua falta. → Potom, ve čtvrtek brzo ráno, **budete-li chtít**, tak si jeďte,
i když mi budete chybět.
Literally: *if you wish*.
João Guimarães Rosa, *Velká divočina* (*Grande Sertão*), transl. Pavla Lidmilová,
Prague: Mladá Fronta – Dauphin, 2003.

(19) Fr.
(...) **en me refusant** le baptême, on eût craint de violenter mon âme ; (...). → (...)
kdyby mi **byli odmítli** křest, byli by se báli, že znásilňují mou duši, (...).
Literally: *if they had refused the baptism to me*.
Jean Paul Sartre, *Slova* (*Les Mots*), transl. Dagmar Steinová, Prague: Svoboda, 1992.

The last meaning of the gerund is signalled lexically: by the adverbs *mesmo* or *embora* in Portuguese:[89]

(20) Pt.

É preciso não relaxar nunca, **mesmo tendo chegado** tão longe (...). → Nikdy nesmíme polevit, **i když dojdeme** tak daleko, (...).
Literally: ***even when we get*** *that far*.
Paulo Coelho, *Alchymista* (*Alquimista*), transl. Pavla Lidmilová, Prague: Argo, 2005.

(21) Pt.

E a sua intervenção parecia ter apenas o propósito de restabelecer o respeito que cada um devia aos camaradas, **embora sabendo** que o brilho das suas palavras provocaria nos outros um ressentido amargor de inferioridade. → A svým zásahem jako by nesledoval jiný cíl než znovu nastolit vzájemnou úctu, **přestože ví**, že lesk jeho slov vyvolá v druhých záštiplnou trpkost méněcennosti.
Literally: ***even though he knows***.
Fernando Namora, *Muž s maskou* (*O Homem Disfarçado*), transl. Pavla Lidmilová, Prague: Svoboda, 1979.

by the adverb *aun* in Spanish:

(22) Es.

Una fuerza instintiva e irrefrenable me impulsaba y habría continuado solo **aun sabiendo** que un turbio destino (y tal vez la muerte) me aguardaban. → Hnala mě instinktivní a nezkrotná síla a byl bych pokračoval, **i kdybych věděl**, že mě čeká temný osud (snad i smrt).
Literally: ***even if I knew***.
Eduardo Mendoza, *Pravda o případu Savolta* (*La verdad sobre el caso Savolta*), transl. Petr Koutný, Prague: Odeon, 1983.

by the adverb *pur* in Italian:

(23) It.

Il professor Broderfons, **pur ammettendo** la correttezza della mia osservazione, non riconosce ad essa alcun significato particolare. → Profesor Broderfons, **i když připustil** správnost mé připomínky, jí nepřisuzuje žádný zvláštní význam.
Literally: ***even if he admitted***.
Alessandro Baricco, *Oceán moře* (*Oceano mare*), transl. Miloslava Lázňovská – Alice Flemrová, Prague: Eminent, 2001.

---

89 We identified even one case of *mesmo* followed by the preposition *em*: *Vejo que o senhor não riu*, **mesmo em tendo vontade**. → *Vidím, že jste se nezasmál,* **přestože jste chtěl**. João Guimarães Rosa, *Velká divočina* (*Grande Sertão*), transl. Pavla Lidmilová, Prague: Mladá Fronta – Dauphin, 2003. Literally: ***even though you wanted***.

and by the adverb *tout* in French (although most of the constructions *tout* + gerund do not convey concession but emphasise the simultaneity of the two processes, see (7)):

(24) Fr.
Tout en lui conservant pour l'éternité une fidélité muette, je m'estimais libéré de lui dès lors que des lecteurs s'en étaient emparés. → **Třebaže jsem** jí **zůstával** navždy věrný, cítil jsem se svobodně, teprve když se jí zmocnili čtenáři.
Literally: ***even though I remained*** *devoted to her forever*.
Pierre Assouline, *Zákaznice* (*La Cliente*), transl. Lubomír Martínek, Prague: Prostor, 2000.

It is worth noting that the concession is almost non-existent in the Czech transgressive (see Dvořák 1978), very probably due to the absence of an explicit lexical signal of this complex meaning. The Czech respondents of the Romance gerund, including the transgressive, will be investigated in detail in the next section.

6.5.2 CZECH RESPONDENTS OF THE ROMANCE GERUND

In our research, we divided the Czech respondents of the Romance gerund into three main groups corresponding to the three levels of the scale of syntactic condensation: finite verb (specified in a coordinate or a subordinate clause), nominalisation (PP or NP, adverb, etc.) and non-finite verb forms (especially the transgressive). **Table 6.4** shows the proportions of these categories:

Tab. 6.4. Types of Czech respondents of the adverbial Romance gerund (PP – prepositional phrase, NP-instr – nominal phrase in the instrumental case, Tg – transgressive, Inf – infinitive)

Type of respondent in Czech	Fr.		It.		Es.		Pt.	
Coordinate finite clause	985	41.70%	1,089	58.67%	903	56.97%	885	54.70%
Subordinate finite clause	591	25.02%	335	18.05%	207	13.06%	232	14.34%
Nominalisations (PP, NP-Instr, adverb)	372	15.75%	179	9.64%	137	8.64%	125	7.73%
Non-finite verb form	56	2.37%	51	2.75%	140	8.83%	220	13.60%
Other	358	15.16%	202	10.88%	198	12.49%	156	9.64%
Total	2,362		1,856		1,585		1,618	

The category of "Other" contains, on the one hand, missing respondents (misaligned segments, zero translations etc.), and special translational solutions on the other (esp. *modulations*[90] ou *dépouillements*[91]). However, due to the high quality of the corpus (translations as well as alignment, see Rosen – Vavřín 2012), the frequency of misaligned or missing segments is very low. As for the special translational solutions, they may be interesting for further research in translation studies but in a contrastive analysis, they are not relevant as only recurrent translation respondents (see Krzeszowski 1990, 27) can reveal the structural, systemic similarities and differences between the languages (see the introductory chapter in this volume). Consequently, the category of "Other" will not be taken into account in the following explanations – with one exception only: the category of verbs of movement conveying the Manner, see **Section 6.5.2.3**).

The most striking finding revealed in **Table 6.4** is the overwhelming proportion of finite respondents of the Romance gerund in Czech, and very low frequency of the other types, especially the non-finite one. In fact, in the four Romance languages, the finite respondents (together with the coordinate and the subordinate ones) represent approximately 70% of all the occurrences analysed in our research.[92] Therefore, the Czech language, in comparison with the four Romance languages, shows a clear tendency to verbal (finite) expression (such as e.g. Norwegian in comparison with German, see Fabricius-Hansen 1998 and 1999). This tendency is most likely caused by the strong stylistic markedness of the Czech converb, the transgressive. Other explanations are also possible, for example, Vachek (1961, 43), observing the same tendency in Czech in comparison with English, explains this by the typological differences between the two languages, stating that "there is certain interdependence between the analytical language structure and the reduced dynamism of the finite verb in English and on the other hand, the synthetic language structure and the strong dynamism[93] of the finite verb in Czech".

In what follows, we will introduce a detailed analysis of the three types of Czech respondents, particularly with respect to the semantic types of the Romance gerund they correspond to. Particular attention will be paid to the transgressive (**Section 6.5.2.3**), the potential (converbal, nonfinite) systemic respondent of the Romance gerund.

---

90   E.g. *A quelle perversion obscure avez-vous cédé* **en fournissant** *à l'humanité, de votre plus belle plume, un acte d'auto-accusation d'une transparence aussi criante?*→ *Jaká ničivá zvrácenost vás přiměla* **sepsat** *pro lidstvo nejčistším stylem, jakého jste schopen, tak křiklavě průhledné sebeobvinění?*
Literally: **to write**.
Amélie Nothomb, *Vrahova hygiena* (*Hygiène de l'assassin*), transl. Jarmila Fialová, Prague – Liberec: Paseka, 2001.

91   E.g. *Un trio se donna des gifles et la jeune fille chanta* **en s'accompagnant** *au luth.* → *Trojice herců se fackovala a děvče zazpívalo* **s** *loutnou.*
Literally: **with**.
Frédéric Tristan, *Hrdinné útrapy Baltazara Kobera* (*Les Tribulations héroïques de Balthasar Kober*), transl. Oldřich Kalfiřt, Prague: DharmaGaia – Dauphin, 2003.

92   A similar proportion of finite respondents was also observed by Malá – Šaldová (2015) in translations of English participial adjuncts in –*ing* into Czech (73%).

93   By the term *dynamism of the finite verb* Vachek means the tendency of the language to convey linguistic contents using finite forms, in opposition to non-finite ones.

6.5.2.1 FINITE VERBS AS RESPONDENTS OF THE ROMANCE GERUND

Finite respondents of Romance gerunds may be divided into two major types: finite verbs in coordinate and subordinate clauses.

The finite respondents represent 66.72% of occurrences in French, 76.72% in Italian 70.03% in Spanish and 69.04% in Portuguese. The analysis of the semantic types of the gerunds corresponding to these main types of Czech respondents revealed a clear correspondence between the gerund conveying the meaning of accompanying circumstance (Type B identified by Halmøy 1982 and 2003a, see **Section 6.2.2**) and the coordinate finite clause in Czech and a strong correlation between a specific adverbial meaning of the gerund (Type A according to Halmøy 2003a) and the subordinate clause. In fact, the adverbial relationship of the gerund conveying the meaning of accompanying circumstance to the main verb is only vague and corresponds to the basic interpretative instruction defined by Kleiber (2007b, 117 or 2009, 19 and **Section 6.2.2** above): the two processes are only juxtaposed, co-occurring. On the contrary, gerunds conveying specific adverbial meanings necessitate the explicitation of the logical relationship between the two processes by a (subordinating) conjunction. In what follows, we intend to analyse the specific types of these two major categories and find to what extent they respect the original meaning of the Romance gerund.

6.5.2.1.1 COORDINATE FINITE CLAUSE AS A RESPONDENT OF THE ROMANCE GERUND

The overwhelming majority of coordinate clauses as respondents of Romance gerunds are related to the other clause (corresponding to the original main clause) by the conjunction *a/and*; see (6) and the following example:

(25) Es.
Campillo lo miraba ahora con fijeza, fruncido ligeramente el ceño, **tamborileando** con los dedos sobre el brazo del sillón. → Campillo na něho teď hleděl upřeně s lehce svraštělým obočím a **bubnoval** prsty na opěradlo křesla.
Literally: *and **he drummed** his fingers*.
Pérez-Reverte, Arturo, *Šermířský mistr* (*El maestro de esgrima*), transl. Bronislava Skalická, Prague: Alpress, 1998.

The cases of asyndetic relation (juxtaposition) were also placed in this category – see (5) and (7). This type of respondents (coordinate and asyndetic clause) represent approximately one-half of the respondents of the Romance gerund in our corpus (the least in French). The advantage of the coordinate clause as a respondent of the Romance gerund is the semantic vagueness of the relationship between the two clauses, which corresponds perfectly to the Romance gerund of this semantic type. The most frequent specification of this meaning in Czech is the adverb *přitom/at the same time*, explicitating the simultaneity of both processes (see (7)). However, the relation of coordination/juxtaposition places the two clauses on the same level of importance, which does not correspond to the meaning of the converb, conveying a process considered to be secondary, circumstantial. In some cases, the translators try to retain the hierarchy of processes by changing the order of the clauses: the respondent of the converb is placed in the first position, and the respondent of the main clause is placed at the end of the sentence in a clearly rhematic position:

(26) Fr.
Là-dessus, elle a pris le tisonnier pour soulever le couvercle de ma cuisinière et elle a jeté votre lettre dedans, **en la froissant** en boule, (...). → Potom vzala pohrabáč, nadzvedla poklop na kamnech, <u>**zmačkala** dopis do kuličky</u> (...).
Literally: ***she crumpled** the letter into a bowl*.
Sébastien Japrisot, *Příliš dlouhé zásnuby* (*Un Long dimanche de fiançailles*), transl. Veronika Sysalová, Prague: Euromedia Group, 2005.

Another potential semantic shift caused by the translation of the Romance gerund by a coordinate clause concerns the temporal relationship between them: in fact, if the two coordinate verbs are perfective in Czech, the meaning of simultaneity may be turned into succession. This type of shift is particularly frequent in introductory clauses:

(27) Es.
—Ya sé, ya sé a quién se parece —sonrió feliz, **mostrando** a Lituma el alto de revistas multicolores. → „Aha, už to mám, komu je podobný!" Šťastně se usmál <u>**a ukázal** Litumovi</u> štos obrázkových časopisů.
Literally: ***and he showed** to Lituma*.
Mario Vargas Llosa, *Tetička Julia a zneuznaný génius* (*La tía Julia y el escribidor*), transl. Libuše Prokopová, Prague: Mladá Fronta, 2004.

6.5.2.1.2 THE SUBORDINATE FINITE CLAUSE AS A RESPONDENT OF THE ROMANCE GERUND

As mentioned above, the subordinate finite clause is the most frequent respondent of gerunds conveying not a simple accompanying circumstance but a specific adverbial meaning (temporal, causal, conditional, etc. - Type A identified by Halmøy 1982, 2003a). This type of respondent for example, in French, represents between 13.06% and 25.02% of the respondents of the Romance gerund (the least in Spanish and the most in French).

This type of respondent explicates the semantic type of the gerund by a subordinating conjunction. Nevertheless, the most frequent conjunction introducing this type of respondent, *když* ('when'), to a certain extent maintains the semantic vagueness of the gerund since it can convey both the temporal meaning (simultaneity – (12)

or anteriority – see (13)) as well as causal or condition nuances (such as (13), (16) or (17) or note 37). The temporal meaning is also rendered in Czech by more specific conjunctions than *když*, such as *zatímco* or *jak* (*meanwhile*, conveying simultaneity, see (28) and note 43) or *jakmile* (*as soon as*, conveying immediate anteriority – see (14)).

(28) It.
Uscendo dalla cucina incontrammo Aymaro. → **Jak jsme vycházeli** z kuchyně, potkali jsme Aymarda.
Literally: ***as we were leaving*** *the kitchen*.
Umberto Eco, *Jméno růže* (*Nome della rosa*), transl. Zdeněk Frýbort, Prague: Odeon, 1988.[94]

After the temporal conjunctions (including the polysemic *když*), the second most frequent specific semantic type rendered by subordinate finite clauses is Manner/Means, introduced in Czech by the compound subordinators *tak, že* ('so that') and especially *tím, že* ('by') (see (11)):

(29) Fr.
Elles savent reproduire artificiellement n'importe quelle phéromone: passeport, piste, communication... juste **en mélangeant** judicieusement des sèves, des pollens et des salives. → Dovedou uměle vytvořit jakýkoli feromon: vstupní, stopovací, komunikační... prostě **tím, že** dovedně **míchají** šťávy, pyl a sliny.
Literally: ***by mixing*** *skilfully*.
Bernard Werber, *Mravenci* (*Les Fourmis*), transl. Richard Podaný, Prague: Euromedia Group – Knižní klub, 2005.

Subordinate finite clauses introduced by the conjunctions conveying the meaning of Manner/Means are quite frequent. For example, in French, they represent 17% of this type of respondent (together with the temporal conjunctions, they represent 85% of the subordinate clauses corresponding to French gerund). The same meaning can also be rendered by a noun phrase (NP in the instrumental case) although this type of respondent is limited by syntactic constraints and especially by the number of gerund complements (see below **Section 6.5.2.2**).

Explicitation of the causal relationship by the conjunction *protože/poněvadž* ('because') is rare, as it is usually rendered by the polysemic conjunction *když/when* (see (13) or (16)). This type of respondent often corresponds to the gerund expressed by a static verb conveying emotions (30) or by *verba opinandi* (31):

---

[94]   Or in French, with the conjunction *zatímco* ('while') as a respondent in Czech: **En attendant** les brioches, ils s'échangeaient puces, poux, morpions, gales... → **Zatímco čekali** na briošky, vyměňovali si blechy, vši, filcky, svrab...
Literally: ***while they were waiting***.
Ferdinand Louis Céline, *Od zámku k zámku* (*D'un château l'autre*), transl. Anna Kareninová, Brno: Atlantis, 1996.

(30) It.

Ancor bambina, mia madre restò incinta di me, — raccontava Torrismondo, — e **temendo** le ire dei genitori quando avessero appreso il suo stato, fuggì dal castello reale di Scozia e andò vagando per gli altopiani. → „Má matka nosila mě pod srdcem ještě jako dívka," vyprávěl Thorismund, „a **protože se obávala**, že by ji rodiče zahrnuli hněvem, kdyby zjistili její stav, prchla ze skotského královského zámku a toulala se po horských pláních."
Literally: ***because she was afraid***.
Italo Calvino, *Naši předkové* (*I nostri antenati*), transl. Zdeněk Digrin – Vladimír Mikeš, Prague: Odeon, 1970.

(31) Pt.

E o bom Ferrão sorria, **sabendo** que, sob aquela ferocidade de ímpio obtuso, havia um santo coração... → A dobrák Ferrão se usmíval, **poněvadž věděl**, že pod divokostí toho zavilého bezbožníka tepe šlechetné srdce...
Literally: ***because he knew***.
José Maria Eça de Queiroz, *Zločin pátera Amara* (*O Crime do Padre Amaro*), transl. Zdeněk Hampl, Prague: SNKLU, 1961.

In comparison with the other Romance languages, the causal relationship conveyed explicitly is even rarer among respondents corresponding to the French gerund because this form in French is considered incompatible with static verbs (see Halmøy 2003a); these verbs are used more in the form of the present participle; thus, the corresponding forms in (30) and (31) in French would be *craignant* and *sachant* and not *?en craignant* and *?en sachant*).

The remaining semantic types – condition and concession – are usually rendered by the corresponding specific conjunctions in Czech: *kdyby* ('if') – see (18) in Pt. and (19) in Fr., and *třebaže* and *i když*, meaning 'although' (signalled by *mesmo* or *embora* in Pt., see (20) and (21), by *aun* in Spanish, see (22), by *pur* in Italian, see (23) and by *tout* in French, see (24) in **Section 6.5.1**.

To summarise, most of the subordinate finite clauses explicate the vague meaning of the non-finite Romance gerund (with the exception of the polysemic conjunction *když*), restraining it to one interpretation only. A similar effect is observed on the other extremity of the scale of the syntactic condensation, in nominalisations.

6.5.2.2 NOMINALISATIONS AS RESPONDENTS OF THE ROMANCE GERUND

Nominalisations represent the second most frequent respondent on the scale of syntactic condensation corresponding to the Romance gerund, after the coordinate and the subordinate clauses (about 10%; the most are in translations from French and the least are in translations from Portuguese). The three most frequent types of nominalisations correspond to the three most frequent meanings of the Romance gerund:

s ('with') + NP

The PP introduced by the preposition *s* ('with') conveys the meaning of accompanying circumstance, e.g. *s úsměvem* ('smiling' It. *sorridendo*, see (8); Fr. *en souriant*; Es. *sonriendo*; Pt. *sorrindo* or 'laughing'/*ridendo* etc.).[95] This type of respondent is particularly frequent in introductory clauses, since it renders, in a condensed way, a circumstance of the reported speech:[96]

(32) Pt.
— E estou tambén com vontade de ir rezar unia estaçãozinha para aliviar cá por dentro —ajuntou, **suspirando**. → „A chci se tam také pomodlit, aby se mému srdci trochu ulevilo," dodala **s povzdechem**.
Literally: *with a sigh*.
José Maria Eça de Queiroz, *Bratranec Bazílio* (*O Primo Basílio*), transl. Zdeněk Hampl, Prague: Státní nakladatelství krásné literatury, hudby a umění (SNKLHU), 1955.[97]

při ('with', 'by') + NP

This type of PP usually corresponds to the gerund conveying the temporal meaning. In the four Romance languages, one of the most frequent gerunds having this respondent in Czech is *při pohledu na* 'looking at' – Fr. *en regardant*, Es. *mirando*, It. *guardando*, Pt. *olhando*:

(33) Fr.
Et tes amis seront bien étonnés de te voir rire **en regardant** le ciel. → Tvoji přátelé se budou strašně divit, až tě uvidí smát se **při pohledu** na nebe.
Literally: *with a look at the sky*.
Antoine de Saint Exupéry, *Malý princ* (*Le Petit prince*), transl. Zdeňka Stavinohová, Prague: Albatros, 1989.

However, other verbs are also possible in this meaning: 'running' (It. *correndo* – Cs. *při běhu*), 'saying that' (Fr. *en disant* – Cs. *při těch slovech*) etc.[98]

---

95 E.g. It. "Perché", gli risponde tuttavia l'altro, **ridendo**, "la bellezza era un trucco, per farci credere al paradiso, quando si sa che tutti noi siamo condannati fino dalla nascita." → „Proč...?" „Protože," odpoví mu král **se smíchem**, „krása je jenom obyčejný trik, abychom uvěřili, že je nějaký ráj, když každý naopak ví, že jsme od narození odsouzeni."
Literally: *with laughter*.
Elsa Morante, *Příběh v historii* (*La storia*), transl. Zdeněk Frýbort, Prague: Odeon, 1990.
96 For example in Italian and in French, this type of respondent represents about 30% of all the nominalisations.
97 Nevertheless, this type of respondent is not limited to the introductory clauses, cf. Émerveillés, les indigènes suivent longtemps les bateaux **en chantant** et **en dansant** au son des tambourins. (Davidson, *Sur les traces d'Alexandre le Grand*, 2002) → Žasnoucí domorodci sledovali dlouho lodě **se zpěvem** a **tancem** za zvuku bubínků.
Literally: *with song and dances*.
Marie Thérèse Davidson, *Po stopách Alexandra Velikého* (*Sur les traces d'Alexandre le Grand*), transl. Vladimír Čadský, Prague: Knižní klub, 2005.
98 The temporal meaning is (less frequently) rendered also by the PP *v* ('in') + NP, e.g. Fr. *en dormant* – Cs. *ve spánku* ('in sleep'), It. *conversando* – *v hovorech* ('in conversations') or *za* + NP (Fr. *en marchant* – *za chůze* ('in walking')).

NP-Instrumental

This type of respondent is typical for the meaning of Manner/Means, see (10) for Spanish or the following example:

(34) It.
E quante ore ho trascorso a fissare il bianco di un foglio di pergamena, **pensando** a ciò che avrebbe potuto prendere vita su quel foglio, se Velthune avesse voluto aiutarmi... → A kolik hodin jsem strávil s pohledem upřeným na bílý list pergamenu **přemýšlením** o tom, co by se na tomto listě mohlo zrodit, kdyby mi Velthune chtěl pomoci...
Literally: **by thinking**.
Sebastiano Vassalli, *Nespočet* (*Infinito numero*), transl. Kateřina Vinšová, Prague – Litomyšl: Paseka, 2003.

In the case of the instrumental, the noun is usually a verbal noun in *-ní*, retaining the verbal meaning (cf. *přemýšlením* 'by the thinking' (34), *odhalením* 'by the revelation' in (10), or *uškrcením* 'by the strangling' in the note 50). Nevertheless, other nouns are also acceptable (e.g. *zradou* 'by the treason' in (10), *láskou* 'by the love', *popisem* 'by the description', *diskusí* 'by the discussion' etc.).

The NPs in the instrumental keep the subordinate character of the gerund. However, their use in Czech is limited in two aspects: it is not able to render long gerundival clauses (the number of complements of verbal nouns in Czech being limited) and for some verbs, the corresponding verbal noun is not available in Czech. The last type of respondent of the Romance gerunds in Czech, the transgressive, does not have these constraints. Nevertheless, due to its stylistic properties, it is the least frequent from all the three members of the scale of syntactic condensation examined in this study.

6.5.2.3 NON-FINITE VERB FORMS AS RESPONDENTS OF THE ROMANCE GERUND

Among the three non-finite verb forms available in Czech, the transgressive is the most frequent among the respondents of the Romance gerund. This prevalence of the transgressive (in comparison with the other non-finite verb forms) reflects its converbal character (see **Section 6.2**). However, as shown in **Table 6.4**, it represents the least frequent type of Czech respondent of the Romance gerund in our corpus. This very low frequency of the transgressive among the respondents of the gerund is provided by its very low frequency in contemporary Czech in general.

In our corpus, the occurrences of the transgressive are limited on the one hand by its stylistic specificity (the present, i.e. the imperfective transgressive is considered bookish; the past, i.e. the perfective transgressive is even archaic), and on the other hand by the overwhelming majority of only one meaning – the accompanying circumstance.

Due to the stylistic specificity, the transgressive especially occurs in texts with specific, e.g. historical, stylisation. In the Italian subcorpus, for example, 59% of all the oc-

currences of the transgressive corresponding to the gerund come from only one text:
I nostri antenati by Italo Calvino:

(35) It.
Dall'olmo, sempre **cercando** dove un ramo passava gomito a gomito con i rami
d'un'altra pianta, si passava su un carrubo, e poi su un gelso. → Z jilmu, **hleda-je** vždy místo, kde větev s větvemi sousedního stromu se proplétala, na rohovník
přelezl a posléze na morušovník.
Literally: *__searching__*.
Italo Calvino, *Naši předkové* (*I nostri antenati*), transl. Zdeněk Digrin – Vladimír
Mikeš, Prague: Odeon, 1970.[99]

By using the transgressive, the translators in (35) intend to render the archaistic
stylisation of the original. Similarly, in the Portuguese subcorpus, most of the transgressives corresponding to Portuguese gerunds are attested in texts written in the 19th
century by Eça de Queiroz (this fact explains the high frequency of non-finite verb
forms in translations from Portuguese, see **Table 6.4**):

(36) Pt.
São o melhor bocadinho deste vale de lágrimas – interrompeu com fatuidade o Savedra, **dando palmadinhas** sobre o estômago. → Jsou nejchutnějším soustíčkem
v tomto slzavém údolí," přerušil ho ješitně Savedra, **poplácávaje** se po břiše.
Literally: *__smacking__ his belly*.
José Maria Eça de Queiroz, *Bratranec Bazílio* (*O Primo Basílio*), transl. Zdeněk Hampl, Prague: SNKLHU, 1955.[100]

Another factor influencing the frequency of transgressives in translation is the idiolect of the translator and the date of creation of the translation. For example, most
of the occurrences of the transgressive corresponding to the French gerund are found
in a translation first published in 1965 (both occurrences of the past transgressive in
translations from French come from this text):

---

99 The only occurrence of past (perfective) transgressive corresponding to the Italian gerund comes from the same
text: E **spartendo** davanti a sé le foglie ognuno dal ramo in cui stava scese a quello più basso, verso il ragazzo col
tricorno in capo. → A každý, **rozhrnuv** před sebou listí haluze, na které seděl, na nižší větev slezl, blíže k chlapci
s třírohákem na hlavě.
Literally: *__having pulled__*.
Italo Calvino, *Naši předkové* (*I nostri antenati*), transl. Zdeněk Digrin – Vladimír Mikeš, Prague: Odeon, 1970.

100 Cf. a similar historical stylisation in the following text: Là-dessus il voulut me mettre dehors **en invoquant**
l'heure tardive et son sommeil troublé. → Načež mě chtěl zase vystrnadit ven na déšť, **odvolávaje se** na pozdní
hodinu a svůj přerušený spánek.
Literally: *__invoking__*.
André Pieyre de Mandiargues, *Vlčí slunce* (*Soleil des loups*), transl. Ladislav Šerý, Prague: Reflex, 1992.

(37) Fr.

(...) plusieurs fois par semaine, il jette sa serviette sur la table et quitte la salle à manger **en claquant** la porte (...). → (...) několikrát v týdnu hodí ubrousek na stůl a odchází z jídelny, **bouchnuv** dveřmi (...).

Literally: ***having slashed*** *the door*.

Jean Paul Sartre, *Slova* (*Les Mots*), transl. Dagmar Steinová, Prague: Svoboda, 1992.

As for the semantic limitation of the occurrences of the transgressive in translations of the Romance gerund, we must point out that despite the capacity of the transgressive to convey various adverbial meanings (see **Table 6.3**), our occurrences are mostly limited to only one semantic type: the accompanying circumstance – see (35), (36) or the following example in translation from Spanish:

(38) Es.

El Consejero y los peregrinos subieron la montaña al atardecer y entraron en el pueblo en procesión, **cantando** Loores a María. → Rádce a poutníci za soumraku vystoupili na kopec a vešli do osady v procesí, **zpívajíce** chvalozpěvy na počest Panny.

Literally: ***singing*** *hymns*.

Mario Vargas Llosa, *Válka na konci světa* (*Lituma en los Andes*), transl. Vladimír Medek, Prague: Odeon, 1989.

The limitation of the transgressive to only one meaning in translations is provided by the dominance of this meaning in fiction – in the Romance originals as well as in non-translated Czech fiction (see **Table 6.3**).[101] Moreover, in contrast to the specific adverbial meanings (Type A of Halmøy 1982, 2003a), the accompanying circumstance cannot be rendered in Czech by a subordinate finite clause. Since the translator has to choose between two extremities (a coordinate finite clause, see **Section 6.5.2.1.1**, and PP introduced by the preposition *s* 'with', see **Section 6.5.2.2**), without the possibility to use the intermediate member of the scale of syntactic condensation (a subordinate clause), the probability of the use of the transgressive is increased. In fact, the transgressive maintains all the characteristics of the Romance converb: not only the vagueness of the meaning and the subordination but also the condensed way of their expression.

In order to find out to what extent the Czech transgressive truly corresponds to the Romance gerund, we conducted an analysis focused solely on this form and on its respondents in the four Romance languages. From the methodological point of view, the research was inspired by Johansson (1998). We expected that the gerund would be the most frequent respondent of the Czech transgressive since both forms belong to the category of the converb. In order to identify (and balance) a potential influence of

---

101   For example, in the French subcorpus, the transgressives corresponding to French gerunds convey the meaning of accompanying circumstance in 80% of cases; in Italian, this proportion is 51%.

Tab. 6.5. *Romance respondents of Czech (present and past) transgressives in translations from Czech into Romance* (PP = prepositional phrase; lexicalised forms = occurrences of lexicalised transgressives in Czech, type *počínaje*; other = special translation solutions, zero translations etc.)

Type of counterpart in Romance	Spanish present transgressive		Spanish past transgressive		French present transgressive		French past transgressive		Italian present transgressive		Italian past transgressive		Portuguese present transgressive		Portuguese past transgressive	
	Abs.f.	Rel.f.	Abs.f.	Rel.f.	Abs.f.	Rel.f.	Abs.f.	Rel.f.	Abs.f.	Rel.f.	Abs.f.	Rel.f.	Abs.f.	Rel.f.	Abs.f.	Rel.f.
gerund	121	50.21%	22	51.16%	207	34.27%	13	12.62%	80	59.26%	3	30.00%	16	45.71%	–	–
present participle	11	4.56%	–	–	144	23.84%	33	32.04%	3*	2.22%	3*	30.00%	2	5.71%	–	–
(Prep+)Inf	35	14.52%	4	9.30%	23	3.81%	3	2.91%	16	11.85%	–	–	6	17.14%	–	–
PP	17	7.05%	–	–	–	–	–	–	8	5.93%	1	10.00%	2	5.71%	–	–
finite verb	33	13.69%	8	18.60%	72	11.92%	25	24.27%	19	14.07%	3	30.00%	9	25.71%	–	–
lexicalised form	5	2.07%	–	–	24	3.97%	–	–	4	2.96%	–	–	–	–	–	–
adjective	–	–	–	–	–	–	–	–	2	1.48%	–	–	–	–	–	–
other	19	7.88%	9	20.93%	134	22.19%	29	28.16%	3	2.22%	–	–	–	–	–	–
Total	241		43		604		103		135		10		35		0	

* – past participle

Tab. 6.6. *Romance respondents of Czech transgressives (present and past) in translations from Romance into Czech* (PP = prepositional phrase; lexicalised forms = occurrences of lexicalised transgressives in Czech, type *počínaje*; other = special translation solutions, zero translations etc.)

Type of counterpart in Romance	Spanish				French				Italian				Portuguese			
	present transgressive		past transgressive		present transgressive		past transgressive		present transgressive		past transgressive		present transgressive		past transgressive	
	Abs.f.	Rel.f.	Abs.f.	Rel.f.	Abs.f.	Rel.f.	Abs.f.	Rel.f.	Abs.f.	Rel.f.	Abs.f.	Rel.f.	Abs.f.	Rel.f.	Abs.f.	Rel.f.
gerund	145	58.70%	63	62.38%	42	17%	0	0%	81	42.86%	14	46.67%	291	60.00%	19	70.37%
present participle	13	5.26%	9	8.91%	88	35%	8	62%	-	-	-	-	41	8.45%	4	14.81%
Prep + Inf	30	12.15%	6	5.94%	2	1%	0	0%	11	5.82%	4	13.33%	29	5.98%	2	7.41%
PP	13	5.26%	1	0.99%	-	-	-	-	12	6.35%	2	6.67%	44	9.07%	1	3.70%
finite verb	14	5.67%	10	9.90%	7	3%	2	15%	2	1.06%	5	16.67%	29	5.98%	1	3.70%
lexicalised forms	18	7.29%	-	-	56	22%	-	-	56	29.63%	-	-	24	4.95%	-	-
adjective	2	0.81%	-	-	58	23%	3	23%	11	5.82%	1	3.33%	10	2.06%	-	-
other	12	4.86%	12	11.88%	-	-	-	-	16	8.47%	4	13.33%	17	3.51%	-	-
Total	247	100	101	100	253		13		189		30		485		27	

the direction of translation, we analysed the transgressives and their Romance respondents both in translations from Czech to Romance (see **Table 6.5**) and from Romance to Czech (see **Table 6.6**).

Tables 6.5 and **6.6** show that in Spanish, Italian and Portuguese, the gerund is effectively the dominant respondent of the Czech transgressive, independently from the direction of translation and of the form of the transgressive (past or present). However, in translations involving French, the gerund in this function is strongly in concurrence with the other V-ant form, the present participle. Moreover, in translations from French into Czech, the transgressive is more frequent as a respondent of the present participle than of gerund (35% against only 17%). This may be caused not only by the concurrence of the two forms in the meaning of accompanying circumstance but especially by the stylistic markedness of the transgressive corresponding to the stylistic characteristics of the French present participle, which is considered formal and typical for written texts.

The following example shows the translation of the Czech present transgressive by the French present participle:

(39) Fr.
Jednou nabili pana Jirouta do kanónu, a když ho vystřelili a pan Jirout dosáhl vrcholu křivky, rozpřáhl ruce a po hlavě **padaje**$_{\text{to.fall'-TRANSGRESSIVE.PRS}}$, zvolna dolů viděl, že už dávno minul trampolínu (...). → Un jour, on chargea M. Jirout dans son canon et lorsqu'on eut fait feu et que M. Jirout eut atteinle sommet de sa trajectoire il écarta les bras et, **tombant** lentement, la tête en bas, il vit qu'il avait déjà dépassé le trampoline; (...).
Bohumil Hrabal, *La Chevelure sacrifiée* (*Postřižiny*), transl. Claudia Ancelot, Paris: Gallimard, 1987.

It is worth noting that among the respondents of the Czech past transgressive in all the four Romance languages, the compound forms of the gerund are rare or not attested, as the anteriority is conveyed by the aspectual characteristics of both verbs.[102] However, in French, one-third of the present participles corresponding to the Czech past transgressive in translations from Czech into French are in compound form, conveying the anteriority explicitly:

(40) Fr.
Doktor Kurka je očistil, prohlédl, a **zjistiv**$_{\text{to.find.out'-TRANSGRESSIVE.PST}}$, že jsou nepoškozené a zdravé, navrhl dívce, že by je mohl vložit zpátky do čelisti, jestliže to snese bez

---

102 In Spanish, for example, we found only one occurrence of compound gerund corresponding to the past transgressive in Czech: (...) zemřel mezi dvěma kliky, provedenými z podporu ležmo za rukama, **dosáhnuv** stáří 48 let. → (...) murió entre dos flexiones realizadas con ayuda de las manos en posición de decúbito, **habiendo alcanzado** la edad de cuarenta y ocho años.
Literally: ***having reached***.
Zdeněk Jirotka, *Saturnino* (*Saturnin*), transl. Eduardo Fernández Couceiro, Prague: Karolinum, 2004.

umrtvení. → Le docteur Kurka les a nettoyées et **ayant constaté** qu'elles étaient intactes, il a proposé à la jeune femme de les remettre à leur place dans la mâchoire, à condition qu'elle supporte l'opération sans anesthésie.
Ludvík Vaculík, *La Clef des songes* (*Český snář*), transl. Jan Rubeš, Arles: Actes de Sud, 1989.

These results show clearly that, especially in French, the contrastive analysis of converbs is not possible without taking into account the other non-finite verb forms in the compared language systems.[103] A thorough analysis may reveal the converbal uses of the present participle in French.

Nevertheless, the results summarised in **Tables 6.5** and **6.6** are limited in several aspects: the frequency of the transgressive is very low (especially for the past transgressive) and limited mostly to the accompanying circumstance (see above). Moreover, in some cases, all the occurrences of the Czech transgressive come from the same text or the same author. Consequently, the use of the transgressive may be influenced by the idiolect of the author, and its Romance respondents by the strategy of the corresponding translator. Therefore, research of larger corpora (including monolingual corpora) is required.

Despite the limitations indicated above, the contrastive analysis of the Czech transgressive revealed three interesting differences between the Czech converb and the Romance gerund:

1) The Czech transgressive easily conveys the negative accompanying circumstance although the dominating respondent in Romance, in this case, is not a converb (rare in negation) but the construction *sans/sine* etc. + inf:

    (41) Fr.
    „Keby boly hory samé papírové a voda atrament, hvezdy písarové (...)," zpíval Jaroslav **nesundávaje**$_{\text{take.out'-TRANSGRESSIVE.PRS.NEG}}$ housle zpod brady (...). → « Si les montagnes étaient en papier – si l'eau se changeait en encre (...) », chantait Jaroslav **sans décoller** le violon de sa poitrine.
    Milan Kundera, *La Plaisanterie* (*Žert*), transl. Marcel Aimonin, Paris: Gallimard, 1975.

2) On the contrary, the Czech transgressive almost never conveys the concessive meaning (see Dvořák 1978, 33 and 39); in Romance, this meaning is not frequent but is well attested. This difference may be explained by the use of explicit lexical signals of the concessive meaning in Romance (see (20) – (24)), rendering the complex concessive meaning clearer.

---

103 Similarly, in Portuguese, it would be necessary to also involve the analysis of the infinitive, concurrencing the gerund in European Portuguese.

3) The Romance gerund may convey the Manner by the lexical relationship between the two verbs, especially in verbs of saying and verbs of movement (Type B of Halmøy 1982, 2003a). In Czech, the Manner may be rendered, for example, by an adverb (Fr. *ajouter* **en chuchotant** – Cs. *dodat* **šeptem** 'to add **in whisper**' in (9)). However, if the meaning of the main verb is fully included in the meaning of the gerund (e.g. Fr. *marcher/boiter* or Fr. *dire/chuchoter*), the use of the transgressive in Czech is problematic (?*kráčel* **kulhaje** – 'he walked **limping**' or ?*řekla* **šeptajíc** – she said **whispering**'). This suggests that in Czech, both processes are conceptualised as separated, whereas in Romance, the converb may convey a simple adverbial specification of the main verb. In the case of verbs of movement, a typological difference between the Romance languages on the one hand, and Czech on the other, comes into play. As mentioned in 6.2.2, Romance belongs to the *verb-framed languages*, conveying the Manner using satellites (gerunds in this case) and the Path by the finite verb (e.g. Fr. *il est arrivé$_i$ en courant$_j$* 'he came running'). Czech, on the contrary, belongs to satellite-framed languages, rendering the Manner by the root and the Path by the satellite (*při$_i$běhl$_j$* 'he came running'). This type of constellation is not very frequent in any of the four Romance languages (a few items in each language only), but it is attested:

(42) Fr.
Une autre sentinelle arrive **en courant** à la porte numéro 5. → K bráně číslo pět se **přiřítila** jiná hlídka.[104]
Literally: *another watch **rushed towards** the gate*.
Bernard Werber, *Mravenci* (*Les Fourmis*), transl. Richard Podaný, Prague: Euromedia Group – Knižní klub, 2005.

(43) Pt.
Quando a sentiu chamar, impacientar-se em cima, subiu, **correndo**. → Když slyšela, že ji paní nahoře volá a je zneklidněna, rychle tam **vyběhla**.
Literally: ***she ran up***.
José Maria Eça de Queiroz, *Bratranec Bazílio* (*O Primo Basílio*), transl. Zdeněk Hampl, Prague: SNKLHU, 1955.[105]

In the examples mentioned above ((42) and (43)), the use of transgressive is not possible, which suggests deeper typological differences between the four Romance languages and Czech in this point.

---

104 Similarly: *Il approcha d'eux* **en clopinant**. → **Přibelhal se** k nim.
    Literally: **he came hobbling**.
    Frédéric Tristan, *Hrdinné útrapy Baltazara Kobera* (*Les Tribulations héroïques de Balthasar Kober*), transl. Oldřich Kalfiřt, Prague: DharmaGaia – Dauphin, 2003.
    Je quittai la salle de contrôle **en vacillant**, *j'avais la tête qui tournait*. → **Vypotácel jsem se** z kontrolní místnosti, motala se mi hlava.
    Literally: **I left staggering**.
    Jean-Philippe Toussaint, *Milovat se* (*Faire l'amour*), transl. Jovanka Šotolová, Prague: Garamond, 2004.
105 Manner is sometimes also specified in Czech by an adverb, such as *rychle* ('quickly') in (43).

6.6 CONCLUSION

The aim of this chapter was to analyse the Romance gerund and its Czech respondents and, on the basis of the cross-linguistic notion of the converb used as tertium comparationis, to find to what extent the Romance gerund corresponds to its potential systemic counterpart in Czech – the transgressive. From the morphological point of view, these non-finite verb forms are different: the Romance gerund, resulting from the Latin ablativus gerundii, is non-congruent whereas the Czech transgressive agrees with its controller in gender and in number. Despite this, all these forms are considered as converbs. From the syntactic point of view, they may be considered the middle member of the scale of syntactic condensation, between the finite verb (in a coordinate or a subordinate clause) and nominalisations.

We first focused our analysis on the Romance gerund only – its frequency, syntactic functions and semantic interpretation. The analysis of the frequency and the syntactic properties of the gerund in the four Romance languages revealed important differences between the Spanish and Portuguese gerunds on the one hand and the Italian and, especially, the French form on the other. In fact, in Spanish and in Portuguese, the gerund is used not only in its adverbial converbal function (including absolute constructions) but adjectival uses (attributive as well as predicative) are also well attested while both languages (especially Spanish) make extensive use of the gerund in verbal periphrases. On the contrary, in Italian and French, the adjectival uses of the gerund are excluded and moreover, in French, the gerund is limited to the non-absolute adverbial use and the only verbal periphrase involving this form (*aller (en) –ant*) is extremely rare. As for the Czech transgressive, it seems closest to the French gerund (with respect to the syntactic properties):

Tab. 6.7. Syntactic properties of the gerund in four Romance languages and of the Czech transgressive

Romance gerund		Es.	Pt.	It.	Fr.	Cs.
non-converbal	verbal periphrases	+	+	+	(+)	–
	adjectival use	+	+	–	–	–
converbal (adverbial)	absolute constructions	+	+	(+)	–	(+)[106]
	non-absolute	+	+	+	+	+

The differences in the syntactic functions of the gerund strongly influence the overall frequency of the gerund in the four languages. In Portuguese and Spanish, the relative frequency of the gerund (in all the uses together) is 8,300 and 7,274 ipm respectively; in Italian, the frequency is lower but still comparable (5,100 ipm) but in French, the relative frequency of the gerund is only 1,572 ipm.

---

106 According to Dvořák (1978), absolute uses were well attested up to the 17th century in Czech, even though in contemporary grammars, they are non accepted.

Observing the differences in the use of gerunds in the four languages, we suggested that in accordance with the classification by Nedjalkov (1995, 104sq.), the gerund in Italian and in French may be considered as a "monofunctional, canonical converb" (as well as the Czech transgressive) while in Spanish and in Portuguese, the gerund belongs more to the category of polyfunctional, potential quasi-converbs.

The analysis of semantic types of converbal uses of the gerund (absolute as well as non-absolute) revealed, on the contrary, striking similarities between the four forms – and also the Czech transgressive (converb). In the five languages, the dominant meaning is the accompanying circumstance, corresponding to the basic interpretative instruction of the gerund (at least 40% of all the occurrences). However, this tendency also reveals the potential limitation of our research: in fact, this meaning is typical for narrative texts, as it allows for the expression of two co-occurring processes without a strict logical relationship. Since our corpus contains mostly fiction (see Nádvorníková this volume), the predominance of this meaning is inevitable. Therefore, future research, aimed at a more complex analysis of the question, should also include other text types, especially non-fiction.

The second similarity in the semantic interpretation of the four Romance gerunds and the Czech transgressive was the *ranking* of the remaining meanings: in all the five languages, the second most frequent semantic type is temporal, followed by manner/means and cause. The remaining semantic types (condition and concession) are rare. The extremely low frequency of concessive meaning can be explained by the high cognitive effort necessary for its decoding.

The thorough analysis of the semantic types of the Romance gerund confirms that this form belongs to the contextual converb category, as already suggested by Haspelmath (1995): its meaning remains vague and is given by the context. On the basis of the research conducted by (Dvořák 1978) in Czech, the same confirmation may be given for the Czech transgressive. Contextual factors participating in the interpretation of the Romance gerund, as well as the Czech transgressive, are multiple: the aspectual and semantic relationship between the gerundival verb and the main verb, mode of the main verb (especially the conditional), position of the form vis-à-vis the main clause (the anteposition facilitates the temporal or causal interpretation) etc. The explicit lexical signals of the meaning are limited to the temporal meaning of the immediate anteriority (*em* in Portuguese and in Spanish) and especially to the concession (*tout* in French, *aun* in Spanish, *mesmo* or *embora* in Portuguese and *pur* in Italian). The lack of an explicit lexical signal may explain the quasi-absence of the concessive meaning in the Czech transgressive.

In the second part of our study, we investigated the potential correlations of the semantic types of the Romance gerund and the types of its Czech respondents. Since the potential systemic counterpart of the Romance gerund, the transgressive, is rare in contemporary Czech and considered very formal and bookish (the imperfective form, conveying simultaneity) or even archaic (the perfective form, conveying anteriority), we expected that the other members of the scale of syntactic condensation will take its place. This hypothesis was confirmed only partially since the overwhelming majority of the respondents of the Romance gerund belong to only one category: finite clause (coordinate clauses being twice or even three times more frequent than subordinate ones). Nominalisations represent only a minor part of the respondents. This result confirms the tendency of Czech for explicit verbal expression, which has also been observed in previous studies.

The research also revealed a strong correlation between the semantic type of the Romance gerund and the type of its Czech respondent: the basic meaning of pure accompanying circumstance is dominantly rendered in Czech by a coordinate finite clause (with the conjunction *a* 'and'), whereas the gerunds conveying more specific adverbial meanings usually have the corresponding adverbial subordinate clause as a respondent. In contrast with specific subordinating conjunctions, the coordinating conjunction *a* retains the vague semantic relationship between the clauses in Romance although the coordination modifies their hierarchy, as it replaces the subordination, typical for converb, and puts both clauses on the same level of importance.

As expected, the non-finite respondent of the Romance gerund, the transgressive, was very rare. The final research focused specifically on the transgressive and its respondents in Romance showed that with the exception of French, the gerund is effectively the dominant respondent of the transgressive. In French, the gerund is strongly in concurrence with the other V-ant form – the present participle. However, these results are limited in several aspects: the low frequency of the transgressive in our corpus and its limitation to only one semantic type (accompanying circumstance), the potential influence of authors' idiolects (in translations from Czech) and the translators' strategies (in the opposite direction of translation) etc.

The limitations of the research carried out on the transgressive are also applicable to the whole research presented in this study. As mentioned in the introductory chapter in this volume, the subcorpora of the four Romance languages under investigation are of different sizes, and in numerous aspects are not representative, especially with regard to the variety of text types. Future research into the Romance gerund and its respondents in Czech, founded on corpora containing not only fiction but also an important sub-corpus of non-fiction or journalistic texts, might bring interesting insights into the different uses of Romance converb. From the contrastive point of view, the present study also revealed the necessity to examine the converb (not only the Romance gerund but also the Czech transgressive) with respect to its *valeur* in the system of the other non-finite forms (infinitives and participles).

7. FORMAL EXPRESSIONS VS ABSTRACT LINGUISTIC CATEGORIES: COMING TO TERMS WITH POTENTIAL (NON-VOLITIONAL) PARTICIPATION, ITERATIVITY, CAUSATION, INGRESSIVITY AND ADVERBIAL SUBORDINATION

PETR ČERMÁK
DANA KRATOCHVÍLOVÁ
OLGA NÁDVORNÍKOVÁ
PAVEL ŠTICHAUER

7.0 INTRODUCTION

Throughout the present monograph, we have analysed five different phenomena that can be found in Spanish, Italian, French and Portuguese. In abstract terms, these phenomena could be defined as an expression of potential (non-volitional) participation, repetition (iterativity), causation, beginning of an action (ingressivity) and adverbial subordination (in the broadest sense of the term). In the Romance languages studied, all these phenomena dispose of a means of expression that is typically associated with them, i.e. expresses these notions in their "purest" form while also being highly productive and frequent. The potential (non-volitional) participation is expressed through the suffix –ble/-bile/-vel, iterativity through the prefix re-/ri-,[107] causativity is expressed through the construction hacer/fare/faire/fazer + infinitive, ingressivity through a wide range of partially synonymous verbal periphrases and non-finite adverbial subordination is typically marked by the gerund.

In the Czech language, the above-mentioned notions are coded in a different manner and their prototypical Romance forms of expression do not always find a clear systemic Czech counterpart. We can imagine a scale ranging from an apparently perfect analogy between the Romance expression and Czech (both in terms of the notions typically attributed to the expression and its formal manifestation), through partial correspondence (either in terms of non-corresponding secondary notions attributed to the expression and/or its formal expression) to an apparently missing form of systemic expression. This initial schema based on Romance and Czech grammars is represented in **Table 7.1**.

The objectives of our study can be subsumed into the following points:
1) While not being our main goal, the decision to consider the above-presented phenomena as generally Romance and put them into contrast with Czech, required at least a brief comparison of their functions across the Romance languages under scrutiny and to pinpoint some general differences.

---

107 In the case of iterativity, the prefix re-/ri- shares a function with the iterative verbal periphrasis Es. *volver a* + infinitive, It. *tornare a* + infinitive, Pt. *voltar a* + infinitive. However, there is no similar verbal periphrasis in French.

Tab. 7.1. Systemic counterparts of the analysed Romance phenomena

Romance expression	Czech systemic counterpart	Notional correspon-dence	Formal correspon-dence	Frequency and combinatory correspondence
suffix *–ble/-bile/-vel*	suffix *-telný*	yes	yes	?
gerund	transgressive	partial	partial	no
ingressive verbal periphrases	prefixes	partial	no	?
hacer/fare/faire/fazer + infinitive	prefix *roz-*	partial	no	no
prefix *re-/ri-*	no systemic correspondence			

2) The main objective of our study was a corpus-based analysis of the Czech respondents of the Romance linguistic phenomena. This focussed primarily on the question as to whether the existence of a partial or apparently absolute systemic Czech counterpart automatically means that this counterpart will be the predominant respondent in the corpus and as to whether Romance phenomena that do not possess any clear Czech systemic counterpart have any dominant Czech respondent(s), which can be structurally defined.

3) The analysis of the Czech respondents and the secondary notions they expressed also enabled us to reformulate some of the original assumptions regarding the semantics of the analysed Romance phenomena.

4) We could evaluate the exploitation possibilities and limitations of parallel corpora and the possible contribution of corpus-based analyses to the discussion regarding the nature of a concrete language phenomenon.

In the following sections, the above-presented points are discussed in greater detail with reference to the conclusions we were able to make in light of the conducted corpus analyses.

7.1 CORRESPONDENCES OF THE ANALYSED PHENOMENA ACROSS ROMANCE LANGUAGES

A data-based comparison among all four of the languages studied proved to be difficult due to the differences in the size of the respective subcorpora with which we worked (see Nádvorníková this volume). The limited amount of Italian, French and Portuguese data (in contrast to the considerably larger Spanish subcorpus) turned out to be especially relevant when analysing the complex words (Štichauer et al. this volume), where no reliable quantitative analysis in terms of affix frequencies and their combinatorics could be made. However, the data also revealed an interesting frequency mismatch worth exploring in a future study. In fact, we noted that the overall frequency of the prefix *re-* was considerably higher in French than in the other Romance languages. In the absence of a further in-depth study, we can only guess that this might be due to the absence of a productive iterative verbal periphrasis in French (as opposed to Spanish, Italian and Portuguese, where verbal periphrases of this type are commonly used, see Kratochvílová – Jindrová et al. this volume).

Nevertheless, based on the corpus data, we can conclude that in terms of combinatory possibilities and overall frequency, there are considerable differences between *hacer/fare/faire/fazer* + infinitive on the one hand and the ingressive verbal periphrases and gerund on the other. While in Čermák – Kratochvílová et al. (this volume, **Section 4.6**), we observed that the causative construction displays similar combinatory possibilities in all four languages studied and the possible differences can be considered to be only isolated phenomena, the analyses made by Kratochvílová – Jindrová et al. (this volume, **Section 5.2.4.1.2**) and Nádvorníková et al. (this volume, **Section 6.2.1**) prove key structural differences in the usage of both the ingressive verbal periphrases and the gerund. These differences can be defined in terms of the lower general frequency of the phenomenon in question in Italian and French and its very high frequency of use in Spanish and Portuguese. While apparently unrelated, these observations might point towards a different behaviour of non-finite verbal forms in the analysed languages. Analyses presented in this monograph indicate a close relationship between the usage of verbal periphrases and the gerund. As observed by Kratochvílová – Jindrová et al. (this volume), the set of French periphrastic constructions is considerably smaller than the Spanish and Portuguese one (Italian being in the middle between these two poles). The general preference for expressing the manner of action in forms other than periphrastic construction is closely related to the limited periphrastic usage of the Italian and especially the French gerund (see Nádvorníková et al. this volume, **Section 6.2.1**), thus influencing the general lower frequency of its usage (see Nádvorníková et al. this volume, **Section 6.4**).

In terms of the semantic notions attributed to the phenomena in question, the largest differences can be observed in the case of ingressive periphrastic constructions, especially when referring to notions other than the mere beginning of an action. Unlike Italian and French, Spanish and Portuguese dispose of a large set of stylistically marked verbal periphrases that underline notions such as [+unexpectancy], [+sheer energy], [+inappropriateness] etc. (see Kratochvílová – Jindrová this volume; Jindrová 2016, Kratochvílová – Jindrová 2017). However, an exhaustive comparison between Spanish and Portuguese proved to be impossible, especially due to the limited extension of the Portuguese subcorpus. Such a comparison requires a considerably larger set of data, as proven by Kratochvílová – Jindrová (2017), who analysed the differences between Spanish and Portuguese ingressive periphrases using the considerably larger CORPES XXI, CETEMPúblico, Araneum Hispanicum Maius and Araneum Portugallicum Maius corpora.

7.2 CZECH RESPONDENTS OF THE ANALYSED PHENOMENA VS SYSTEMIC COUNTERPARTS

As can be observed in **Table 7.1**, the suffix *-ble/-bile/-vel* was the only analysed phenomenon with a clearly defined Czech counterpart (the suffix *-telný*), which apparently corresponds to the Romance element both in the form (suffix) and the semantic features (potential participation). While this respondent type, indeed, proved to be the most frequent (see Štichauer et al. this volume, **Sections 3.4.2** and **3.6**), it was used only in approximately 58% of all analysed translations (see **Table 3.2**). This suggests differences both in the combinatorics of the Czech and Romance suffix (a systemic comparison is impossible due to the limited amount of data contained in InterCorp) and, perhaps more importantly, in the behaviour of the abstract category of potential (non-volitional) participation in Romance and in Czech, its definition and formal manifestation.

The question of how precisely it is possible to define semantic notions attributed to an affix becomes even more important when analysing the prefix *re-/ri-*, which lacks any clear Czech counterpart. The great heterogeneity of the Czech respondents and the dominance of respondent types where iterativity either resulted from a larger context or was apparently not expressed at all (see Štichauer et al. this volume, **Sections 3.5.2** and **3.6**) give rise to questions regarding not only the organisation of the iterativity category in Czech but also the combinations of iterativity with other notions in the matrix of the Romance prefix on one hand and the possible lexicalisation of a prefixed word, i.e. the semantic emptiness of the prefix, on the other.

It is interesting to observe that very similar problems, i.e. the inherent presence of the notion attributed to the Romance phenomenon in the very semantics of the Czech respondent or in the meaning of an utterance as a whole rather than in a concrete formal respondent and the combination of the notions traditionally attributed to the phenomenon in question with others that proved to be hard to define, also became an important topic when analysing the causative constructions. While the prefix *roz-*, which is generally considered to be a prototypical means of expressing causativity in Czech, proved to be rather a marginal respondent of *hacer/fare/faire/fazer* + infinitive, in approximately 60% of cases, causativity was not overtly expressed in the Czech respondent and resulted either from the meaning of a verb or from syntax. The third most frequent Czech respondent is an analytic causative construction which, nevertheless, always includes secondary notions such as [+forcing], [+command], [+allowance] etc. (see Čermák – Kratochvílová et al. this volume, **Section 4.7**), which, on the contrary, were not overtly expressed in the Romance original and resulted from the context.

However surprising, probably the greatest systemic similarities between Romance languages and Czech can be found when analysing the ingressive verbal periphrases and the Czech respondents. Prefixes, such as *roz-*, *vy-* or *za-*, which are generally considered ingressive, were not the clearly dominant respondent type and analyses revealed that ingressivity in Czech is also systematically coded through verbal and verbo-nominal constructions, see Kratochvílová – Jindrová et al. (this volume). However, the Czech respondents of concrete periphrases could generally express not only the beginning of an action but also secondary semantic notions, such as [+quick beginning], [+previous retention], [+energy] etc., which can also be attributed to Romance periphrases. The analyses revealed that both the Romance languages and Czech tend to express these notions cumulatively, both the Romance languages and Czech also dispose of a set of partially synonymous expressions that accentuate different facets of the beginning of a process. In the analysed Romance languages, these constructions display large formal similarities (the construction of a semi-auxiliary verb + infinitive); in Czech, the forms of expressing ingressive MoA are less coherent (prefixes and verbal or verbo-nominal constructions), nevertheless, the tendency to express the initial stage of a process through a relatively clearly defined set of productive linguistic features can also be observed. On the other hand, especially with regard to Czech, where ingressivity is traditionally associated solely with prefixes, the analyses clearly show that, just like in the case of causativity, iterativity and the expression of action carrier, identifying the analysis of the beginning of an action solely with one formal manifestation, clearly impedes us from viewing the category in its complexity.

Finally, in light of the presented analyses, we can state that observations regarding the deep and complex nature of the category in question, which were made with reference to potential (non-volitional) participation, iterativity, causation and ingressivity, also apply when referring to the gerund. Despite the large systemic similarities between the Romance gerund and the Czech transgressive (see Nádvorníková et al. this volume), the stylistic features attributed to the Czech transgressive, such as "archaic" and "obsolete", made this apparently ideal typological counterpart appear very rarely in the corpus (even in literary texts that constituted the main part of our data). If restricted to its non-periphrastic, i.e. converbal use, the Romance gerund shows striking semantic similarities in the four Romance languages under scrutiny in this study (see **Section 7.1**). If we base the definition of the main function of the gerund on its most frequent kind of usage, we can identify it with a highly abstract notion of adverbial subordination, more concretely with the expression of accompanying circumstance. Being the most frequent Czech respondent of this type of gerund, a coordinate clause with the conjunction *a* ('and'), it might seem tempting to conclude that Czech respondents do not reflect the main syntactic feature of gerund (i.e. subordination), thus changing the relationship between the main process (expressed through a finite verbal form in Romance) and its accompanying circumstance (expressed through the gerund). However, leaving aside the purely formal syntactic features of a Romance sentence with a gerund and its most frequent Czech respondent, i.e. a coordinate clause, we can also observe that *a* is the most frequent and, consequently, also the most neutral, conjunction in the Czech language. Returning to the question of the semantic properties of the Romance prefix *re-/ri-* and its semantic non-transparency (possibly even emptiness) in some contexts, we might ask whether the conjunction *a* does not serve in many contexts as a neutral way of connecting two verbal contents without overtly pointing out the hierarchical relationship between them. In this way, we can also conclude that the notion of accompanying circumstance, which is explicitly expressed through the form of the gerund in Romance, is once again present in the very semantics of the Czech respondent or in the context.

7.3 EXPLOITING THE PARALLEL CORPUS IN SEARCH OF LANGUAGE UNIVERSALS AND ABSTRACT CATEGORIES

The analyses presented throughout this monograph and the results lead us to the conclusion that, even when counting on relatively small data-sets for all analysed languages (with the possible exception of Spanish), a systemic contrastive analysis of concrete language phenomena and their Czech respondents can offer interesting insights both when concentrating on the typology of Czech translations and when observing the semantic features of the Romance construction in question, in the light of its Czech respondents. All the presented analyses clearly demonstrate that notions attributed to the Romance phenomena under scrutiny are very common in language and, often, the Czech speaker does not even realise their presence (for example, in the case of inherent iteratives and causatives or in the case of the commonly used ingressive prefix za-). On the other hand, the analyses also reveal a similar tendency in the case of the Romance phenomena we analysed. The large amount of non-transparent uses of the prefix re-/ri-, the combination of stylistically neutral ingressive verbal periphrases with a verb that clearly expressed the beginning of an action in its internal MoA or the high frequency of the circumstantial gerund that was translated through a neutral coordinate construction, suggest that an overt expression of iterativity, ingressivity and adverbial circumstance is, actually, redundant in these cases and might be explained on the grounds that these forms are often lexicalised or considered a neutral form of expression rather than a marked emphasising of the above-mentioned notions.

We consider the observed non-transparency of the analysed categories (both in Romance languages and in Czech) probably the most important general conclusion that can be drawn from our study. Parallel corpora proved to be a useful tool for revealing non-transparent, non-systematic or covert expressions of potential (non-volitional) participation, iterativity, causation, ingressivity and abstractly conceived adverbial circumstance. In this aspect, the presented analyses clearly shed new light on the nature of the categories the analysed phenomena express and on the organization of these categories both in Romance and in Czech, which proves to be much more complex, more abstract and less delimited by the formal manifestation than it is generally assumed. While our analyses concentrated on morphology and morphosyntax, the categories under scrutiny proved to also be connected on a purely semantic level (for example, in the case of inherent iteratives or causatives) and to hypersyntax and pragmatics (for example, in the case of causative and circumstantial relationship or the expression of the potential participation, which resulted from the context of the analysed utterance rather than from one concrete element).

BIBLIOGRAPHY

Aijmer, K. 2008. "Parallel and Comparable Corpora". In *Corpus Linguistics: An International Handbook*. Vol. 1, edited by A. Lüdeling and M. Kytö, 275–92. Berlin: Walter de Gruyter.

Alarcos Llorach, E. 1994. *Gramática de la lengua española*. Madrid: Espasa.

Albertuz, F. J. 1995. "En torno a la fundamentación lingüística de la Aktionsart". *Verba* 22:285–337.

Alsina, A. 1992. "On the Argument Structure of Causatives". *Linguistic Inquiry* 23 (4): 517–55.

Altenberg, B., and Granger, S. 2002. *Lexis in Contrast. Corpus–Based Approaches*. Amsterdam: John Benjamins.

Araújo, S. 2012. "Pour une caractérisation syntaxique et sémantico–pragmatique de la construction causative en *faire/fazer* inf. en français et en portugais". *Studii de gramatică contrastivă* 17:7–28.

Arnavielle, T. 1997. *Le morphème en –ant: Unité et diversité. Étude historique et théorique*. Louvain – Paris: Peeters.

Arrais, T. 1985. "As construçoes causativas em português". *Alfa* 29:41–58.

Baker, M. 1993. "Corpus Linguistics and Translation Studies: Implications and Applications". In *Text and Technology: In Honour of John Sinclair*, edited by M. Baker, G. Francis, and E. Tognini-Bonelli, 233–50. Amsterdam – Philadelphia: John Benjamins.

Baker, M. 1996. "Corpus Linguistics and Translation Studies: Implications and Applications". In *Terminology, LSP, and Translation: Studies in Language Engineering in Honour of Juan C. Sager*, edited by J. Sager and H. Somers, 175–186. Amsterdam: John Benjamins.

Barlow, M. 2008. "Parallel Texts and Corpus-Based Contrastive Analysis". In *Current Trends in Contrastive Linguistics: Functional and Cognitive Perspectives*, edited by M. Á. Gómez González, J. L. Mackenzie, and E. M. González Álvarez, 101–22. Amsterdam: John Benjamins.

Baroni, M. 2007. "I sensi di ri-. Un'indagine preliminare". In *Miscellanea di studi linguistici offerti a Laura Vanelli*, edited by R. Maschi, N. Penello, and P. Rizzolatti, 163–171. Udine: Forum.

Barroso, H. 1988. "O Aspecto Verbal Perifrástico em Português Contemprâneo". Ph.D. diss. Braga, Universidade do Minho.

Barroso, H. 1994. *O Aspecto Verbal Perifrástico em Português Contemporâneo: visão funcional/sincrónica*. Porto: Porto Editora.

Barroso, H. 1999. "Das perífrases verbais e/ou dos complexos verbais perifrásticos enquanto meio de expressão privilegiado de alguns valores aspectuais e/ou temporo–aspectuais em Português". *Diacrítica* 13–14:331–87.

Barroso, H. 2000. "Das perífrases verbais como instrumento expressivo privilegiado das cateorias de natureza temporo-aspectual e simplesmente aspectual no sistema verbal do português de hoje". In *Estudos de gramática portuguesa*. Vol. 3, edited by E. Gärtner, C. Hundt, and A. Schönberger, 89–103. Frankfurt: TFM.

Barroso, H. 2016. "<Pôr-se a + infinitivo> no português europeu". In *Língua Portuguesa. Unidade na Diversidade*. Vol. 1, edited by B. Hlibowicka-Węglarz, J. Wiśniewska, and E. Jabłonka, 109–124. Lublin: Wydawnictwo Uniwersytetu Marie Curie-Skłodowskiej.

Bauer, L. 2017. *Compounds and Compounding*. Cambridge: Cambridge University Press.

Bechara, E. 2009. *Moderna Gramática Portuguesa*. Rio de Janeiro: Editora Nova Fronteira.

Begioni, L. 2012. "Aktionsart et aspect verbal en français et italien". In *L'aspect dans le langues naturelles. Approche comparative*, edited by C. Bracquenier and L. Begioni, 11–37. Rennes: Presses Universitaires de Rennes.

Bertinetto, P. M. 2001. "Il verbo". In *Grande grammatica italiana di consultazione*. Vol. 2., edited by L. Renzi, G. Salvi, and A. Cardinaletti, 1–163. Bologna: Il Mulino.

Bisetto, A. 2009. "Italian Adjectives in –*bile*". In *Ročenka textů zahraničních profesorů / The Annual of Texts by Foreign Guest Professors*. Vol. 3, 23–41. Prague: Faculty of Arts, Charles University.

Blum-Kulka, S. 1986. "Shifts of Cohesion and Coherence in Translation". In *Interlingual and Intercultural Communication: Discourse and Cognition in Translation and Second Language Acquisition Studies*, edited by J. House and S. Blum-Kulka, 17–35. Tübingen: Gunter Narr.

Bourciez, É. 1946. *Éléments de linguistique romane*. Paris: Librairie C. Klincksieck.

Bratánková, L., and P. Štichauer. 2011. "Italský iterativní prefix ri- a jeho české protějšky / The Italian Iterative Prefix ri- and its Czech Respondents". In *Korpusová lingvistika Praha 2011*. Vol. 1, *InterCorp*, edited by F. Čermák, 136–43. Prague: Nakladatelství Lidové noviny.

Campos, H. 1999. "Transitividad e intransitividad". In *Gramática descriptiva de la lengua española*, edited by I. Bosque and V. Demonte, 1519–74. Madrid: Espasa.

Camus Bergareche, B. 2004. "Perífrasis verbales y expresión del aspecto en español". In *El pretérito imperfecto*, edited by L. García Fernández and B. Camus Bergareche, 511–72. Madrid: Gredos.

Cano Aguilar, R. 1977. "Las construcciones causativas en español". *Boletín de la Real Academia Española* 57 (211): 221–258; 57 (212): 323–49.

Carvalho, P. de (2003): "'Gérondif', 'participe présent' et 'adjectif verbal' en morpho–syntaxe comparative". *Langages* 37 (149): 100–26.

Chen, P. H. 2015. "La construction factitive 'faire + Vinf' en français et ses équivalents en chinois: aspects linguistiques et didactiques". Diploma thesis. Grenoble, Université Stendhal.

Chlumská, L. 2013. "Není korpus jako korpus: Korpusy v kontrastivní lingvistice a translatologii / Not All Corpora are Equal: Corpora in Contrastive Linguistics and Translation Studies". *Časopis pro moderní filologii* 96 (2): 221–32.

Chlumská, L. 2017. *Překladová čeština a její charakteristiky / Translated Czech and Its Characteristics*. Prague: Nakladatelství Lidové noviny.

Chromý, J. 2018. "Experimentální výzkum gramatického vidu a způsobu slovesného děje: situační modely / Experimental Research on Grammatical and Lexical Aspect: Situation Models". *Naše řeč* 101 (3): 121–37.

Ciutescu, E. 2013. "Micro-Parametric Variation in Romance Causative Constructions". *Bucharest Working Papers in Linguistics* 15 (2): 45–60.

Comrie, B. 1976. *Aspect*. Cambridge: Cambridge University Press.

Comrie, B. 1989. *Language Universals and Linguistic Typology. Syntax and Morphology*. 2nd ed. Chicago: University of Chicago Press.

Corbin, D. 1987. *Morphologie dérivationnelle et structuration du lexique*. Niemeyer: Tübingen.

Croft, W. 2012. *Verbs. Aspect and Causal Structure*. Oxford – New York: Oxford University Press.

Cuesta, P. V., and M. A. M. da Luz. 1980. *Gramática da Língua Portuguesa*. Lisbon: Edições 70.

Cunha, C., and L. Cintra. 1999. *Nova Gramática do Português Contemporâneo*. Lisbon: João Sá da Costa.

Cvrček, V., and L. Chlumská. 2015. "Simplification in Translated Czech: A New Approach to Type-Token Ratio". *Russian Linguistics* 39 (3): 309–25.

Cvrček, V., A. Čermáková, and M. Křen. 2016. "Nová koncepce synchronních korpusů psané češtiny / A New Design of Synchronic Corpora of Written Czech". *Slovo a slovesnost* 77 (2): 83–101.

Cvrček V., and V. Kodýtek. 2013. "Ke klasifikaci morfologických variant / On the Classification of Morphological Variants". *Slovo a slovesnost* 74 (2): 139–45.

Čechová, M. et al. 1996: *Čeština – řeč a jazyk / Czech – Speech and Language*. Prague: ISV.

Čermák, F. 2001. *Jazyk a jazykověda / Language and Linguistics*. Prague: Karolinum.

Čermák, F. 2010. "Parallel Corpora: The Case of *InterCorp*". In *InterCorp: Exploring a Multilingual Corpus*, edited by F. Čermák, P. Corness, and A. Klégr, 10–18. Prague: Nakladatelství Lidové noviny.

Čermák, F., and A. Rosen. 2012. "The Case of *InterCorp*, a Multilingual Parallel Corpus". *International Journal of Corpus Linguistics* 17 (3): 411–27.

Čermák, P. 2013. "Las posibilidades del estudio ofrecidas por los corpus paralelos: el caso del prefijo español *re*–". *AUC Philologica. Romanistica Pragensia* 19 (2): 123–36.

Čermák, P., and O. Nádvorníková et al. 2015. *Románské jazyky a čeština ve světle paralelních korpusů / The Romance Languages and Czech in the Light of Parallel Corpora*. Prague: Karolinum.

Daneš, F., and Z. Hlavsa et al. 1981. *Větné vzorce v češtině / Sentence Patterns in Czech*. Prague: Academia.

Davies, M. E. 1995. "The Evolution of the Spanish Causative Construction". *Hispanic Review* 63 (1): 57–77.

Dietrich, W. 1983. *El aspecto verbal perifrástico en las lenguas románicas: Estudios sobre el actual sistema verbal de las lenguas románicas y sobre el problema del origen del aspecto verbal perifrástico*. Madrid: Gredos.

Dixon, R. M. W. 2000. "A Typology of Causatives. Form, Syntax and Meaning". In *Changing Valency*, edited by R. M. W. Dixon and A. Aikhenvald, 332–83. Cambridge: Cambridge University Press.

Dowling, L. H. 1981. "A Investigation of the Spanish Causatives". *Hispania* 64 (4): 588–94.

Drzazgowska, J. 2011. "As perífrasis verbais no português europeu". *Romanica Cracoviensia* 11: 107–15.

Dušková, L. (2012): "Vilém Mathesius and Contrastive Studies, and beyond". In *A Centenary of English Studies at Charles University: From Mathesius to Present-Day Linguistics*, edited by M. Malá and P. Šaldová, 21–48. Prague: Faculty of Arts, Charles University.

Dvořák, E. 1970. *Vývoj přechodníkových konstrukcí ve starší češtině / Development of Transgressive Constructions in Old Czech*. Prague: Charles University.

Dvořák, E. 1978. *Přechodníkové konstrukce v nové češtině / Transgressive Constructions in Modern Czech*. Prague: Charles University.

Enghels, R., and E. Roegiest. 2012. "La causación negativa y el argumento causado: la sintaxis de *dejar* y *laisser* en contraste". *XXVIᵉ congrès international de linguistique et de philologie Romanes. Proceedings* 2:159–70.

Enghels, R., and E. Roegiest. 2013. "*Dejar*: Entre verbo causativo y verbo de control". *Bulletin of Hispanic Studies* 90 (5): 505–22.

Escoubas-Benveniste, M.-P. 2013. "Usages du gérondif et du participe present en français parlé et écrit: Étude comparée basée sur corpus". *TIPA: Travaux interdisciplinaires sur la parole et le langage* 29: not paginated.

Fabricius-Hansen, C. 1996. "Informational Density: A Problem for Translation and Translation Theory". *Linguistics* 34:521–65.

Fabricius-Hansen, C. 1999. Information Packaging and Translation: Aspects of Translational Sentence Splitting (German – English / Norwegian). In *Sprachspezifische Aspekte der Informationsverteilung*, edited by M. Doherty, 175–214. Berlin: Akademie Verlag.

Fente Gómez, R., J. Fernández Álvarez, and L. Feijó. 1994. *Perífrasis verbales*. Madrid: Edelsa.

Fernández Ordóñez, O. 1999. "Leísmo, laísmo y loísmo". In *Gramática descriptiva de la lengua española*, edited by I. Bosque and V. Demonte, 1317–97. Madrid: Espasa.

Fernández Pérez, M. 1993. "Sobre la distinción aspecto vs. Aktionsart". *ELUA. Estudios de Lingüística* 9:265–93.

Fogsgaard, L. 2002. *Algunas perífrasis aspectuales del español*. Alicante: Universidad de Alicante.

García Fernández, L. et al. 2006. *Diccionario de perífrasis verbales*. Madrid: Gredos.

Gettrup, H. 1977. "Le gérondif, le participe présent et la notion de repère temporel". *Revue Romane* 12 (2): 210–71.

Gilquin, G. 2015. "Contrastive Collostructional Analysis: Causative Constructions in English and French". *Zeitschrift für Anglistik und Amerikanistik* 63 (3): 253–72.

Gilquin, G. 2017. "A Collostruction-Based Approach to the Integrated Contrastive Model: The Idiomaticity of Causative Constructions in English, French and French Learner English". Paper presented at the Idiomaticity Workshop 1–2 September 2017. Oslo.

Głowicka, M. 2013. "La perífrasis incoativa *empezar a* + infinitivo y sus equivalencias en polaco". *Estudios Hispánicos* 21:75–86.

Goddard, C., and A. Wierzbicka. 2008. "Universal Human Concepts as a Basis for Contrastive Linguistic Semantics". In *Current Trends in Contrastive Linguistics: Functional and Cognitive Perspectives*, edited by M. Gómez González, J. L. Mackenzie, and E. M. González Álvarez, 206-27. Amsterdam: John Benjamins.

Gómez Torrego, L. 1988. *Perífrasis verbales*. Madrid: Arco Libros.

Gómez Torrego, L. 1999. "Los verbos auxiliares. Las perífrasis verbales de infinitivo". In *Gramática descriptiva de la lengua española*, edited by I. Bosque and V. Demonte, 3323-89. Madrid: Espasa.

Gómez Torrego, L. 2006. *Hablar y escribir correctamente*. Vol. 2, *Gramática normativa del español actual*. Madrid: Arco Libros.

Gonçalves, A., and I. Duarte. 2001. "Construções causativas em Português Europeu e em Português Brasileiro". In *Actas do XVI Encontro Nacional da Associação Portuguesa de Linguística*, 657-71. Lisbon: APL.

Gosseline, L. 2011. "L'aspect de phase en français: le rôle des periphrases verbales". *French Language Studies* 21:149-71.

Gougenheim, G. 1929. *Étude sur les périphrases verbales de la langue française*. Paris: Les Belles Lettres.

Granger, S. 1996. "From CA to CIA and back: An Integrated Approach to Computerized Bilingual and Learner Corpora". In *Languages in Contrast: Papers from a Symposium on Text-Based Cross-Linguistic Studies (1994)*, edited by K. Aijmer, B. Altenberg, and M. Johansson, 38-51. Lund: Lund University Press.

Granger, S., J. Lerot, and S. Petch-Tyson. 2003. *Corpus-Based Approaches to Contrastive Linguistics and Translation Studies*. Amsterdam – New York: Rodopi.

Grevisse, M., and A. Goosse. 2007. *Le bon usage*. Bruxelles: De Boeck – Duculot.

Grevisse, M., and A. Goosse. 2008. *Le bon usage*. Bruxelles: De Boeck – Duculot.

Grossmann, M., and F. Rainer. 2004. *La formazione delle parole in italiano*. Tübingen: Niemeyer.

Guidère, M. 2011. *Introduction à la traductologie. Penser la traduction: Hier, aujourd'hui, demain*. Bruxelles: De Boeck – Duculot.

Halmøy, O. 1982. *Le gérondif. Éléments pour une description syntaxique et sémantique*. Trondheim: Tapir.

Halmøy, O. 1994. "Subordination et insubordination: Gérondif, sujet logique et fantaisie". *Travaux de linguistique* 27:151-65.

Halmøy, O. 2003a. *Le gérondif en français*. Paris: Ophrys.

Halmøy, O. 2003b. "Le gérondif: Une originalité du francais?" In *La syntaxe raisonnée. Mélanges de linguistique générale et française offerts à Annie Boone à l'occasion de son 60ᵉ anniversaire*, edited by P. Hadermann, A. Van Slijcke, and M. Berré, 267-278. Bruxelles: De Boeck – Duculot.

Hamplová, S. 1994. *K problematice vidovosti v italštině / Problems of Aspect in Italian*. Prague: Charles University.

Haspelmath, M. 1995. "The Converb as a Cross-Linguistically Valid Category". In *Converbs in Cross-Linguistic Perspective: Structure and Meaning of Adverbial Verb Forms – Adverbial Participles, Gerunds*, edited by M. Haspelmath and E. König, 1-57. Berlin – New York: Mouton de Gruyter.

Haspelmath, M., and E. König, eds. 1995. *Converbs in Cross-Linguistic Perspective: Structure and Meaning of Adverbial Verb Forms – Adverbial Participles, Gerunds*. Berlin – New York: Mouton de Gruyter.

Haton, S. 2005. "L'intégration des périphrases verbales dans les «champs sémantiques multilingues unifiés» – illustration par la périphrase *se mettre à*". In *Les périphrases verbales*, edited by H. B.-Z. Shyldkrot and N. Le Querler, 397-406. Amsterdam – Philadelphia: John Benjamins.

Havránek, B., and A. Jedlička. 1981. *Česká mluvnice / Grammar of Czech*. Prague: SPN.

Havu, E., and M. Pierrard. 2008. "L'interprétation des participes présents adjoints: Converbalité et portée du rapport entte prédications". In *Congrès Mondial de Linguistiuqe Française – CMLF'08*, edited by J. Durand, B. Habert, and B. Laks, 2519-29. Paris: Institut de Linguistique Française.

Heidinger, S. 2015. "Causalness and the Encoding of the Causative-Anticausative Alternation in French and Spanish". *Journal of Linguistics* 51 (3): 562-94.

Hernanz, M. L. 1999. "El infinitivo". In *Gramática descriptiva de la lengua española*, edited by I. Bosque and V. Demonte, 2197-356. Madrid: Espasa.

Hu, X. 2018. "Explorer la structure interne des constructions causatives du français". *Canadian Journal of Linguistics / Revue canadienne de linguistique* 63 (1): 70-99.

Jalenques, M. P. 2002. "Étude sémantique du préfixe RE en français contemporain: À propos de plusieurs débats actuels en morfologie dérivationnelle". *Langue française* 133:74–90.

Jindrová, J. 2016. *Perifrastické konstrukce v portugalštině / Periphrastic Constructions in Portugese*. Prague: Karolinum.

Johansson, S. 2007. *Seeing through Multilingual Corpora: On the Use of Corpora in Contrastive Studies*. Amsterdam – Philadelphia: John Benjamins.

Karlík, P., M. Nekula, and J. Pleskalová, eds. 2002. *Encyklopedický slovník češtiny / Encyclopaedic Dictionary of Czech*. Prague: Nakladatelství Lidové noviny.

Karlík, P. , M. Nekula, and Z. Rusínová, eds. 1995. *Příruční mluvnice češtiny / Hanbook of Czech Grammar*. Prague: Nakladatelství Lidové noviny.

Katelhoen, P. 2011. "Kausative Verbalperiphrasen im italienisch-deutschen Sprachvergleich". *Inntrans. Innsbrucker Beiträge zu Sprache, Kultur und Translation* 4:637–50.

Kemmer, S., and A. Verhagen. 1994. "The Grammar of Causatives and the Conceptual Structure of Events". *Cognitive Linguistics* 5 (2): 115–156.

Kenny, D. 2001. *Lexis and Creativity in Translation: A Corpus-Based Study*. Manchester: St. Jerome.

Kleiber, G. 2007a. "En passant par le gérondif, avec mes (gros) sabots". *Cahiers Chronos* 19:93–125.

Kleiber, G. 2007b. "La question temporelle du gérondif: Simultanéité ou non?" In *Travaux linguistiques du Cerlico*. Vol. 20, *Les formes non finies du verbe 2*, edited by F. Lambert, C. Moreau, and J. Albrespit, 109–123. Rennes: Presses Universitaires de Rennes.

Kleiber, G. 2009. "Gérondif et relations de cohérence: Le cas de la relation de cause". In *Recherches ACLIF: Actes du Séminaire de Didactique Universitaire*. Vol. 6, edited by E. Comes and F. Hrubaru, 9–24. Cluj: Editura Echinox.

Komárek, M., J. Kořenský et al. 1986. *Mluvnice češtiny 2. Tvarosloví. / Grammar of Czech 2. Morphology*. Prague: Academia.

König, E., and J. van der Auwera. 1990. "Adverbial Participles, Gerunds and Absolute Constructions in the Languages of Europe". In *Toward a Typology of European Languages*, edited by J. Bechert, G. Bernini, and C. Buridant, 57–95. Berlin – New York: Mouton de Gruyter.

König, E. 1995. "The Meaning of Converb Constructions". In *Converbs in Cross-Linguistic Perspective: Structure and Meaning of Adverbial Verb Forms – Adverbial Participles, Gerunds*, edited by M. Haspelmath and E. König, 57–97. Berlin – New York, Mouton de Gruyter.

Kortmann, B. 1991. *Free Adjuncts and Absolutes in English: Problems of Control and Interpretation*. London: Routledge.

Králová, J. 2006. "El enfoque contrastivo: El complemento circunstancial en español desde la óptica del hablante checo". In *Análisis del discurso: lengua, cultura, valores. Actas del I congreso internacional*, edited by M. Casado Velarde, R. González Ruiz, and M. V. Romero Gualda, 1961–74. Pamplona: Universidad de Navarra.

Králová, J. 2012. *Vybrané problémy španělské lingvistiky na pozadí češtiny / Selected Problems of Spanish Linguistics with Czech as a Background*. Prague: Faculty of Arts, Charles University.

Kratochvílová, D., and J. Jindrová. 2017. "Ingressive Verbal Periphrases in Spanish and Portuguese". *Linguistica Pragensia* 27 (1): 38–56.

Krzeszowski, T. P. 1990. *Contrasting Languages: The Scope of Contrastive Linguistics*. Berlin: Mouton de Gruyter.

Křen, M., V. Cvrček, T. Čapka, et al. 2016. "SYN2015: Representative Corpus of Contemporary Written Czech". In *Proceedings of the Tenth International Conference on Language Resources and Evaluation (LREC'16)*, edited by N. Calzolari, K. Choukri, T. Declerck, et al., 2522–8. Portorož: European Language Resources Association (ELRA).

Labelle, M. 2017. "Causative and Perception Verbs". In *Manual of Romance Morphosyntax and Syntax*, edited by A. Dufter and E. Stark, 299–331. Berlin – Boston, MA: De Gruyter.

Laca, B. 2002. "Spanish 'Aspectual' Periphrases: Ordering Constraints and the Distinction between Situation and Viewpoint Aspect". In *From Words to Discourse: Trends in Spanish Semantics and Pragmatics*, edited by J. Gutiérrez Rexach, 61–93. Oxford: Elsevier.

Laviosa, S. 2002. *Corpus-Based Translation Studies: Theory, Findings, Applications*. Amsterdam: Rodopi.

Lázaro Carreter, F. 1953. *Diccionario de términos filológicos*. Gredos: Madrid.

Leeman, D., and S. Meleuc. 1990. "Verbes en tables et adjectifs en -*able*". *Langue française* 87:30–51.

Lieber, R. 2004. *Morphology and Lexical Semantics*. Cambridge: Cambridge University Press.

Lopes, M. G., and V. M. C. de Menezes. 2018. "A formação do subesquema argumental causativo no português brasileiro". *Confluência* 1 (54): 90–112.

Luque, R. 2008. "Las perífrasis verbales: un planteamiento contrastivo entre español e italiano". *Romanica Cracoviensia* 8 (1): 61–9.

Luque, R. 2015. "La traducción de las perífrasis de infinitivo del español al italiano". *Rivista internazionale di tecnica della traduzione* 17:107–23.

Macháčková, E. 1982. "Vztah příčiny a následku vyjádřený slovesy *způsobit, vést k, vyvolat* aj. / Relation of Cause and Consequence Expressed by the Verbs *způsobit, vést k, vyvolat*, etc.". *Slovo a slovesnost*, 43 (2): 119–24.

Malá, M. 2013. Translation Counterparts as Markers of Meaning. The Case of Copular Verbs in a Parallel English-Czech Corpus. *Languages in Contrast* 13 (2): 170–92.

Malá, M. 2014. *English Copular Verbs: A Contrastive Corpus-Supported View*. Prague: Faculty of Arts, Charles University.

Malá, M., and P. Šaldová. 2015. "English Non-Finite Participial Clauses as Seen Through Their Czech Counterparts". *Nordic Journal of English Studies* 14 (1): 232–57.

Maldonado, R. 2007. "Soft Causatives in Spanish". In *On Interpreting Construction Schemas: From Action and Motion to Transitivity and Causality*, edited by N. Delbecque and B. Cornillie, 229–60. Berlin: Mouton de Gruyter.

Martín García, J. 1998. *La morfología léxico-conceptual: Las palabras derivadas con RE-*. Madrid: Ediciones de la Universidad Autónoma de Madrid.

Mateus, M. H. M. et al. 2003. *Gramática da Língua Portuguesa*. Lisbon: Caminho.

Mathesius, V. 1961. *Obsahový rozbor současné angličtiny na základě obecně lingvistickém / Content Analysis of Contemporary English Based on General Linguistics*. Prague: Nakladatelství Československé akademie věd.

Mauranen, A. 1999. "Will 'Translationese' Ruin a Contrastive Study?". *Languages in Contrast* 2 (2): 161–85.

May, R. 1997. "Sensible Elocution: How Translation Works in & upon Punctuation". *The Translator* 3 (1): 1–20.

Michálková, V. 1962. "Přechodníkové vazby ve východomoravských nářečích / Transgressive Constructions in East Moravian Dialects". *Sborník Matice moravské* 81:200–6.

Mok, Q. 1964. "Le préfixe RE- en français moderne: Essai d'une description synchronique". *Neophilologus* 48 (2): 97–114.

Moortgat, B. 1978. "Participe et gérondif. Étude de l'opposition entre la présence et l'absence de EN devant la forme en -*ant*". PhD. diss. Metz, Université de Metz.

Nádvorníková, O. 2009. Que font les personnages des romans en parlant? (dit-il en souriant). Typologie des constructions gérondives accompagnant les verbes de dire dans les propositions incises. In *La perspective interdisciplinaire des études françaises et francophones*, edited by A. Kieliszczyk and E. Pilecka, 89–98. Łask: Oficyna wydawnicza LEKSEM.

Nádvorníková, O. 2010. "The French Gérondif and Its Czech Equivalents". In *InterCorp: Exploring a Multilingual Corpus*, edited by F. Čermák, P. Corness, and A. Klégr, 83–96. Prague: Nakladatelství Lidové noviny – Ústav Českého národního korpusu.

Nádvorníková, O. 2012. "Korpusová analýza faktorů sémantické interpretace francouzského gérondivu / A Corpus Analysis of the Semantic Interpretation Factors of the French Gérondif". Ph.D. diss. Prague, Faculty of Arts, Charles University.

Nádvorníková, O. 2013a. "Paul se rase en chantant, dit-il en bafouillant: Quels types de manière pour le gérondif en français?". *Acta Universitatis Carolinae Philologica. Romanistica Pragensia* 19 (2): 31–44.

Nádvorníková, O. 2013b. "Francouzský gérondif a český přechodník: kontrastivní analýza a jazykové korpusy / French Gerondif and Czech Transgressive: Contrastive Analysis and Language Corpora". *Jazykovědné aktuality* 50 (3–4): 80–96.

Nádvorníková, O. 2016. "Le corpus multilingue InterCorp et les possibilités de son exploitation". In *Actes du XXVIIᵉ Congrès international de linguistique et de philologie romanes (Nancy, 15–20 juillet 2013)*.

Section 16: Projets en cours. Ressources et outils nouveaux, edited by D. Trotter, A. Bozzi, and C. Fairon, 223–237. Nancy: ATILF/SLR.

Nádvorníková, O. 2017a. "Le corpus multilingue InterCorp: Nouveaux paradigmes de recherche en linguistique contrastive et en traductologie". *Studii de Lingvistica* 7:67–88.

Nádvorníková, O. 2017b. "Pièges méthodologiques des corpus parallèles et comment les éviter". *Corela - cognition, représentation, langages* 15 (1): not paginated.

Nádvorníková, O. 2017c. "Les proportions des verbes SAY/DIRE/ŘÍCI dans les propositions incises et leurs équivalents en traduction: étude sur corpus parallèle". *Linguistica Pragensia* 28 (2): 35–58.

Nádvorníková, O. (forthcoming a). "Le gérondif et le participe présent en français contemporain: Différence revisitée a la lumière de leur compatibilité avec les verbes de perception". In *La Perception en langue et en discours*, edited by F. Marsac. Paris: L'Harmattan.

Nádvorníková, O. (forthcoming b). "Differences in Types of Reporting Verbs in French, English and Czech Fiction and Their Consequences in Translation". *Languages in Contrast.*

Nedjalkov, V. P. 1995. "Some Typological Parameters of Converbs". In *Converbs in Cross-Linguistic Perspective: Structure and Meaning of Adverbial Verb Forms - Adverbial Participles, Gerunds*, edited by M. Haspelmath and E. König, 97–137. Berlin - New York: Mouton de Gruyter.

Nosek, J. 1964. "Notes on Syntactic Condensation in Modern English". *Travaux linguistiques de Prague* 1:281–8.

Nübler, N. 2017. "Způsob slovesného děje / Aktionsart". In *CzechEncy - Nový encyklopedický slovník češtiny* [online], edited by P. Karlík, M. Nekula, and J. Pleskalová. Accessed December 6, 2018. https://www.czechency.org/slovnik/ZPŮSOB SLOVESNÉHO DĚJE.

Olbertz, H. 1998. *Verbal Periphrases in a Functional Grammar of Spanish*. Berlin - New York: Mouton de Gruyter.

Olohan, M. 2004. *Introducing Corpora in Translation Studies*. London: Routledge.

Olohan, M., and M. Baker. 2000. "Reporting that in Translated English: Evidence for Subconscious Processes of Explicitation?" *Across Languages and Cultures* 1 (2): 141–58.

Panevová, J., and P. Karlík. 2017. "Reflexivní sloveso / Reflexive Verb". In *CzechEncy - Nový encyklopedický slovník češtiny* [online], edited by P. Karlík, M. Nekula, and J. Pleskalová. Accessed August 21, 2018. https://www.czechency.org/slovnik/REFLEXIVNÍ SLOVESO.

Pápai, V. 2004. "Explicitation: A Universal of Translated Text?" In *Translation Universals: Do They Exist?*, edited by A. Mauranen and P. Kujamäki, 143–64. Amsterdam - Philadelphia: Benjamins.

Pauly, É. 2005. "Des emplois spatiaux de partir à ses emplois périphrastiques (*partir à* + infinitif)". In *Les périphrases verbales*, edited by H. B. Z. Shyldkrot and N. Le Querler, 407–28. Amsterdam - Philadelphia: John Benjamins.

Pawlak, A. 2008. "Sobre los orígenes y las confusiones terminológico-conceptuales de los términos de aspecto y de Aktionsart". *Studia Romanica Posnaniensia* 35:257–66.

Perissutti, A. M. 2010. "Analytické kauzativní konstrukce v češtině / Analytical Causative Constructions in Czech". In *Karlík a továrna na lingvistiku / Karlík and Linguistics Factory*, edited by A. Bičan, J. Klaška, P. Macurová, and J. Zmrzlíková, 355–67.

Perissutti, A. M. 2017. "Analytická kauzativní konstrukce / Analytical Causative Construction". In *CzechEncy - Nový encyklopedický slovník češtiny* [online], edited by P. Karlík, M. Nekula, and J. Pleskalová. Accessed August 21, 2018. https://www.czechency.org/slovnik/ANALYTICKÁ KAUZATIVNÍ KONSTRUKCE.

Pešková, J. 2005. "Slovesné vazby s infinitivem a gerundiem jako prostředek k vyjádření povahy slovesného děje v současné španělštině / Verb infinitive and gerund as a means of expressing the nature of the verbal action in contemporary Spanish". Ph.D. diss. Prague, Faculty of Arts, Charles University.

Pešková, J. 2018. *Kontrastivní analýza vybraných významů povahy slovesného děje v češtině a ve španělštině / Contrastive Analyses of Selected Meanings of Manner of Action in Czech and Spanish*. České Budějovice: Episteme.

Peters, C., E. Picchi, and L. Biagini 2000. "Parallel and Comparable Bilingual Corpora in Language Teaching and Learning". In *Multilingual Corpora in Teaching and Research*, edited by S. P. Botley, A. M. McEnery, and A. Wilson, 73–85. Amsterdam: Rodopi.

Pires de Oliveira, R., and F. Ngoy. 2007. "Notas sobre a semântica do sufixo -*vel:* A expressão da modalidade no PB". *Revista Letras* 73:185–201.

Pîrvu, E. 2010. "La costruzione italiana *fare con l'infinito* e le modalità della sua traduzione in romeno". *Analele Universității din Craiova. Seria Științe Filologice. Lingvistică* 22 (1–2): 338–44.

Real Academia Española (RAE). 2009. *Nueva gramática de la lengua española*. Madrid: Espasa.

Reichler-Béguelin, M.-J. 1995. "Les problèmes d'emploi du gérondif et des participiales en français contemporain". In *Le français langue étrangère à l'université: Théorie et pratique*, edited by K. Zaleska and A. Cataldi, 243–60. Warsaw: University of Warsaw.

Reichzieglová, A. 2010. "K distribuci a funkci ingresivního významu u předponových sloves / On the distribution and function of ingressive meaning in prefixed verbs". *Slovo a slovesnost* 71 (2): 83–115.

Renzi, L., G. Salvi, and A. Cardinaletti, eds. 2002. *Grande grammatica italiana di consultazione*. Bologna: Il Mulino.

Riegel, M., J.-Ch. Pellat, and R. Rioul. 2008. *Grammaire méthodique du français*. Paris: PUF.

Robustelli, C. 2000. *Causativi in italiano moderno e antico*. Modena: Il Fiorino.

Rosen, A., and M. Vavřín. 2012. "Building a Multilingual Parallel Corpus for Human Users". In *Proceedings of the Eight International Conference on Language Resources and Evaluation (LREC'12)*, edited by N. Calzolari, 2447–52. Istanbul: European Language Resources Association (ELRA).

Said Ali, M. 2001. *Gramática Histórica da Língua Portuguesa*. São Paulo: Editora Melhoramentos.

Salvi, G., and L. Vanelli. 2004. *Nuova grammatica italiana*. Bologna: Il Mulino.

Sánchez Montero, M. C. 1993. *Perífrasis verbales en español e italiano*. Trieste: Lint.

Shibatani, M. 1976. "The Grammar of Causative Constructions: A Conspectus". In *The Grammar of Causative Constructions*, edited by M. Shibatani, 1–42. New York: Academic Press.

Shibatani, M., and P. Pardeshi. 2002. "The Causative Continuum". In *The Grammar of Causation and Interpersonal Manipulation*, edited by M. Shibatani, 85–126. Amsterdam: John Benjamins.

Silva Soares da, A. 1998. "Prototipicidad y cambio semántico: El caso ibérico de *deixar/dejar*". In *Estudios de lingüística cognitiva*. Vol. 1, edited by J. L. Cifuentes Honrubia, 279–94. Alicante: Universidad de Alicante.

Silva Soares da, A. 2001. "Comparaison de la grammaticalisation des constructions causatives dans les langues romanes". In *XXIII Congreso Internacional de Lingüística y Filología Románica*, edited by F. Sánchez Miret, 441–56. Salamanca: Niemeyer.

Silva Soares da, A. 2004. "Verbos y construcciones causativas analíticas en portugués y en español". In *Estudios de lingüística: el verbo*, edited by J. L. Cifuentes Honrubia and C. Marimón Llorca, 581–98. Alicante: Universidad de Alicante.

Silva, Soares da, A. 2005. "Revisitando as construções causativas e perceptivas do Português: Significado e uso". In *Actas do XX Encontro Nacional da Associação Portuguesa de Linguística*, 855–74. Lisbon: Associação Portuguesa de Linguística.

Simone, R., and D. Cerbasi. 2001. "Types and Diachronic Evolution of Causative Constructions in Romance Languages". *Romanische Forschungen* 113:441–73.

Skytte, G., and G. Salvi. 2001. "Frasi subordinate all'infinito". In *Grande grammatica italiana di consultazione*. Vol. 2, *I sintagmi verbale, aggettivale, avverbiale. La subordinazione*, edited by L. Renzi, G. Salvi, and A. Cardinaletti, 483–569. Bologna: Il Mulino.

Smith, C. 1997. *The Parameter of Aspect*. Dodrecht – Boston – London: Kluwer.

Stosic, D. 2012. "En passant par: Une expression en voie de grammaticalisation?" *Corela*, HS-12: not paginated.

Škrabal, M., and M. Vavřín. 2017. "Databáze překladových ekvivalentů Treq / The Translation Equivalents Database (TREQ)". *Časopis pro moderní filologii* 99 (2): 245–60.

Štícha, F. 1981. "Poznámky k pojmu kauzace / Notes on the Causation Term". *Slovo a slovesnost* 42 (1): 41–9.

Štícha, F. et al. 2013. *Akademická gramatika spisovné češtiny / Academic Grammar of Standard Czech*. Prague: Academia.

Štícha, F. et al. 2018. *Velká akademická gramatika spisovné češtiny*. Vol. 1, *Morfologie. Druhy slov. Tvoření slov. / Comprehensive Grammar of Standard Czech*. Vol. 1, *Morphology. Parts of Speech. Word Formation*. Prague: Academia.

Štichauer, P., and P. Čermák. 2011. "Španělská a italská adjektiva se sufixem -ble/-bile a jejich české ekvivalenty / Spanish and Italian Adjectives with the -ble/-bile Suffix and Their Czech Equivalents". In Korpusová lingvistika Prague 2011. Vol. 1, InterCorp, edited by F. Čermák, 124–35. Prague: Nakladatelství Lidové noviny.

Šustrová, N. 2010. "Analyse sémantique du gérondif français dans la proposition incise". Diploma thesis. Brno, Faculty of Arts, Masaryk University.

Talmy, L. 1988. "Force Dynamics in Language and Cognition". Cognitive Science 12 (1): 49–100.

Talmy, L. 2000. Toward a Cognitive Semantics. Vol. 1, Typology and Process in Concept Structuring. Cambridge, MA: MIT Press.

Tekavčić, P. 1972. Grammatica storica dell'italiano. Vol. 3. Bologna: Il Mulino.

Toops, G. H. 1992. "Causativity in Czech: The Verbs Dá(va)t and Nech(áv)at". Canadian Slavonic Papers / Révue canadienne des slavistes 34:39–56.

Toops, G. H. 2013. "The Morphosyntax of Causative Relations in Czech and Upper Sorbian: A Contrastive, Descriptive Analysis". The Slavonic and East European Review 91 (3): 401–30.

Topor, M., A. Fernández, and G. Vázquez. 2006. "Perífrasis verbales del español y rumano, correspondencias y vacíos léxicos". In Studies in Contrastive Linguistics, Proceedings of the 4th International Contrastive Linguistics Conference, edited by C. Mourón Figueroa, T. Moralejo Gárate, and A. Álvarez Rodríguez, 1061–7. Santiago de Compostela: Universidad de Santiago de Compostela.

Topor, M., A. Fernández, and G. Vázquez. 2007. "La perífrasis verbal incoativa ponerse a + INF y las equivalencias en rumano". In 25 años de lingüística aplicada en España: Hitos y Retos, edited by R. Monroy Casas and A. Sánchez Péres, 1122–8. Murcia: Universidad de Murcia.

Topor, M., A. Fernández, and G. Vázquez. 2008. "Diccionario de perífrasis verbales español-rumano". Ianua: Revista philologica romanica 8:101–11.

Vachek, J. 1955. "Some Thoughts on the So-Called Complex Condensation in Modern English". Sborník prací Filozofické fakulty brněnské univerzity 4 (A3): 1955, 63–77.

Vachek, J. 1961. "Some Less Familiar Aspects of the Analytical Trend of English". Brno Studies in English 3:9–78.

Val Álvaro, J. F. 1981. "Los derivados sufijales en -ble en español". RFE 61:185–198.

van der Auwera, R. 1985. Dutch Novels Translated into English: The Transformation of a "Minority" Literature. Amsterdam: Rodopi.

Varela, S., and J. Martín García. 1999. "La prefijación". In Gramática descriptiva de la lengua española, edited by I. Bosque and V. Demonte, 4994–5040. Madrid: Espasa.

Varga, D. et al. 2005. "Parallel Corpora for Medium Density Languages". In Recent Advances in Natural Language Processing IV, edited by N. Nicolov, K. Bontcheva, G. Angelova, and R. Mitkov, 247–58. Amsterdam – Philadelphia: John Benjamins.

Vavřín, M., and A. Rosen. 2008. "InterCorp: A Multilingual Parallel Corpus Project". In Proceedings of the International Conference Corpus Linguistics – 2008, 97–104. St. Petersburg: St. Petersburg State University.

Vecchiato, A. 2003. "The Italian Periphrastic Causative and Force Dynamics". USC Working Papers in Linguistics. Vol. 1, edited by N. Ketrez, J. Aronoff, M. Cabrera, et al., 91–109.

Veenstra, H. D. 1946. Les formes nominales du verbe dans la prose du treizième siècle. Participe présent, gérondif, infinitif. Rotterdam: W. L. & J. Brusse.

Vendler, Z. 1967. Linguistics in Philosophy. Ithaca – New York: Cornell University Press.

Verroens, F. 2011. "La construction inchoative se mettre à: Syntaxe, sémantique et grammaticalisation". Ph.D. diss. Gent, Universiteit Gent.

Vesterinen, R. 2008a. "Direct, Indirect and Inferred Causation: Finite and Infinitive Complements of Deixar and Fazer". Journal of Portuguese Linguistics 7 (1): 23–50.

Vesterinen, R. 2008b. "Complementos finitos e infinitivos dos verbos causativos deixar e fazer – causação directa vs. indirecta e a noção de controlo". Studia Neophilologica 80 (1): 75–98.

Vesterinen, R. 2012. "Control and Dominion: Factivity and Mood Choice in Spanish". Language and Cognition 4 (1): 43–64.

Vilela, M. 1994. Estudos de Lexicologia Portuguesa. Coimbra: Almedina.

Vinay, J.-P., and J. Darbelnet. 1995. *Comparative Stylistics of French and English: A Methodology for Translation*. Amsterdam: John Benjamins.

Vondřička, P. 2014. "Aligning Parallel Texts with InterText". In *Proceedings of the Ninth International Conference on Language Resources and Evaluation (LREC'14)*, 1875–9. Reykjavík: European Language Resources Association (ELRA).

Wilmet, M. 1997. *Grammaire critique du français*. Louvain-la-Neuve: Duculot.

Xiao, R., and M. Yue. 2009. "Using Corpora in Translation Studies: The State of the Art". In *Contemporary Corpus Linguistics*, edited by P. Baker, 237–62. London: Continuum.

Zavadil, B., and P. Čermák. 2010. *Mluvnice současné španělštiny*. Prague: Karolinum.

Zieliński, A. 2017. "Perífrasis verbales". In *Gramática constrastiva español–polaco*, edited by W. Nowikow, 179–237. Łódź: Wydawnictwo Uniwersytetu Łódzkiego.

Zubizarreta, M. L. 1985. "The Relation between Morphophonology and Morphosyntax: The Case of Romance Causatives". *Linguistic Inquiry* 16 (2): 247–89.

Online corpora

Čermák, P., and M. Vavřín. 2013. *Korpus intercorp_es, Release 6 of 8 April 2013*. Institute of the Czech National Corpus, Faculty of Arts, Charles University: Prague. http://www.korpus.cz.

Chlumská, L. 2013. *JEROME: Jednojazyčný srovnatelný korpus pro výzkum překladové češtiny / JEROME: Monolingual Comparable Corpus for the Research of Translated Czech*. Institute of the Czech National Corpus, Faculty of Arts, Charles University: Prague. http://www.korpus.cz.

Jindrová, J., and M. Vavřín. 2013. *Korpus intercorp_pt, Release 6 of 8 April 2013*. Institute of the Czech National Corpus, Faculty of Arts, Charles University: Prague. http://www.korpus.cz.

Křen, M. , V. Cvrček, T. Čapka, A. Čermáková, M. Hnátková, L. Chlumská, T. Jelínek, D. Kováříková, V. Petkevič, P. Procházka, H. Skoumalová, M. Škrabal, P. Truneček, P. Vondřička, and A. Zasina. 2015. *SYN2015: Reprezentativní korpus psané češtiny / SYN2015: Representative Corpus of Written Czech*. Institute of the Czech National Corpus, Faculty of Arts, Charles University: Prague. http://www.korpus.cz.

Nádvorníková, O., and M. Vavřín. 2013. *Korpus intercorp_fr, Release 6 of 8 April 2013*. Institute of the Czech National Corpus, Faculty of Arts, Charles University: Prague 2013. http://www.korpus.cz.

Real Academia Española (RAE): Banco de datos (CORPES XXI): *Corpus del Español del Siglo XXI (CORPES)*. http://www.rae.es.

Štichauer, P., and M. Vavřín. 2013. *Korpus intercorp_it, Release 6 of 8 April 2013*. Institute of the Czech National Corpus, Faculty of Arts, Charles University: Prague. http://www.korpus.cz.

Institute of the Czech National Corpus, Faculty of Arts, Charles University. 2013. *InterCorp: Český národní korpus – InterCorp / InterCorp: Czech National Corpus – InterCorp*. Prague. <http://www.korpus.cz>.